Anschluss an B...

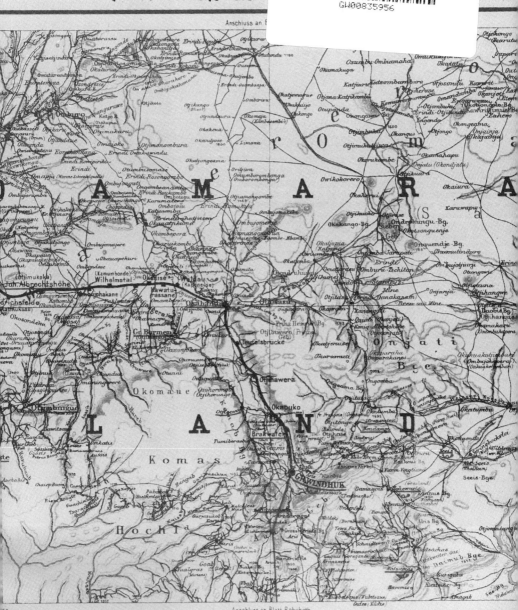

Anschluss an Blatt Rehoboth

Station Bahn im Betrieb ════ Bahn im Bau —— Wege ∼ Flussbetten (nur zeitweise nach heftigem Regen Wasserführend) ◡ Quellen
...sbruch des Aufstandes militärisch besetzte Plätze ⊕ Missionsstationen ⊙ von Weissen bewohnte Orte ∼∼∼ Heliographenlinien ⚬ Postämter Age...
...en in Klammern, ohne Ortszeichen (Eisenheim) = Farmen   Station st.W. = stets Wasser, zw.W. = zeitweise Was...

Maßstab 1:800 000

drift Furt	kolk Wasserloch	• Dampferlinien (Woermann)	rivier Fluss
fontein Wasserloch, Quelle	kopp, kopje Bergkuppe, Hügel	hoogte Hochebens	reld Feld, Ebene, Weide- u. Jagdfeld
klip Stein, Felsen	laagte Niederung, weites Flusstal	pan Salzpfanne	rlei zur Regenzeit Wasserführende
klopf Schlucht, Kluft	modder Morast	put, pits gegrabener Brunnen, Wasserloch	werft Wohnplatz, Ansiedelung
neus Nase		riet Schilfrohr	

URGENT IMPERIAL SERVICE

GERALD L'ANGE

URGENT IMPERIAL SERVICE

SOUTH AFRICAN FORCES
IN GERMAN SOUTH WEST AFRICA
1914-1915

ASHANTI PUBLISHING
(PTY) LIMITED
P.O. Box 10021 Rivonia 2128

Published in 1991 by Ashanti Publishing (Pty) Ltd
A Division of Ashanti International Films Gibraltar
P.O. Box 10021
Rivonia 2128

ISBN 1 874800 22 7 Standard Edition
      1 874800 29 4 Collectors Edition
      1 874800 30 8 De Luxe Edition in full leather

First published 1991
© Gerald L'Ange
© Richard Wood
© End-Paper Maps courtesy Namibia Archives

Typeset: Adcolour Durban
Printed by CTP Book Printers, Cape Town

BK2483

. . . If your ministers at the same time desire
and feel themselves able to seize such part
of German South West Africa as will give
them command of Swakopmund, Luderitzbucht
and the wireless stations there or in the
interior, we should feel that this was a
great and urgent Imperial service.

--From British Government cable to Prime
Minister Louis Botha of South Africa,
August 6 1914.

AUTHOR'S NOTE

This is possibly the most comprehensive book yet written about the campaign in German South West Africa. It nevertheless does not pretend to be the definitive work, which remains to be written. It attempts to tell the story in human rather than in military terms but at the same time to give an accurate account of the campaign.

I have drawn extensively on the few first-hand accounts that are available, both published and unpublished, and have acknowleged these sources as fully as possible in the text as well as in the notes. If the borrowing has at times been heavy it is in the belief that those from whom the material was taken, nearly all now dead, would have given their approval in the interests of having their stories revived before a fresh and wider audience and in this way helping to preserve the honour that is due to those who fought in this marvellous 'sideshow' of the First World War.

In researching and writing this book I was continually moved to admiration of the spirit and courage of those men and I hope that the retelling of their stories will serve as a posthumous salute to them.

The stories would not be available for the retelling if they had not been preserved by those often unsung servants of history, the archivists and librarians, and this work is offered also as a tribute to them.

In this note I record my debt and my gratitude to those from whose material I have drawn and to Barbara Worby and Bettie de Lange of the library of the Museum of Military History in Johannesburg; to Sandra Rowoldt of the Cory Library at Rhodes University, Grahamstown; to Brigitta Lau of the National Archives of Namibia in Windhoek; to Commandant S du Preez at Defence Headquarters in Pretoria; to the director and staff of the South African Defence Force Archives in Pretoria; to Commander W M Bissett of the Museum of Coast and Anti-Aircraft Artillery, Fort Wynyard, Cape Town; to the Cape Archives in Cape Town; to the Naval Historical Branch of the War Department in London; to Norman Fairbairn of *The Star* Archives; to Gordon McGregor and Gunther von Schumann of Windhoek for historical guidance and to Rex Sevenoaks for assistance with research.

The spelling of some of the place-names in this book is different from that in use now because some names have changed since the campaign was fought. The original spelling has been used wherever there is a disparity. Thus, Windhoek is Windhuk throughout the book.

There are also variances in the punctuation of German Southwest Africa and South-West Africa. For consistency I have used (German) South West Africa.

The measurements in use at the time have been preserved in the interests of authenticity.

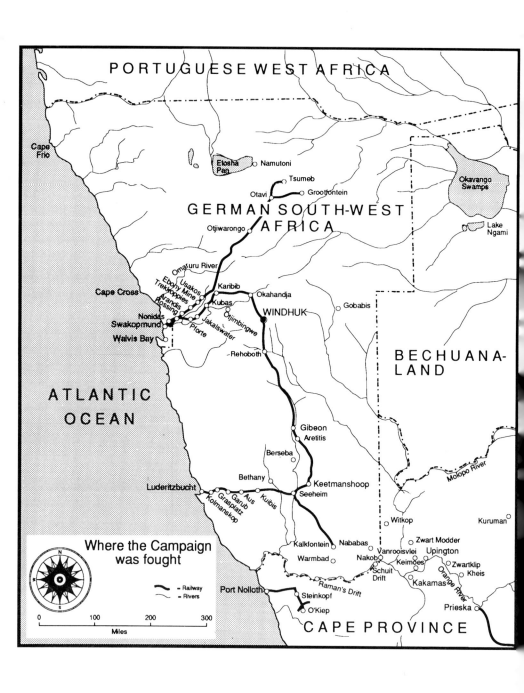

PORTUGUESE WEST AFRICA

Cape Frio

Etosha Pan

Namutoni

Tsumeb

Otavi ○ Grootfontein

GERMAN SOUTH-WEST AFRICA

Otjiwarongo

Okavango Swamps

Lake Ngami

Omaturu River

Cape Cross

Usakos
Ebony Mine
Trekkoppies
Arandis
Rossing
Nonidas
Swakopmund
Walvis Bay

Karibib

Kubas

Okahandja

Jakalswater
Orjimbingwe
Pforte

Gobabis

WINDHUK

Rehoboth

BECHUANA-LAND

ATLANTIC OCEAN

Gibeon
Aretitis

Berseba

Bethany

Luderitzbucht

Kolmanskop
Grasplatz
Garub
Aus
Kubis

Keetmanshoop
Seeheim

Molopo River

Witkop

Kuruman

Kalkfontein
Warmbad

Nababas
Nakob
Schuit Drift
Raman's Drift

Zwart Modder
Vanrooisvlei Upington
Keimoes
Zwartklip
Kheis
Kakamas

Orange River

Port Nolloth
Steinkopf
O'Kiep

Prieska

CAPE PROVINCE

Where the Campaign was fought

N
W — E
S

── = Railway
── = Rivers

0   100   200   300

Miles

CONTENTS

1

An Extraordinary Army

The day had begun with a battle and it ended, inevitably, with a burial. It was an unusual burial, even for a battlefield.

The sun was low when the survivors lined up beside the 26 new graves in the little cemetery at Sandfontein in German South West Africa on September 26 1914. On one side of the graves stood Germans and on the other side stood their enemies, the South Africans.

First they buried the South African dead. For, although the Germans were the victors on the day, their commander had ordered that the enemy dead should be buried before his own as a tribute to the fight that they had put up against great odds.

Only terse soldierly accounts have been left by the survivors, but the scene can be reconstructed from them.

The ranks of the South Africans were probably ragged from weariness and wounds, for they had fought all day under the desert sun with little food and water. Lying in their schanzes – low walls of stones hastily thrown up to shield them from enemy fire – they had sucked pebbles to ease their thirst and throughout the day they had kept firing back at the Germans who had encircled them and were pouring artillery, machine-gun and rifle fire into their position round the kopje at Sandfontein.

The Germans, too, must have been weary as they stood in the cemetery, for they had fought in the same conditions, though with freedom of movement and with access to food and water. In their bulky uniforms – jackboots and big broad-brimmed hats flapped up on one side and secured with a large red and black metal badge – they looked somehow larger than the South Africans in their riding-breeches and leggings and pith helmets.

The contrast was extended, though in a slightly different way, to the two commanders. Colonel Joachim von Heydebreck, Commander-in-Chief of the German forces in South West Africa, was an amply proportioned tough-looking man. The South African commander at the battle of Sandfontein, Lieutenant-Colonel Ronald Charles Grant, was slender, dapper and fair. Photographs show him with a long, aggressive moustache that looks slightly incongruous on a face unusually ascetic for a military man.

He had been wounded in one leg during the battle and it is not certain whether he conducted the burial service. He probably did, with someone helping him to stand, for he was a brave and conscientious man.

Because of the hour and the weariness and the wounds he would have kept his burial service brief. Still, the sun was going down when it ended and the young bugler of the South African Mounted Riflemen raised his bugle and, no doubt, struggled to find saliva to moisten his cracked lips. Then the clear, unutterably moving notes of the Last Post floated out over the graves and over the battlefield.

They echoed, perhaps, from the kopje that earlier had thrown back the savage rattle of machine-guns and rifles and the roar of cannon and crash of exploding shells and the screams of the horses as the shells burst among them.

Then darkness closed over the carnage, the empty schanzes and the thousands of cartridge cases and shrapnel fragments littering the South African positions. But the smell of cordite and high explosives would still have lingered in the still evening air as the German dead, some of them barely cold, were buried by lamplight, near the South Africans and the old graves of German settlers already in the cemetery.

Colonel RC Grant, Commander of the South African Mounted Riflemen at the Battle of Sandfontein. (Picture courtesy Cory Library, Rhodes University)

Colonel Joachim von Heydebreck, Commander-in-Chief of the German forces in South West Africa. (Courtesy Namibia Archives, Windhoek)

It is probable that the Germans and the South Africans stood at attention for the burial of each other's dead, for there seems to have been at the close of that day the sense of respect, even of kinship, that grows when men who have fought each other hard and well are brought together afterwards.

But when they turned away from the graves it was as victor and vanquished, as captors and prisoners of war. For Colonel Grant and the 288 survivors of his detachment of the South African Mounted Riflemen the campaign to conquer German South West Africa was over after the first battle.

But their role in the campaign, though brief, had been an honourable one, for despite having had to raise the white flag of surrender they had left the German commander astonished at the end of the day to learn that his forces had been held off for so long by so few men.

The Germans were to be surprised often again in the campaign, for the soldiers from South Africa were an unusual breed and they waged war with a unique flair.

★ ★ ★ ★ ★

It was, in fact, an extraordinary army that went off in 1914 to fight the Germans in South West Africa.

It was not only that every man was a volunteer that made it remarkable, nor that it was led by the Prime Minister himself – sometimes riding a large white horse at the battlefront – or even that it was setting out on the only campaign planned, conducted and completed by the armed forces of any Dominion of the British Empire entirely on its own in the First World War. What was most remarkable about this army was the nature of the men in it.

Nearly half of the army consisted of Dutch-speaking commandos, the same commandos that only 12 years earlier had defied the might of Victorian Britain in the Anglo-Boer War.

These were the men who, with little more than their horses and rifles, had kept the most powerful army in the world at bay for four years in an effort to stop Britain from seizing their republics; these were the fighting farmers whose successful tactics had changed the nature of warfare; the men who had seen the British generals, unable to defeat them in the field, resort in frustration to burning their farms and locking up their women and children in concentration camps, where many died long before their time.

Some of the bitterness left by these things had waned by the time victorious Britain, with a magnanimity not unmixed with self-interest, brought the conquered Transvaal and Orange Free State republics together with the Cape and Natal colonies to form the Union of South

Africa in 1910. But there was still bitterness among the Dutch-speaking people, who were now calling themselves Afrikaners, when, only four years later, Britain called on the Union to join with the other Dominions to help it to fight its war against Germany.

There was enough bitterness to make thousands of Dutch-speaking South Africans refuse to fight in the war or to see their country fight in it and to make ten thousand of them rise in rebellion.

Then Boer fought Boer in the land that they had defended together against the British; Afrikaner killed Afrikaner, commando fought commando and English-speaking fought Dutch-speaking South Africans until there were more South Africans dead on their own soil than were later to die in the campaign in South West Africa.

And now the Boer commandos, having put down the rebellion by their kinsmen and buried the dead, were going off side by side with their English-speaking countrymen – many of whom had fought against them in the Boer War – to fight under the Union Jack against the Germans, with whom many Afrikaners felt a greater affinity than with the British.

And when they won the victory they joined their commanders, those famous Boer generals, Louis Botha and Jan Smuts, in giving three cheers for His Majesty the King!

Some of the Dutch-speaking South Africans were in the war because they supported Botha's views. They shared his belief that, having made a pact with the British at the Treaty of Vereeniging at the end of the Boer War and joined the British Empire, they were in honour bound to help it to fight its wars. Others were in it purely out of loyalty to Botha and, to some extent, for the sheer love of a fight, like the colourful Boer general Coen Brits who, when asked by Botha to join in the war, responded: 'My men are ready; who do we fight – the English or the Germans?'

An extraordinary army, indeed. It was perhaps not surprising that it fought an extraordinary campaign.

Not only had the South Africans to fight the Germans but they had to fight the country as well. They marched across scorching desert plains where the rocks cut through their boots and over sands where men and horses sank to their knees, where cavalrymen sometimes had to heave a horse over the edge of a steep dune when the animal refused to descend it. They suffered blazing heat and freezing cold and, always, thirst – often made harder to bear at wells of clear water that could not be drunk because it had been poisoned by the enemy.

Except for some similarities with the fighting in the desert in the Middle East, the South West Africa campaign was like no other fought in the First World War.

Unlike the entrenched stagnation of the Western Front and Galli-

Cape Town docks are alive with military bustle as cavalrymen prepare to board a troopship to take them to South West Africa. (Cape Archives Depot – Elliott Collection)

poli, it was one of wide, sweeping cavalry movements, of the charge by mounted riflemen firing from the saddle that had been made famous and feared by the Boers in the South African War and of astonishing forced marches by the infantry.

Again and again the Germans were forced to retreat in haste from strongly fortified positions when these were outflanked by marches by the South Africans across terrain that the Germans had considered impassable by such large forces in so short a time.

In South West Africa the commandos and their generals used the same tactics against the Germans that they had used against the British in the Boer war; and with greater success, for this time they were on the stronger side.

Their superb combination of mobility, cohesion and initiative, their ability to cover vast distances quickly and with little sustenance, were qualities for which the Germans had no counter. That, and the readiness of the infantry regiments (composed almost entirely of English-speaking South Africans) to keep undertaking seemingly impossible marches and to complete them in times that were hardly credible.

At the beginning of the campaign, some of those who volunteered to fight with the infantry did not know that they would be going to South West Africa; many thought they were going to France. And some in the commandos were not fully aware that they would be fighting under the Union Jack.

But when they found that they would be campaigning in South West Africa and in the name of the British Empire they all gave their best in often cruel conditions, and this is perhaps the most distinctive aspect of the campaign: the dedication with which it was fought by all the South African soldiers.

CHAPTER

2

Choosing Sides

When Britain declared war on Germany in August 1914, official eyes in London were focused on maps of the oceans rather than the land. If there was one thing on which there was no disagreement in the Cabinet, the War Office and the Admiralty, it was on the absolute dependence of Britain on its navy. For the island nation, the defeat of its navy would mean disaster, for not only would its shores be opened to invasion but it would be cut off from foreign supplies and from its Empire.

The British had to think not only of the German fleets in the North Sea but also of German warships operating in distant oceans and threatening the countries and supply lines of the Empire.

It was primarily in that light that strategists in London looked at German South West Africa.

The colony had two seaports: Luderitzbucht and Swakopmund, which, though unsuitable for big ships or heavy traffic, could be used to refuel, supply and repair German warships operating in the South Atlantic. The best harbour on the coast, Walvis Bay, was a British enclave in the German colony but it was not defended and in fact it was seized by the Germans at the outbreak of war. It had only rudimentary port facilities, however, and the British were not greatly concerned about its being used by the Germans.

In London they were more concerned about something else. At Windhuk, high on the central plateau stood the second largest wireless station is the world. From its masts towering 350 feet above the town the station could maintain contact with Berlin in favourable weather conditions. In bad weather communication was maintained through a relay station in the German colony of Togo in West Africa.

There were smaller wireless stations at Luderitzbucht and Swakopmund, and the three could maintain contact between Berlin and German warships in distant waters, including the South Atlantic and the vital route round the Cape of Good Hope that was a lifeline between Britain and much of her Empire.

General Louis Botha, Prime Minister of the Union of South Africa and Commander-in-Chief of its armed forces. (SADF Archives)

Depriving the Germans of the use of the South West African ports and wireless stations became an important objective in London from the day that war was declared on Germany on August 4.

On that same day the Prime Minister of the Union of South Africa, General Louis Botha, sent a message to the British government suggesting that the British garrison then based in the Union should be withdrawn and sent into the fight against Germany. South Africa would if necessary defend itself with its own army, he said.

Acceptance of the offer was cabled only two days later. With it came an inquiry about whether South Africa would be willing to capture the wireless stations in German South West Africa.

If South Africa would undertake that, said the Secretary of State for the Colonies, it would be 'a great and urgent Imperial service'. On August 10 the Union cabinet agreed to send an expedition against the German colony and, only four years after South Africa had become a nation, its fledgeling army had been morally committed to a conflict beyond its borders.

Obtaining political ratification of the commitment was more difficult. It was got only at the cost of tearing the new nation apart. Only five weeks after the decision by the cabinet the first Union forces crossed the Orange River, under the command of Brigadier-General Tim Lukin, to open the South African invasion, and two days after that the first seaborne landing took place at Luderitzbucht.

And within weeks the northern part of South Africa was aflame with rebellion as opponents of the invasion took up arms against it.

The rebellion had a sputtering start, for there was much uncertainty among the public about what their Government had committed them to. South Africa's entry into the war had been almost furtive. When Lukin landed at Port Nolloth most South Africans were unaware of it. They remained in ignorance as he assembled his force at Steinkopf for the advance to the Orange River.

Most South Africans did not even know about the decision to invade German South West. Weeks afterwards, it had not been reported in the press. It was only when the matter came before Parliament a month later that the public got confirmation of what most had only guessed.

As early as August 15 General Jacobus (Koos) de la Rey, one of the heroes of the Anglo-Boer War, called a meeting at Treurfontein in the Transvaal to discuss the danger of South Africa becoming involved in an invasion of German South West Africa.

The papers had been full of news from the European front and patriotic fervour had been rising, at least among the English-speakers, many of whom were preparing to join up to fight the Germans. Many thought that the fighting would be in France or

The prime target: The wireless station at Windhuk. The picture shows one of the masts and the buildings housing the generating plant and the wireless equipment. (National Museum of Military History [War Museum], Johannesburg)

Belgium, although there were occasional references in the newspapers to the danger posed by the existence of a German colony on the South African border.

The failure of the newspapers to inform their readers fully about the drift of South Africa into war was probably due mainly to the reluctance of Botha's government to be frank with the public and the press about its actions. The newspapers may even have been intimidated by the prosecution under the Defence Act of the editor of *The South African News*, F C Donovan, who was hauled into court in Cape Town on August 13, only two days after his newspaper ran a story about troop movements. He was charged with publishing information about the disposition of Imperial troops while a state of war existed between the King and Germany.

Despite his argument that the news had been cabled from Britain and passed by the military censors, Donovan was convicted, the first South African editor to suffer this fate under the Defence Act. He was, however, given a nominal fine of five pounds rather than the maximum of 100 pounds.[1]

A week later South Africans were left in little doubt that they were going to war when a proclamation was issued announcing that as war had been declared between Britain and Germany, parts of the Defence Force might be called up for active service 'anywhere in South Africa, within or outside the Union'. Precisely what was meant by this apparent contradiction of geographic reality was not explained.

Some may have seen a clue, however, in the news announced next day: German forces, it was said, had invaded Union territory from South West Africa.

It was the lead story in the biggest South African newspaper, *The Star* in Johannesburg on August 21 and was headlined in what was probably its largest type. Headlines did not scream in those days, but *The Star* announced in its most stentorian typographical tone: 'German Invasion of Union Territory.'[2]

It was the first time since the war had begun that the news from the European front was not the main item in the paper. Below the big headlines the report was terse: 'It is officially notified for information that German troops from German South West Africa have crossed the border in the neighbourhood of Nakab [sic] and have invaded Union territory, where they are now entrenching themselves.'

The report, obviously based on an official news release, gave few details of the 'invasion'. It turned out later that it was hardly a serious offensive: a detachment of German troops had occupied a kopje overlooking the waterhole near Nakob.

Nakob is on the border some distance from where it makes a right-angled turn from the Orange River and runs north along longitude 20, an imaginary line running through vast, empty reaches of country varying from semi-desert to outright desert.

A prospector, Fred Cornell, had come across the Germans digging trenches on the kopje. He had taken photographs and, according to a report in *The Cape Times*, had 'escaped by crawling and wriggling away'.

The water hole was in German territory but the kopje on which they had dug fortifications to defend it was in South Africa. The Germans said later that they did not know the kopje was not on their side of the border; but if Botha was looking for something to justify his Cabinet's decision to invade South West, the photographs brought back by Cornell were all that he needed in the atmosphere then prevailing in the Union.

Patriotism was flowing strongly among English-speaking South Africans, who had no difficulty giving their allegiance to the British Crown. In Albert Park in Durban, named after Queen Victoria's consort, fêtes were being held to raise money for comforts for the British tommies, and in Johannesburg a large shop was advertising Union Jacks – 'a children's special' – at sixpence each.

There was other important news on the day when the German 'invasion' was reported: newspaper readers learned that various regiments of the Active Citizen Force had been called up.

Another report said that news had reached Cape Town that the Germans had evacuated Swakopmund after blowing up the jetty, sinking hulks in the approaches to the harbour and shifting the navigational buoys.

When the National Reserve units were called up on August 24, *The Star* commented that this step had evidently been taken to enable the Government to call out the National Reserve 'in the districts affected by the German invasion of the Union'.

News now came in, by way of a telegram from the SAMR in Upington , of an incident that exacerbated bellicose feelings. On August 21 a group of Dutch South African farmers who had been living in South West just across the Orange River were ordered by the Germans to leave the border region and go with their cattle to the Keetmanshoop district. They refused, and began crossing back into South Africa. German troops tried to stop them, and there was an exchange of shots. The only casualty was a German soldier killed – and he thus became the first casualty of the conflict – but the incident strengthened Botha's hand.

It was reported on August 28 that the Transvaal Horse Artillery had left Johannesburg 'quietly and unobtrusively' but no hint was given of where it had gone. And two hundred railway engineers had left for 'an unknown destination'.

In Pretoria the National Party was holding its annual congress in a hotel, and misgivings about the situation were voiced by delegates. Outside the hotel, police arrested a man who had been displaying a picture showing British tommies looting a burning Boer farmhouse, which was flying a white flag, while Boer women looked on and wept. He was charged with incitement.

Tension was growing.

Amid more reports of troops leaving by train for undisclosed destinations, the Commandant-General of the Union Defence Force, General Christiaan Beyers, went to the military camp at Booysens, near Johannesburg, and watched the Imperial Light Horse, the Rand Light Infantry and the Transvaal Scottish perform military exercises.

Beyers had also fought with distinction on the Boer side in the Anglo-Boer War. At the end of the exercise he addressed the assembled troops and concluded by saying: 'I now bid you to remove your headdress and give three cheers for His Majesty the King.'[3]

The soldiers cheered. But they might not have cheered so lustily if they had known what Beyers would be doing in the coming weeks.

By the end of August talk of a German invasion of South Africa was becoming more open, despite the fact that the German forces in South West Africa were hardly strong enough to take on the army that South Africa was capable of putting into the field. But if the South African authorities were aware of that they probably suspected that German strategists were counting on the Dutch part of the population rising in rebellion in sympathy with a German invasion. There were, in fact, signs at that point that this might be the case.

Or perhaps Sir Percy Fitzpatrick simply did not know the German strength in South West when he told a reporter who interviewed him in Cape Town on September 2, on his return from a visit to Britain, that there was a danger of a German invasion of the Union.

Fitzpatrick is best remembered for his tales of the goldfields transport riders in his classic book, *Jock of the Bushveld*. In 1914 he was a prominent member of Parliament in Botha's government. He told the interviewer that the Germans were on South Africa's borders 'ready to attack', and that the threat of invasion from German South West Africa had in fact been an important factor in bringing about union in 1910. Fitzpatrick, though not a member of Botha's cabinet, was no doubt privy to its thinking; certainly the newspapers seemed to think he was specially well-informed. He suggested that the security of South Africa was dependent on the Royal Navy and said this was one of the privileges of belonging to an Empire with powerful naval forces.

'We, like England, are fighting for our existence', he said. 'The fate of Brussels and Louvain might be ours.'[4]

Next day Fitzpatrick explained in another interview why South African troops were being moved to the north: because the railways in German South West had been built 'not for the development of that country but to take ours'.

At least the people of South Africa now had a clearer idea of why their armed forces were being mobilised. But most still did not know the country was committed to invading South West Africa.

Most did not even know that South African troops had sailed from Cape Town and landed at Port Nolloth on August 31 and were marching north towards the German border. Nor did they know that an invasion force was being assembled at Cape Town for a landing at Luderitzbucht.

General de la Rey did little to clarify the confusion when he addressed the troops at Booysens camp on September 6, and exhorted them to 'obey their superiors in all instances'.[5] De la Rey was not a serving officer in the UDF, and presumably was allowed to address the troops on the strength of his status as a senator.

More troops now moved off to join the war. Units of the Transvaal Scottish, wearing Canadian Mountie hats, khaki tunics and tartan riding breeches, marched to the station past cheering crowds. They were followed by the RLI and the ILH. The women of South Africa were probably still uncertain whether their sons and husbands were going to fight in Europe or were only going to defend the border. Few English-speakers seemed to think it made much difference. It was only some of the Dutch-speakers who thought it did.

South Africans who looked to the opening of Parliament for

clarification of where their country stood on the question of war were disappointed when the Governor-General, Lord Buxton, in his opening speech on September 9 said only that the outbreak of war between Britain and Germany had led to the mobilisation of part of the Union Defence Force 'for the purpose of cooperating with His Majesty's government in guarding the welfare of the Empire'.

Botha at last put an end to doubts the next day in a speech frequently interrupted by cheers.[6]

Never, he said, had Parliament been called together at a more critical time. The view among some South Africans that the storm in Europe did not threaten the Union was 'a most narrow-minded conception'. South Africa was part of the British Empire and an ally in it, and, that empire being involved in a war, South Africa was *ipso facto* also at war with the common enemy.

Only two courses were open to South Africa, he said. One was that of faith, duty and honour; the other was that of dishonour and disloyalty.

The people of South Africa had never attempted to create anything by treason, he said.

Botha told Parliament about the offer by the Government to allow the British garrison in South Africa to be withdrawn and said that acceptance of this offer had made it necessary to call up part of the UDF. The Imperial Government had stated that warlike operations in German South West Africa were considered to be of strategic importance, and if the Union could undertake them it would be considered of great service.

The Union Government had decided to comply with this request in the interests of South Africa as well as those of the Empire. The mode of operations could not be discussed in the House. But the House could not be held responsible for them; they must trust the men who were responsible.

Botha said the Government had been told, even before there was any question of mobilisation, that there were armed forces on the borders of the Union, in large numbers at several points. They had taken up a position at Nakob that they had never taken up before and had entrenched themselves there. One force had crossed the border and taken possession of a kopje in Union territory. Botha referred also to the clash between the German troops and the Dutch South Africans whom they had tried to stop crossing the Orange.

Botha emphasised that Britain had tried to avoid war with Germany. If ever Britain had entered a war with clean hands it was this one.

The outcome on the battlefields of Europe would affect the Union one way or the other. He wanted the House to understand, however, that whatever steps the government took there was no desire whatever to acquire fresh possessions.

14

"Right!"

A propagandistic cartoon published in the *SA Railways and Harbours Magazine* in January 1915 showed symbolic Boer and Briton railways joining to go on to 'German West Africa'. But before the year was much older the Union was being racked by rebellion ignited by the decision to invade German South West. (Railway Museum, Johannesburg)

During the Boer War the white races had fought against each other; but now there was great cooperation. Appealing for greater tolerance than ever, he said he believed they would rather be under the British than the German flag.

Botha moved that the House assure the King of its continuing loyalty and support and endorse all measures necessary to cooperate with the Imperial Government to 'maintain the security and integrity of the Empire'.

The leader of the opposition, Sir Thomas Smartt, supported the motion and assured Botha of the backing of the Unionist Party in bringing 'the struggle to a successful conclusion'.

Nobody was surprised when General Hertzog expressed the opposition of the National Party to the motion by moving adjournment of the debate. He was defeated by 85 votes to 12, but he went on to argue that South Africa had no obligation to declare war on German South West Africa. The people needed time to consider the matter.

Botha's motion, he said, amounted to a request by the Government for authority to send an expeditionary force into German South West Africa. Yet the Prime Minister had said the Government did not intend to secure fresh territory.

How, Hertzog asked, would the invasion help the Empire? He said his first duty was to his people, not to the Empire. What would happen if the Allies lost the war? Who could say in a war who was right?

No one had the right, said Hertzog, to ask the Union, which had hardly closed the door on the miseries of the last war, to do more than any other Dominion had done.

He challenged Botha's assertion that the people would rather live under the British flag than the German. The government should consult the people. Botha's views were certainly not those of the people of the Free State, he said.

The debate was adjourned overnight, and in its report next day *The Star* left no doubt about its own views with the headlines: 'Premier's Great Speech' and 'Hertzog's Curious Speech'.

In a leading article *The Star* said that Germany was 'only waiting for a chance to bring Africa into the general upheaval and obliterate existing boundaries'. The Windhuk wireless station was a danger to British shipping and to South African trade.

'We feel assured,' it said, 'that our Dutch fellow-subjects will be as ardent as the British section of the population in their support of General Botha's policy.'

When the debate was resumed the leader of the Labour Party, Colonel Frederic Cresswell, asserted that the war had been avoidable, but if South Africa were to take part it should send troops to Europe rather than to South West Africa.

When General Smuts entered the debate he too made much of the German threat. But first he attacked the notion of Boer-German kinship, recalling that when President Paul Kruger of the old Transvaal Republic had gone to Germany to plead the cause of the two Boer republics the Germans had threatened to arrest him, whereas the French had given him a warm reception.

Then he called up old loyalties: 'Our mother countries have been attacked . . . we have Belgian, French and English blood.'

At the signing of the Treaty of Vereeniging, he said, he had stated that South Africa had fought for its liberty and it had been guaranteed. Now it was a free nation and 'opposed to us there is a military autocracy which is threatening to suppress and isolate [and is] doing its best to annihilate the smaller nations . . . If we act as cowards and shirk from our duty, then we do not deserve the liberty which we enjoy.'

Germany had entrenched itself on South African soil, Smuts declared, and German cruisers were in South African waters and communicating with Germany through the South West African wireless stations. If it were not for the protection of the British fleet, it would not be safe to send goods from South Africa. The South African coast would not be safe until the wireless communication had been stopped and all the points he had referred to were in the possession of South Africa.

Smuts appealed to members not to listen to 'the German advocates who stood up in this house'. German sympathies had been spread by German agents and dealers who 'were placing a dagger in the heart of South Africa which they were eager to press home'.

He said that the Government had information that clearly showed that the German government had had its eyes on South Africa for many days.

South Africa was not the aggressor; it had been attacked and it was the duty of South Africans to repel [the attack], Smuts said, and sat down amid loud cheers.

At 8.55 that evening the House of Assembly adopted Botha's motion by a vote of 92 to 12, and South Africa was openly committed to war with Germany.

References

1. *The Star,* August 14 1914.
2. *Ibid.*
3. *Ibid,* August 29 1914.
4. *Ibid,* September 3 1914.
5. *Ibid,* September 7 1914.
6. *Ibid,* September 10 1914.

CHAPTER

3

Marching North

'The long treks across this God-forsaken country are like a hideous nightmare . . . The country now is simply rock and sand, rock and sand . . . Some parts are absolutely devoid of vegetation, while here and there one sees a few cacti. A few of the horses give in occasionally, but none of the men. The latter sometimes fall off their horses while asleep.'

Through accounts like this one, published in *The Nongquai*, the magazine of the South African Police, South Africans snugly abed in the Union got glimpses of the kind of war their troops were going into in South West Africa.

The commander of the troops heading north to the Orange River from Port Nolloth, Brigadier-General Sir Henry Timson Lukin, was one of the most experienced soldiers in South Africa. His force of 2 420 men was made up of the 1st, 2nd, 3rd, 4th and 5th Regiments of the

South African cavalry at drill: Some were on their way to invade German South West Africa over the Orange River before South Africa had formally entered the conflict.
(Cape Archives – E)

South African Mounted Riflemen (all Permanent Force); the 10th Infantry (the Witwatersrand Rifles, a Citizen Force regiment); the 2nd and 4th Permanent Force Batteries of artillery; the 8th Citizen Force Battery (Transvaal Horse Artillery); a section of engineers and an ammunition column. Altogether he could field 1 800 rifles and eight artillery pieces.

While Lukin's force had been able to send its supplies on the railway from Port Nolloth to Steinkopf, from there to the Orange River the only transport was by horse and by waggons drawn by mules or even donkeys – hardy little beasts that, when harnessed in sufficient numbers to a waggon, could haul it over rough desert country with less water or food than a mule would need. Most of the waggons were drawn by mules, however.

On the 60 waterless miles from Steinkopf to the Orange the column had to make a long side-trek to a well to water the animals, and the troops got an unpleasant taste of what was to come across the border. They marched at night because of the heat and to avoid giving the enemy gratuitous information about the strength of Lukin's force (a German aircraft flew over the column on one day of the march.)

Night marches became routine not only in the northern Cape but also in South West. Their rigours were described by the Reuters correspondent with the Namaqualand Force.

'We, with certain guns and escort, left camp at half past three on the first afternoon in order to make a water-hole by sundown and to get a fair start on our night's job of 40 miles of waterless desert, feet deep in dry sand, a flowerless, lifeless, Godless land,' he wrote.

'Happily the night was cool and we greeted the uprising of the great yellow moon with the ringing notes of the "Boot and Saddle", and in ten minutes the escort swung out into the skyline. The guns commenced to rumble forward, waggons straining and creaking as the mules responded to the crack of the whip and urgent cries of the native drivers. Much use of the road had covered the surface of sand with a fine, white, closely-ground granular powder that rose in great white clouds around us.

'At first the column moved enthusiastically on its way. Songs enlivened the night, ragtime choruses rose on dusty air. But as the hours dragged on, silence fell and, nerving themselves to the task, animals and men plodded slowly but surely forward. Nothing broke the silence but the soft 'scrunch, scrunch' of the animals' feet in the gritty sand and an occasional cry of the drivers or the neighing shriek of some protesting horse or mule hurt and angry at the indignities and burden of labour put on him by his master.

'Onward till the lights of a water-boring camp at work in the dry watercourse shone brightly and five miles further on midnight brought

The infantry, some of whom are shown here at inspection, landed in South West from the sea. (War Museum)

a halt. Old soldiers snatch a moment's sleep anywhere, but some of us found coffee more sustaining and spent two hours round a hastily improvised fire of brushwood.

'At two o'clock, "Boot and Saddle" again and the dusty, merciless road once more. Throats choked, eyes blinded, ears filled with acrid powder as we dragged ourselves and the animals so wearily forward. We entered on the worst portion of the march as daybreak approached. Grey lights hung over the distant kopjes and fires shone ahead of us, but how far off can one see fires at night and how far those fires were! Now the column had begun to struggle. Some men, more thoughtful of the horses than of themselves, dismounted and led the utterly exhausted cattle.

'Just as we unlimbered in the Valley of Dry Bones, red dawn broke, but there was no sound of dawn, no twittering of birds, just the same silence of the desert that reigned at night. We flung off our saddles and fed the cattle, too tired to eat, and for ourselves lay down too tired to sleep. Our task was not yet done. Another twelve miles lay before us, but before we could attempt them it was necessary to send every animal eight miles to water and bring it back, adding sixteen miles to the march of all the animals and most of the men.

'The Valley of Dry Bones is a huge lake of sand with neither verdure nor any living thing within its borders. It is scattered with the white bones of animals who, having got so far, were so exhausted that they could not walk the extra few miles to water. Here we lay in torrid heat, dirt and discomfort all day. At noon a hot, blasting desert wind sprang up.

'Four-thirty of the second and last afternoon saw us once more in the saddle, climbing to Hell's Gate. I adopt the SAMR geographical nomenclature; it is more poetic than local names and the censor does not object to it. Night closed down on us as we neared our destination but we were to be instantly restored to cheerful energy by the news that we had established a record for the distance over a desert.'[1]

On patrols, the SAMR squadrons travelled lighter. 'Each man carries a greatcoat and, if possible, a blanket under the saddle,' the Reuters correspondent reported. 'Two days' rations for a full-grown man consists of five biscuits, one pound of bully beef and a small issue of coffee.'

Up to the time when Parliament endorsed the invasion of South West Africa, Botha could, if pressed, have justified the presence of Lukin's force by the need to defend the border against a possible German incursion across the Orange River. Once Parliament had given its support to Botha, Lukin wasted no time in taking the initiative.

Three days after the vote in Parliament, Lukin's force crossed the Orange and attacked the German blockhouse at Raman's Drift. According to Reuter's reporter, Lukin had learned that a strong German force was marching south towards the drift, and he decided to secure the vital crossing before they got there.

He sent Colonel Dawson with the 4th SAMR on a forced march from Steinkopf. Marching by night and 'hiding by day', Dawson's force took the garrison at the blockhouse by surprise.

Cavalrymen take their horses past Cape Town's city hall on their way to the docks to board ship for the invasion. (Cape Archives – E)

A German account states that there were only three soldiers guarding the drift, and when they saw a whole regiment crossing the river in the moonlight they wisely departed without firing a shot. But the Reuters report says that there was 'a sharp skirmish' during which one of the South Africans was killed before the garrison surrendered on September 14.

In the ensuing weeks there were more such skirmishes along the borders.

This description in *The Nongquai* was typical of the encounters between Union and German patrols: 'Early in the week, our men ambushed a German patrol, capturing two prisoners and five horses. A

Against a backdrop of Cape Town's landmark mountains, pith-helmeted troops file on board the transport that will take them to South West Africa. (Cape Archives – E)

spoor of blood showed that others of the enemy had been wounded. Three days later a third member of the patrol surrendered. He was driven to do so by thirst. He said that his wounded comrades were in the hills dying of thirst, but they were afraid to surrender lest they might be summarily executed.

'Reassured on this point, the prisoners communicated their whereabouts, and they, with one man hit in the foot and an emaciated horse, were brought into our camp. They showed great gratitude for the kindly treatment, which they evidently did not expect.

'There are still three Germans wandering about on foot, probably wounded and suffering agonies of thirst. According to the prisoners, the enemy must be finding the water difficulty very serious, especially as they have themselves destroyed most of the really important water-holes.' [2]

Four days after the seizure of Raman's Drift, the first seaborne invasion conducted by South African forces came ashore at Luderitzbucht. It met only token opposition, the German forces withdrawing on the landward side of the town as the Union forces came in from the sea.

But at Defence Headquarters in Pretoria there was concern that the Germans might try to retake the port. To prevent them from massing their forces for the purpose it was decided that Lukin should push northwards from the Orange and so force the Germans to divert some of their troops to try to stop him.

Lukin's first objective was the town of Warmbad, 40 miles from Raman's Drift. To get there he had first to secure the wells at Sandfontein to ensure a supply of water for his force.

A squadron of the SAMR sent to reconnoitre the area found Sandfontein, 24 miles from Raman's Drift, undefended. There was not much there – three wells, a pumphouse and a few sheds clustered beneath a kopje 200 feet high – but it was the water that made it important. The South Africans constructed rudimentary defences on the hard, stony slopes of the kopje by piling stones in short, low double walls between which a rifleman could lie and get some protection from enemy fire. They had no idea as they worked in the bright, still desert how they would value those schanzes in a few days time.

Five days after his advance units had occupied the place, Lukin got word of German troop movements towards Sandfontein. He sent reinforcements – a second squadron of the SAMR and two guns of the Transvaal Horse Artillery – from the force at Raman's Drift.

Lukin, a veteran who had fought against the Zulus at Ulundi and in the Anglo-Boer War, had been reluctant to cross the Orange until his troops and supplies were in place south of the river. Inadequate transport had left his advance forces still short of supplies when he received orders to press ahead to Warmbad.

Knowing the risk of the move, he reluctantly ordered Colonel Grant, the officer commanding the reinforcements, to push on to Sandfontein ahead of his supply waggons to ensure that he got there before any German attack was launched on the place.

His misgivings were justified, for, although he did not know it, he was sending Grant and his force into a trap.

Officers of Lukin's force were astonished to learn after the campaign that Defence Headquarters actually had the information that would have warned Lukin of the trap but failed to pass it on to him in time. Intelligence had been received of substantial German troop movements by train southwards towards the railhead at Kalkfontein (Karasburg) and of other movements by road. Instead of telegraphing this information to Lukin immediately, somebody at Defence Headquarters put it in the post![3]

By the time it reached him through the mail the battle of Sandfontein was long over.

References

1. The *Nongquai*, 1914; p. 327.
2. *Ibid*, p. 328.
3. Collyer, J J, *The Campaign in German South West Africa*, 1914-1915; Government Printer, Pretoria, 1937; p. 48.

4

First Blood

'It seemed like hell let loose. There was an infernal din of shrieking, splitting, sickening shells, an interminable rat-a-tat of machine-guns, a cracking of rifles that rose in waves but never died down entirely.

'All this noise was intensified beyond measure because it was caught up in the hollow of the basin and reverberated again and again until the echoes in their clash almost threatened to drown the original noise. I thought my head would burst and if it had done so it would only have been in harmony with the song of the day.'[1]

★ ★ ★ ★ ★

That was how a survivor recalled the battle of Sandfontein, as the Germans poured artillery and machine-gun fire at the kopje around which they had trapped Colonel Grant's SAMR squadrons.

Lukin and Grant on that day became victims of bad intelligence on the South African side and clever planning by the German commander-in-chief.

Their information was that there were substantial German forces in the region, but nothing too strong for Grant's force, supported if necessary by reinforcements from Raman's Drift.

Their intelligence was hopelessly wrong. The reality was that Colonel von Heydebreck had rushed every soldier he could spare at short notice to the vicinity for an attack on Sandfontein. He had brought troops by train from Keetmanshoop to the north and he had called in forces that had been posted on the eastern border, bringing them to Sandfontein by forced marches.

Von Heydebreck attached more importance to Sandfontein than its strategic value as the only watering point between the Orange and Warmbad. He hoped that by inflicting a severe defeat on the South Africans while they were still crossing the Orange he could set back their advance by several months.

Time was everything to the Germans at this stage, for they were

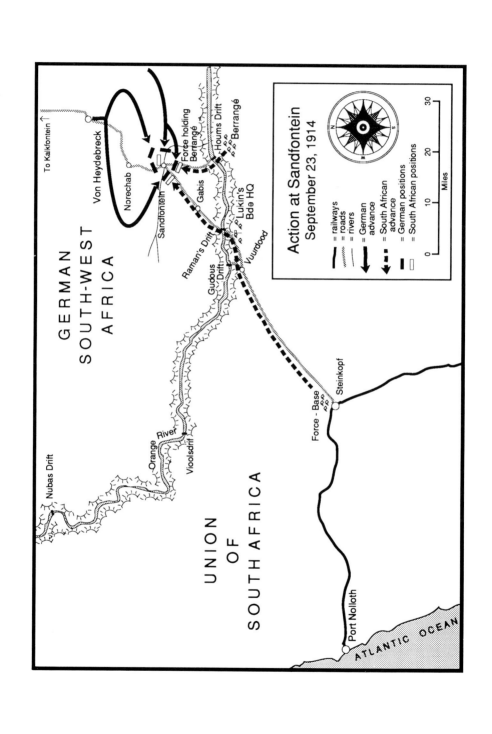

Action at Sandfontein
September 23, 1914

= railways
= roads
= rivers
= German advance
= South African advance
= German positions
= South African positions

Miles
0   10   20   30

To Kalkfontein ↑
Von Heydebreck
Norechab
Force holding Berrangé
Houms Drift
Berrangé
Sandfontein
Gabis
Lukin's Bde HQ
Raman's Drift
Vuurdood
Gudous Drift
GERMAN SOUTH-WEST AFRICA
Nubas Drift
Orange River
Vioolsdrift
Steinkopf
Force - Base
UNION OF SOUTH AFRICA
Port Nolloth
ATLANTIC OCEAN

The Cape Field Artillery at Raman's Drift. Within days of this picture being taken, men of the CFA were engaged in the first battle fought by the South African Defence Force: the battle of Sandfontein. (Museum of Coast and Anti-Aircraft Artillery, Fort Wynyard, Cape Town)

confident that their armies would quickly defeat the British and their allies in Europe, forcing the South Africans to seek peace. Von Heydebreck had decided not to defend Luderitzbucht but to pull up the railway line from the port inland across the desert to hamper an advance from the coast while he concentrated on fighting off Lukin's overland invasion across the Orange – and encouraging a Boer rebellion in South Africa to keep the Union forces busy there.

He knew from his intelligence –which, with the help of an aircraft for aerial reconnaissance, was better than that of the South Africans at that time – Lukin had landed at Port Nolloth with a relatively strong force. He knew that most of them had travelled along the railway to Steinkopf and some had then marched north to Raman's Drift on the Orange.

Obviously the next move would be to occupy the wells at Sand-fontein to secure the water for the advance on Warmbad. Von Heyde-breck decided to lure the South Africans forward by seeming to abandon Sandfontein and then to spring a trap on them.

Thus when the South African invasion force landed at Luderitz-bucht on September 18 it met only token resistance. But when the first detachment of the SAMR occupied Sandfontein on September 19 a large German force was secretly being gathered in the surrounding hills to close the trap.

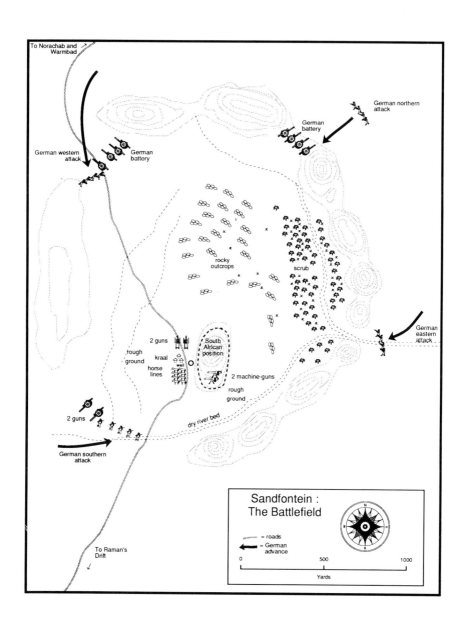

To Norachab and Warmbad

German northern attack

German battery

German western attack

German battery

rocky outcrops

scrub

German eastern attack

2 guns

South African position

tough ground

kraal

well

horse lines

2 machine-guns

rough ground

2 guns

dry river bed

German southern attack

To Raman's Drift

Sandfontein :
The Battlefield

= roads
= German advance

0   500   1000

Yards

On September 24 the commander of the single SAMR squadron at Sandfontein, Captain Welby, spoke to Lukin over a telephone line that had been linked to Raman's Drift and confirmed the first assessment of the place: that it would be impossible to defend unless the surrounding heights were denied to an attacker. The stony ground made it difficult to construct gun pits. Welby also pointed out that his rations were 36 hours overdue and expressed concern at having his line of retreat unguarded.

Lukin assured Welby that his rear would be covered by the forces at Raman's Drift and that Grant would be there in the morning with reinforcements, which would be followed by supplies.

But Welby's uneasiness increased when a patrol that he had sent out at 4 a.m. on September 26 failed to return. Only later did he learn that it had been cut of by a hidden German force with a machine-gun and its leader killed and the rest captured.

After riding through the night, Grant's weary detachment arrived at Sandfontein at 7.30 a.m., bringing the South African strength at the position to 257 men, two machine-guns and two thirteen-pounder guns of the Transvaal Horse Artillery. They did not yet know it, but a force of 1 187 Germans with six machine-guns and ten artillery pieces was closing around them.

Before Grant's men had even dismounted, a lookout on top of the kopje overlooking Sandfontein reported that an enemy column was approaching from the north-east and that the SAMR patrols sent out from Sandfontein were returning.

Just then the signaller ran up to say that the telephone line to Raman's Drift had been cut.

Grant quickly climbed the kopje to assess the situation. He arrived panting at the top to see two more columns closing in, one from the east and another from the west. A few minutes later a fourth column was seen coming up from the south-west, cutting off the line of retreat.

Within twenty minutes of his arrival Grant found himself completely surrounded by a greatly superior force that had been deployed with great swiftness and skill.

The patrols that Welby had sent out were already under severe pressure from the advancing Germans and were fighting delaying actions as they came in. So close were the Germans behind one patrol that the troops at Sandfontein for a moment confused them with the Germans and nearly opened fire on them.

Von Heydebreck was following the course of events through reports sent by wireless and heliograph to his command-post at Aleurisfontein and knew that victory was in his grasp, provided he could prevent the South Africans from receiving reinforcements from Raman's Drift; and he had made plans for such an eventuality.

The rocky slopes of the kopje at Sandfontein, where South African riflemen and gunners held out until hope had gone. (Fort Wynyard Museum)

What he did not know was how well the South Africans might fight. Grant for his part knew that he could do nothing but make the best of a bad situation. He had no choice but to position his guns in the open at the western foot of the kopje. His machine guns he placed on the southern spur, which gave them a field of fire in all directions but north. Grant himself remained on the top of the kopje, where he set up his command post.

Within half an hour of Grant's arrival his men were in action, with the South African guns, under Lieutenant Fritz Adler, opening fire on the Germans to the south. They immediately came under fire from four German guns on a ridge to the north-east and shortly afterwards by another battery of four guns on the west and two more guns on the south-west.

Meanwhile German troops had deployed on foot among rocks and dongas that provided good cover round the Union position, which was soon being swept by rifle and machine-gun fire from all sides and by the German artillery from three sides.

The South Africans were posted in a thin line surrounding the kopje. Those who had arrived with Grant had had time only to collect a few stones with which to throw together their schanzes before the onslaught began.

Lying in their schanzes, they kept up such an accurate fire that the Germans were unable to advance despite the hail of shot and shell poured onto the South African position.

The German artillery fire was concentrated mainly on the Union guns in an attempt to silence them. Adler, skilfully moving his guns and switching targets, made the most of his shots until one of his guns was put out of action. Then one of the two Union machine-guns was knocked out.

At 11 a.m. Adler reported that most of his gun crews were dead or wounded and that he could no longer work the remaining gun. He was ordered to withdraw with the surviving gunners, which he did, but not before removing the breech-blocks of both guns, under heavy fire, to make them unusable by the Germans if captured.

Captain Welby later recorded his admiration for the way in which the gunners had fought under fire and recalled that 'most of them were boys hardly out of their teens who had never seen an angry shot fired before and they behaved like veterans.'

One of those who survived the fight, P J Young, described how 'the German shots made a thick rain on the hill, while their field guns struck at the two guns of the Transvaal Horse Artillery, round which figures were lying still . . . The young artillerymen's courage was grand.'[2]

Smiling survivors of Sandfontein, some with bandaged wounds, march into captivity. (Namibia Archives)

With the South African guns out of action the German artillery fire was now concentrated on the SAMR horse lines, presumably to prevent any attempt by the Union force to try to break out and escape. The lines were soon a shambles, the ground strewn with dead and wounded horses and mules.

'The horses on picket lines near the foot of the hill were frantic with fear as shells burst round them,' Young recalled. 'The poor, helpless creatures stood in rows having their guts blown out, and it looked as if their riders would be soon treated in a like manner.'

Then the German artillery concentrated heavy shrapnel fire over the Union position to provide cover for an attempt by the German riflemen to storm it. According to one account 1 200 shrapnel shells were fired in one hour. But still the rifle fire from the schanzes was too steady and accurate, and the German attempt failed.

Some accounts tell of a German cavalry charge being beaten off but they do not make it clear at what stage point the action it took place.

Grant had been hit in one leg by a piece of shrapnel and tried to hand over command to Welby. With shrapnel and bullets sweeping the position no movement was possible within it and the adjutant had to shout the order to Welby at the foot of the kopje. However, the intense fire prevented Welby from climbing to the top of the kopje, where he had to be to exercise effective command, and Grant was obliged to resume it.

Colonel Grant, wounded in the left leg, is carried on a stretcher after being taken prisoner by the Germans. (Namibia Archives)

At Raman's Drift nothing had been heard from Sandfontein since the telephone line had gone dead – soon after the detachment there had used it to report that there was no sign of the enemy!

When gunfire was heard soon afterwards from the direction of Sandfontein Lukin ordered a squadron (100 men) of the SAMR from Raman's Drift and another from Houm's Drift further east (which had been occupied by Lieutenant-Colonel C A L Berrange) to ride to Sandfontein in case Grant needed help.

The squadron from Raman's Drift came across the waggons that had been carrying Grant's supplies and reserve ammunition, standing burned out in the road where they had been ambushed by a detachment with a machine-gun placed by von Heydebreck to intercept any reinforcements sent to Sandfontein.

Soon the reinforcements from Raman's Drift were under attack by the same force and found themselves pinned down by the well-placed machine-gun.

Over to the east the relieving force from Houm's Drift had also run into an ambush. The Germans at Sandfontein, given advance warning by the cloud of dust raised by the force, had sent a detachment of riflemen with two machine-guns to intercept them.

Pinned down and suffering heavy losses, the force sent a rider back to Houm's Drift with news of the ambush, which was immediately relayed to Lukin at Raman's Drift.

Lukin had already learned of the ambush of Grant's supply waggons from one of the escorting party who had escaped wounded.

He must also have received a report from a scout named Burgher who had been captured at the site of the ambush but managed to escape. The scout had been left in the charge of three German soldiers. When one was wounded, one of the others went off to get help. Seeing that the remaining guard was distracted by the nearby action, Burgher picked up a large rock and hit him on the head with it, knocking him out. Then he made a run for it and successfully made his way through the gunfire back to the Union forces.

It was only when Lukin received these reports that he realised that the Germans were between him and Sandfontein.

He later recalled that from Raman's Drift it had sounded as though only two guns were in action and they were assumed to be Grant's.

The news of the ambush of the relieving party from Houm's Drift, together with its report that at least four guns had been heard in action at Sandfontein, made it clear to Lukin that Grant was involved in something more than just a probing attack. He immediately moved out with 130 men of the SAMR – all that could be spared – and the remaining two guns.

About three miles from Sandfontein he came across the reinforce-

Under the eye of beefy German guards, some of the Sandfontein captives prepare to board a train to be taken to a prison camp. (Cape Archives)

ments that he had sent out earlier from Raman's Drift, still pinned down by machine-gun fire from von Heydebreck's skilfully placed blocking force.

The German commander's perfectly laid trap was now well and truly sprung.

At Sandfontein Grant's men had heard the sound of gunfire from the south and knew that relief forces were on the way. But when the sound of the distant gunfire died down and the Germans kept plastering the kopje with shrapnel Grant knew he and his men were on their own.

They were in a bad way. They were running out of ammunition – each man had arrived at Sandfontein with only the 120 rounds in his bandolier – and had no food. More than half the men had not eaten since the previous day and all were exhausted from lack of sleep.

Most of the wounded were lying where they had fallen, for the heavy German fire raking the position made it impossible to move them even after the medical orderlies had attended to them.

In mid-afternoon the defenders at Sandfontein saw heliograph signals from a hilltop in the direction of Raman's Drift but could not reply because of the heavy enemy fire.

Although he had the South Africans trapped, von Heydebreck was becoming worried as the afternoon wore on. He suspected that there were strong South African forces south of the Orange River, either at

Raman's Drift or on the way from Steinkopf, and he feared that if he could not capture Sandfontein quickly some of those forces might be brought up to the rescue.

In fact, Lukin had insufficient forces at his disposal to launch a powerful attack. At that point he had only 600 men: 200 guarding Houm's Drift and 170 guarding Raman's Drift and his line of retreat and the remaining 230 pinned down by the German forces blocking the way to Sandfontein.

Lukin had already done all he could to rescue Grant and his men. But the German commander did not know that. He ordered an intensified artillery bombardment preparatory to a bayonet charge of the Union positions.

Grant uses a crutch to walk among his German captors, presumably after getting off the train in the background. The man supporting him on his right appears to be wearing a South African tunic and may be his batman, Rifleman Scholl of the Transvaal Horse Artillery. (Namibia Archives)

Just then a white flag was seen waving from the kopje. Grant had bowed to the inevitable and surrendered. Not all the Germans saw the flag, it seems, for the heavy firing continued for fifteen minutes after it was first raised and the lieutenant holding it was wounded in the leg.

Grant said afterwards that he had held on as long as possible in the hope that 'some unexpected turn of events might bring relief but as the evening approached he realised that there was no such hope. The enemy, although repeatedly driven back, had worked themselves to positions close to the Union lines.

'The men had displayed great fortitude for ten hours under most trying conditions and I felt that to commit them to a hand-to-hand struggle in the dark against overwhelming numbers would mean their certain annihilation and a useless sacrifice of life, as no military objective was to be gained by further resistance.'

Grant admitted that he did not know at the time the extent of his casualties, although he knew they were heavy. He had in fact lost a third of his force. That the losses were not greater under the devastating fire poured on the kopje was attributed to the effectiveness of the schanzes built by the defenders and to the steadiness of their own fire.

The Germans actually had more men killed than the South Africans – 14 as against 12. The Union forces had 40 men wounded and the Germans 25.

So impressed was von Heydebreck by the brave fight of the SAMR that he paid them the supreme tribute of ordering their dead to be buried before his own. He allowed their captured comrades to attend the burial, and in a short speech at the graveside he praised the skill and courage of the South Africans, especially the artillerymen.

The German commander kept two South African doctors, Captain Holcroft and Captain Dalton, to look after the Union wounded whom he was taking into captivity, but he allowed an ambulance to return to Raman's Drift with some of the seriously wounded men.

He allowed his prisoners to write hasty letters to be taken with the returning ambulance. They were censored by a German officer who could speak English. In one letter, mentioning that a German shell had blown up one of the South African ambulances, the censoring officer inserted the words 'by accident'.

In return for these favours, von Heydebreck asked that the returning ambulance might take letters from his men to their families in Germany. When these reached Raman's Drift it was found that most of them had been addressed to Germany by way of New York for the United States was then still neutral.

Von Heydebreck's last act was to blow up the wells. Then he gathered his force and his prisoners and marched off to Warmbad, leaving Sandfontein to Lukin and the dead.

★ ★ ★ ★ ★

Lukin did not immediately reoccupy Sandfontein. He withdrew his forces back across the Orange River. His own commanders now suspected what had made it possible for von Heydebreck to launch an attack in such strength on Sandfontein: that the Germans knew that they would not have to face an attack from the Union forces in the Upington sector because the commander of those forces was about to rebel against his government and go over to the German side. This was why von Heydebreck had felt confident enough to withdraw his troops from his eastern border, leaving it unguarded, and throw them into the attack on Sandfontein.

Within a few weeks Lukin and much of his force had temporarily abandoned the war against the Germans to fight in South Africa against the rebels.

References

1. Rayner, W S (with O'Shaughnessy W W), *How Botha and Smuts Conquered German South West;* private publication, 1915.
2. Young, P J, *Boot and Saddle,* Maskew Miller, Cape Town, 1955; p. 159.

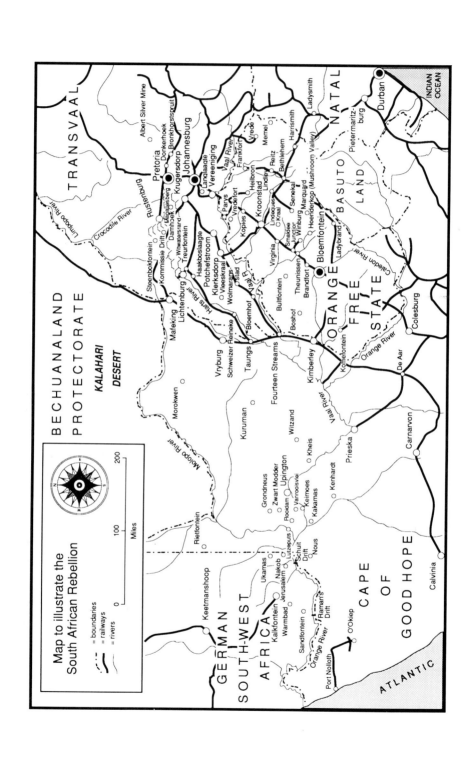

Map to illustrate the
South African Rebellion

- · - · - = boundaries
_____ = railways
~~~~~~~ = rivers

N

W   E

S

0   100   200

Miles

CHAPTER

5

Blood Against Blood

The Union was very young, only four years old, when its unity was put to the cruel test of rebellion.

For three months the country hung in uncertainty, not knowing whether it would be plunged into full-scale civil war or whether the nation would survive in its existing form. Armed men rode in the night, some inspired to rebellion by a latter-day prophet. Towns were attacked, occupied or besieged, shops looted, stores commandeered, railway lines sabotaged and telephone lines cut. Loyal troops hunted the rebels across the Transvaal, through the Orange Free State and the northern Cape Province, while newspapers reported the growing roll of dead.

Communities were split. Families feuded as fathers and sons and brothers took opposing sides for or against the rebellion.

In the infant Union, loyalties tended to be to the known past rather than to the uncertain present. Scars still fresh from the Boer War burst and bled as English-speaking South Africans, most of them intensely loyal to the Crown, rallied to the call of London while many of their Dutch-speaking countrymen turned angrily away; and some looked to Berlin.

The split was deeper and more painful among the Dutch-speaking people themselves than it was between them and the English-speakers. Many Dutch-speakers had never supported the Act of Union. They were still bitterly resentful of the British conquest of the republics that their people had made for themselves after generations of trying to escape from the imperial grasp. They felt no loyalty to the Crown and saw no reason to fight England's wars.

For some of these people the outbreak of war between Britain and Germany was an opportunity to throw off the 'British yoke' and restore the republics of the Transvaal and the Orange Free State.

Some thought that their Dutch origin made them closer kin to the Germans than to the English, and they felt greater sympathy for the cause of Berlin than that of London. Far from seeing themselves as traitors, some of those who rose in rebellion saw Botha as the traitor, betraying his forebears and his compatriots.

Hurt though he undoubtedly was at finding himself the central figure in a dispute splitting his own people, Botha was in no doubt about the rights and wrongs of the question, and events were to show that he had the majority of the Dutch-speakers on his side.

Botha tried desperately to quell the dissension. Hearing of De la Rey's intention to call the meeting at Treurfontein, Botha visited his old friend and comrade-in-arms and argued and knelt in prayer with him in an attempt to persuade him to oppose rebellion.

De la Rey had great respect for Botha, but he was also strongly influenced by a farmer, Niklaas van Rensburg, who was widely reputed in the Lichtenburg district to be a seer. De la Rey had come to have much faith in Van Rensburg's oracular powers after he had made some apparently veridical prophecies in the Boer War. Among a series of visions which Van Rensburg claimed to have had there was one in which the old Boer Republics would be restored. The figure fifteen appeared prominently in one vision, and it certainly turned out later to have a momentous connotation; but not in the way that the seer predicted.

While public controversy raged over the Government's apparent intention to take South Africa into the war, the Government itself was quietly going ahead with its preparations.

On August 21 the South African military commanders met at Defence Headquarters in Pretoria to plan a strategy for the invasion of South West Africa.[1] General Smuts, as Minister of Defence, presided. Others at the table included the commanders of the two branches of the Union Defence Force: Brigadier-General C F Beyers, Commandant-General of the Citizen Force (which consisted of the men undergoing training in the Active Citizen Force and the trained men in the Reserves) and Brigadier-General Lukin, commander of the Permanent Force, which consisted of the five regiments of the South African Mounted Riflemen. Only one of these regiments, the Cape Mounted Riflemen, had a full military background; the others had been formed from mounted police units.

Also present at the meeting were Sir Duncan McKenzie, formerly Commandant-General in Natal; Colonel P S Beves, the Commandant of Cadets; Colonel P C B Skinner, a British Army officer on loan to the UDF as an instructor; and Sir William Hoy, general manager of the South African Railways.

It was decided that an invasion force should be landed at Luderitz-bucht to seize the wireless station, while the Royal Navy would be asked to destroy the wireless station at Swakopmund by bombardment. Lukin would land with another force at Port Nolloth and march north to take the pressure off the Luderitzbucht force. A third force, under Lieutenant-Colonel S F Maritz, commander of UDF units in the northern Cape, would assemble at Upington to threaten the eastern border of South West Africa.

General Beyers must have been a troubled man as he sat and listened to the invasion plans, for he was opposed to them. Yet he did not declare his opposition and was assumed to support the plans. Nobody at the meeting, except perhaps Beyers himself, could foresee that within a few weeks he would be leading a rebellion against the government, or that he would die in doing so.

The lawyer-turned-soldier from the Cape was one of the most tragic figures of the rebellion. When the Boer War broke out Beyers was only twenty and practising law in Pretoria. His qualities of leadership quickly took him to the upper ranks of the Boer command, and when the opposing sides met at Vereeniging to sign the treaty ending the war he was appointed chairman of the conference.

Afterwards, when the British gave responsible government to the Transvaal, he became Speaker of its Parliament. At Union he is said to have hoped to become Speaker of the Union Parliament, but when he failed to get the appointment he accepted the post of Commander of the UDF Citizen Forces. As such he was expected to play a leading

'Manie' Maritz in the field with some of his rebels, most of whom seem to be wearing civilian clothing. (SADF Archives)

part in the hostilities when South Africa entered the war against Germany.

That he ended up leading the rebels opposed to that declaration showed the depth of the fissure that was struck in South African society by entry into the war.

It was later suspected that Beyers was aware as he sat at the meeting in Pretoria that the man who was to lead the third force at Upington, Lieutenant-Colonel Maritz, was already planning rebellion. But there is no certain evidence of that.

Maritz had almost certainly already sought help from the Germans in South West. He was well placed to do so as commander of SADF forces in the north-western Cape, which borders on South West. Evidence emerged after the rebellion that he had been negotiating with the Germans since 1912 for help in an uprising in South Africa.

Even if Beyers had not told him of the planned invasion of South West he could guess that it was coming, and he clearly had no intention of cooperating in it.

On August 23 he went to Schuit Drift, ostensibly to investigate the incident of the South African farmers. Crossing over the river to the police post on the German side, he telephoned to the German army commander at Keetmanshoop, apologised for the shooting of the German soldier by the farmers, and asked for arms and ammunition for an uprising in South Africa.

Political opposition to the invasion continued to increase in South Africa. Outright condemnation of any form of warlike action against German South West was expressed on August 26 by the National Party, which had been formed only in January by General J B M Hertzog, after he had split from Botha's South African Party over the question of the protection of Afrikaner identity.

Now another of the leading players in the rebellion showed his hand. Major Christoffel Kemp, commander of the SADF training camp at Potchefstroom in the Eastern Transvaal, handed in his resignation after a meeting with General Beyers in Pretoria. Much more was to be heard of this able soldier in the coming weeks.

Beyers himself resigned two days later, on September 15, after receiving an envoy from Maritz. His action came as a shock to the Government, which had been suspicious of Maritz but not of Beyers.

Apparently believing that the Government would try to suppress publication of his letter, Beyers released it to the press on the day when he handed it to Smuts. The Minister of Defence appears nevertheless to have succeeded in delaying publication of the statement to enable his own response to be published simultaneously. Both letters appeared in the newspapers on September 21, without any explanation of why the press had agreed to hold up Beyers's letter.[2]

He reminded Smuts in his letter that he had told him and Botha in August that he was opposed to 'sending commandos to German South West Africa to conquer it'. He had been about to resign then, but had delayed because Parliament was soon to open. Although Parliament had supported the decision of the Government, he was convinced that the great majority of the Dutch-speaking people strongly objected to crossing the frontier. He challenged the Government to appeal to the people and obtain any other result.

Recalling that the Government had referred to barbarous acts by the Germans in Europe, Beyers said: 'We have forgiven but not forgotten all the barbarities perpetrated in this, our own country, during the South African War. With few exceptions, all farms, not to mention many towns, were Louvains, of which we now hear so much'.

Beyers accused the Government of trying falsely to intimidate the public by claiming to have information that Germany intended to annex South Africa. But any annexation would be hastened if South Africa invaded South West Africa without provocation.

Beyers then made a statement that seems strange in the light of Maritz's subsequent treachery. He said the Government's allegations that the border of the Union had been violated by the Germans had been disproved by Maritz, who was near the frontier and therefore in a position to know.

Whatever happened in South Africa, he said, the war would be decided in Europe. If Germany won there, and then attacked South Africa, and Britain were unable to defend the Union 'we should at least have a sacred and clean cause in defending our country to the utmost provided we stay within our own borders'.

There were only seven thousand German troops in South West Africa, not enough for an attack on the Union. But if it were attacked, 'Boer and Briton will defend this country side by side', and he would be willing to lead them.

Beyers said he had accepted his post under the Defence Act, which stipulated that South African troops could serve only in defence of the Union. That could not be changed by an informal resolution of Parliament.

The Defence Act 'does not allow us to go and fetch the enemy over the frontier and to light the fire in that way, but should the enemy penetrate into our country it will be our duty to drive him back and pursue him in his own territory'.

Beyers protested strongly against units of the Citizen Force being sent across the border: 'Who can tell where the fire the Government has decided to light, will end?'

Formally resigning his post as Commandant-General and his commission, Beyers said: 'For me, this is the only way of faith, duty and

South African defectors Chris Kemp (left) and 'Manie' Maritz (right) pose for the camera, with a third defector whose identity is uncertain. The photograph must have been taken in South West Africa, for the two on the left are wearing German tunics. (War Museum)

honour towards my people, of which mention was made by General Botha. I have always tried to do my duty according to my best convictions and it sorely grieves me that it must end this way.'

Smuts's response was scathing. He said he knew that Beyers objected to war operations in German South West but had not thought he would resign. All the information that the Government possessed had been given to Beyers, all its plans had been discussed with him and his advice had largely been followed. The plan now being followed was essentially that recommended by Beyers at the officers' conference.

Smuts recalled that before going to Parliament he had instructed Beyers to go to the German border. It had been well understood that

Beyers would take chief command of the operations in German South West.

Smuts said Beyers had thought that Parliament would refuse to approve the Government's action: yet 'now you make your disappointment your reason for your unexpected action'.

Beyers had given the reasons for his resignation to the press before they had even reached the Government. His resignation had 'made a most unpleasant impression on my colleagues and myself'.

Smuts castigated Beyers for attacking Britain over its actions during the Boer War while he was commanding the army of a Dominion. His reference to barbarous acts during that war could not justify the criminal devastation of Belgium 'and can only be calculated to sow hatred and division among the people of South Africa'.

Since the Boer War, said Smuts, Britain had given South Africa its freedom under a constitution 'which allows you to write with impunity a letter for which you would without doubt be liable in the German Empire to the extreme penalty'.

Neither Britain nor South Africa was the aggressor. Now 'our coast is threatened, our mailboats are arrested and our borders are invaded by the enemy'.

Smuts rejected assertions that the German violation of the Union border had been involuntary and denied that any apology had been received by the Government.

He took special umbrage at a veiled suggestion in Beyers's letter that a seven-million-pound loan to the Union Government from Britain was a bribe.

'It only shows the extent to which your mind has become obscured by political bias,' Smuts wrote. 'You speak of duty and honour. My conviction is that the people of South Africa will in these dark days, when [they and] the Government are put to the supreme test, have a clearer conception of duty and honour than is to be deduced from your letter and action.

'For the Dutch-speaking section in particular, I cannot conceive of anything more fatal and humiliating than a policy of lip-loyalty in fair weather and a policy of neutrality and pro-German sentiment in days of storm and stress.'

There might be a limit to what the Government could do, but Smuts was convinced that the people would support the Government in the way that was 'the only legitimate one to fulfil their duty to South Africa and to the Empire and maintain their dearly-won honour unblemished for the future'.

Smuts ended his letter with a curt: 'Your resignation is hereby accepted.'

Although the letters were not published until some time afterwards,

Beyers's resignation became known immediately on September 15. It was one of two developments on that momentous day that were to make the prophet Van Rensburg's words ring eerily in the memories of his listeners.

References

1. Collyer, p. 27.
2. *The Star,* September 21 1914.

CHAPTER

6

The Storm Breaks

On the evening of the day he resigned, Beyers left in haste by car for Potchefstroom with De la Rey, whom he had summoned to Pretoria.

Near Johannesburg they came to a roadblock set up by police hunting for a notorious band of criminals, the Foster gang, who had that morning murdered a detective and fled in a car.

Earlier that evening a medical doctor, Gerald Grace, had been shot dead at another roadblock when he ignored the police order to stop. Beyers and De la Rey did the same but were luckier; the police refrained from shooting. But luck ran out for De la Rey when, in a blinding dust-storm, they came to another roadblock at Langlaagte and again ignored the order to halt.

After one policeman had tried unsuccessfully to stop the car by thrusting his bayonet between the spokes of a rear wheel, another policemen fired at a rear tyre. The shot hit the road and the ricochetting bullet went through the rear of the car and struck De la Rey in the back.

De la Rey said to Beyers in Dutch, 'That has hit me'. Then, Beyers said later, he 'stretched himself backwards with a groaning noise three or four times', then died.[1]

His death shocked the nation, for he was widely respected on all sides. De la Rey had helped capture the Jameson raiders and had been one of the most brilliant generals in the Boer War. He had been one of the signatories of the peace treaty that ended it and he had attended the National Convention and helped draft the Union constitution. At union he had been appointed a senator and had become a leading political figure. During the 1914 strike on the Witwatersrand he had efficiently commanded the government forces that had quelled it.

When De la Rey was shot Beyers abandoned the journey to Potchefstroom and its purpose has remained an intriguing mystery ever since. Many believed he and De la Rey were going to join Kemp in starting a rebellion.

Most of the members of a judicial commission appointed to inquire into the incident found that there were good grounds for believing it was so. The chairman of the inquiry was convinced that it was.

The British historian, Sir Charles Lucas, in a review written shortly after the end of the war, said: 'The plain facts of the case were that the late Commandant-General of the armed forces of the Union, having divested himself of his official duties to the government, having issued a manifesto, for which, as General Smuts told him in the plainest words, he would in the German Empire have been liable to the extreme penalty, having had the latest first-hand information from his traitorous subordinate on the German frontier, was hurrying, in company with the man whose name and character carried most weight in the Western Transvaal, to a camp whose commandant, having taken counsel with him, had also thrown up his charge, and where fifteen hundred young men under arms had been inoculated with the disloyal talk of their officers.'[2]

Later, on September 27, in a courtroom 'crowded to suffocation', Beyers told the commission of inquiry that he and De la Rey had been on their way to Lichtenburg by way of Potchefstroom to hold meetings at both places. The intention was to tell the people what was going on and to leave the matter in their hands. Beyers said he had also intended to go to the army camp at Potchefstroom to tell the men there about his resignation and about Parliament's action. He was convinced, he said, that the Government was suppressing his letter.[3]

Beyers testified that De la Rey had told him he was against the decision to invade South West Africa. In response to a question, Beyers said he was not aware that De la Rey had voted in Parliament in favour of the resolution supporting the invasion.

Beyers's evidence was contradicted on a crucial point by the Deputy Commissioner of Police, Colonel Douglas, who testified that immediately after the shooting Beyers had told him that he and De la Rey had been on their way to spend a holiday on De la Rey's farm.

Senator G G Munnik told *The Star* in an interview that on the day he died De la Rey had told him that he was not going to join the Hertzogites but was fighting against what he thought was a wrong principle (in the decision to invade South West).[4] De la Rey had said that the territory was bound to come into the melting-pot at the end of the war and that no lives should be sacrificed for it.

Whatever De la Rey's intentions had been, his death came as a shock to the country in which he was a universally respected figure. It was widely mourned – and exploited politically.

Condolences and tributes came from all over the country and from abroad, the British Government included. Thousands filed past his body as it lay in the Dutch Reformed Church in Koch Street. Many of those who came were Boers who had fought under him in the Anglo-Boer

War and who remembered, among his many exploits, how he had pioneered the mounted charge by Boers firing from the saddle.

A service conducted in the church was attended by Prime Minister Botha, who, according to newspaper accounts, seemed 'greatly affected by the death of his old friend'. The officiant at the service, the Rev H S Bosman said that the Union had never experienced such critical times. The foundations of church, state, school and home were being shaken. It was the duty of the people to obey their rulers, the preacher said. He was opposed to mutiny and he believed De la Rey was, too.

After the service the coffin was carried 'through streets thickly lined with people' to the railway station to be taken to Lichtenburg for the funeral.[5]

On the day of the funeral, September 29, the car in which De la Rey had died appeared in a prominent position in the market square at Lichtenburg. It had clearly been put there for political purposes, for it was not De la Rey's car but belonged to Beyers, if not to the Union Defence Force.

In a speech at the graveside, Beyers gave no overt support to rebellion. There were angry mutterings, however, among the western Transvalers inspecting the bullet hole in the car and the bloodstains on the seat. The next day the car was used as a speakers' platform at a public meeting to discuss the war issue.[6] A copy of Beyers's letter of resignation was pasted on the windscreen. Kemp, acting as chairman, urged moderation and when a flag of the old Orange Free State Republic

Nakob Police Station, bullet-riddled and ransacked after being stormed by the Vrij Korps. (Cory Library)

was unfurled he asked that it be put down. Later somebody waved the Transvaal Republic flag but Beyers told the crowd: 'We don't want any of that nonsense here.'

Now another Boer War hero, General Christiaan de Wet of the Free State, made his entry into the controversy. Climbing onto the car, he told the crowd: 'We are not going to soil our hands by taking part in an unjust war'. When someone said it might be too late, since the Germans were already fighting, De Wet replied: 'Rather be too late than one minute early in an unjust war.'

Beyers, responding to a suggestion that all UDF officers be called on to resign, said that that had never been his intention; they should stay at their posts. He said he was sorry that the Government was suppressing the contents of his letter of resignation. Rebellion was the thing furthest from his mind and he hoped everyone would obey the laws.

With only a minority of those present voting, the meeting adopted a resolution declaring that the Government had decided to invade German South West Africa without consulting the people, and the members of the UDF who had been sent across the border should be recalled.

At similar meetings in the next few days at Klerksdorp in the western Transvaal and at Kopjes in the Free State, resolutions were adopted opposing the campaign in South West. At the meeting at Kopjes the local magistrate read out a telegram from the Government saying that it would not call out the National Reserve. But De Wet said there was no guarantee that burghers would not be called up if the army could not get enough volunteers.

Botha soon made it clear that only volunteer forces would be used in the campaign; but his clarification came too late for many who might otherwise have balked at rebellion.

The clarification was given on September 28 at a public meeting at Bank Station, where Botha addressed a large audience.[7]

He declared that Germany was looking for a place to send its surplus population and South Africa looked to them like 'a fat lamb waiting to be killed'. German agents had already done great harm with seditious talk.

Botha said he had information about German ambitions in South Africa that would make people's hair stand on end. But he did not tell his audience what the information was.

Some said that the Government should have consulted the public before agreeing to capture the wireless stations in South West Africa, he said, but what was the good of a government that was not prepared to accept its responsibilities? Surely the Government was there to give the lead? If the Government had refused the British request it would have had no alternative but to resign.

The British might then have asked the Australians to do the job or they might even have sent Indian troops to South West and after the war it might have told the Indians they could settle in the territory. Botha asked whether that would have been in South Africa's interest.

Declaring that the Government had taken the only course that was honest and manly, Botha said: 'The British government must be able to look straight into our eyes and be able to see what is in our minds.'

He denied that there was any question of aggrandizement or annexation behind the decision. However, after pointing out that the war would be decided on the battlefields of Europe, he went on to say: 'But if it is decided in the end that German South West is to become British then we shall want to have a say in the matter, that it shall become part of the Union. And what say should we have if we were to sit here with our arms folded in neutrality?'

Repeating the assertion that the Germans coveted South Africa, Botha asked why, if they had never crossed the border, the magistrate of Rietfontein was now a prisoner of the Germans. What Botha did not disclose (perhaps he did not yet know it himself) was that Rietfontein had been captured not by the Germans but by the Vrij Korps, a force made up of dissident Boers who had refused to accept British rule after the Anglo-Boer War and had gone into exile in South West Africa. It was led by Andries de Wet.

Botha made it clear, however, that the Government's decision to invade South West had been dictated not by the German incursions but by the British request to seize the wireless stations.

Rejecting assertions that the Defence Act prohibited Union troops from crossing the border, Botha said that the Act specified that they might serve 'inside or outside the Union'.

The Prime Minister expressed regret at Beyers's resignation and described his letter as nothing but a political manifesto.

A resolution supporting the decision to invade South West was put to the meeting, those in favour being asked to stand on the right of the platform and those against on the left. Newspaper reports said those supporting the motion outnumbered those against by at least ten to one.

Similar support was expressed at other public meetings in the Transvaal and the Free State.

By the beginning of October the public knew of Lukin's crossing of the Orange, of Grant's defeat at Sandfontein and of the South African landing at Luderitzbucht. The Government had in addition published the contents of a manifesto being circulated by De Wet of the Vrij Korps among Dutch-speaking citizens in the northern Cape. The manifesto declared that the Germans were willing to help the Dutch to throw off the British yoke and were placing artillery, gunners, rifles, ammunition, horses, saddles and all other necessary equipment at the disposal of the Korps.

The Star told its readers that Germans in South West Africa were being told in an official notice that thousands of Dutch South Africans were joining the Germans to help to make the whole of South Africa a German colony.[8]

This danger had been foreseen years ago, the newspaper said, by 'Onze Jan' Hofmeyr when he had protested against the British government allowing Germany to annex South West Africa.

The public temper was now thoroughly inflamed, as was dramatically shown on October 3 when De Wet and Kemp addressed about eight hundred people in the Lyric Bioscope Hall in Potchefstroom.[9] A large crowd of Government supporters gathered outside and, finding that the doors had been barricaded, flung dead cats, rotten eggs and bricks through the open windows. Then the main door was battered down and fists flew as those inside the hall tried to repel the invaders.

'Pandemonium reigned supreme,' *The Star* reported, until someone turned the lights out in the hall. De Wet announced that the meeting would continue outside the Dutch Reformed Church. As he and his audience left more rotten eggs were thrown at them.

At the church there was a peaceful and picturesque scene. It was Nagmaal, when countryfolk came into town for the periodic celebration of communion, and ox-waggons and tents were clustered beneath the spire, bathed in moonlight. Into this quiet setting marched De Wet and his followers, and behind them came their noisy opponents.

De Wet stood on a cart and, in a speech interrupted by hooting and singing, condemned the invasion of South West. His supporters adopted a resolution supporting this sentiment and dispersed. Not so the opposition, which marched through the town to the market square singing 'We are Soldiers of the King', 'Britons Never Shall be Slaves' and 'God Save the King'. Botha and Smuts were cheered and De Wet booed.

The public were now sharply divided over the question of invasion. Most English-speakers and a majority of Dutch-speakers were behind Botha; some Dutch-speakers were opposed to the invasion and some were still uncertain, even after the Bank Station speech, whether the government intended to use conscripts in the campaign.

The matter was of no consequence to those who, like Maritz, were concerned not so much with the morality of the invasion as with its value as a trigger for a rebellion aimed at breaking up the Union and restoring the old republics.

Smuts, by now thoroughly suspicious of Maritz, tried a stratagem to test his loyalty, or force his hand. By telegram, he asked whether Maritz could post a strong force near Schuit Drift to support Lukin's advance on Warmbad. Maritz replied that his forces were inadequate for the task and he personally would rather resign than lead them across the border. Smuts's suspicions about Maritz's intentions were heightened, if not confirmed.

Grant's defeat at Sandfontein was welcome news to advocates of rebellion. Coming at a time when the Allies were suffering setbacks against the Germans in Europe, it raised hopes of a German victory in the war and tipped the scales for many Dutch-speakers still uncertain about whether to support rebellion.

The spark of rebellion had already been fanned by the news of the capture of the Nakob police station on September 16, although it was not generally known at the time that it had been captured by Andries de Wet's Vrij Korps and not the Germans. The Government was for obvious reasons giving it out that it was the Germans.

Three days after seizing Nakob, the Vrij Korps captured Rietfontein, an even more isolated police post farther north on the border. The Germans had given the Korps a couple of artillery pieces (and presumably German gunners to operate them) and two machine-guns, and they were now quite a formidable little force. When they went into action against the Union forces they were led by Andries de Wet, with a large, black ostrich feather in his hat, and the Vierkleur flag of the old Transvaal Republic in the van.

While Maritz was obviously encouraged by these events, he kept his intentions hidden for the present. Smuts played for time. Forcing Maritz's resignation at that point would probably have precipitated the rebellion when Maritz had under his command nearly 3 000 men, most of whom might have joined his cause, before the Government had been able to get trustworthy troops to the area, first to stop Maritz taking his men across the border to join the Germans and then to put down his rebellion.

Botha felt that if there were to be a rebellion among the Dutch-speaking South Africans it was better for the sake of national unity that it should be put down by fellow Dutch-speakers than by English-speaking troops. Of the 30 000 Union soldiers deployed against the rebels, more than 20 000 were Dutch burghers in the Boer commandos. The Government nevertheless deemed it necessary to send English-speaking units, such as the Durban Light Infantry, to the northern Cape, and there were fights between them and Maritz's rebels after his insurrection had begun.

Ostensibly the additional troops being sent to the border area under Colonel Wylie of the DLI were reinforcements in the event of a German attack; but Maritz probably had no illusions about their true purpose, or of Smuts's appointment of Colonel (later General) Coen Brits to the overall command of the region.

While the Government was still waiting for the loyal troops to reach the area it received confirmation from loyal officers serving with Maritz that he had made an agreement with the German Governor of South West, Dr Seitz, and concern in Pretoria deepened.

As the loyal troops neared Upington, Smuts summoned Maritz to Pretoria but the instruction was ignored. On October 2 Maritz marched 900 of his troops westwards, ostensibly in compliance with the earlier proposal to station a strong force near Schuit Drift in support of Lukin. But on October 9, while camped at Vanrooisvlei (also known as Van Rooyen's Vlei) near the German border, he went into open rebellion. He read out to his assembled men his treaty with the Germans and declared that South Africa was now independent of the British Empire and at war with England.

Loyal forces hoist the Union Jack over a building in Keimoes after driving out the rebels. (Cape Archives)

That Maritz should have been placed by the UDF in a position to carry out this move is astonishing in the light of his background. During the Anglo-Boer War Salomon 'Manie' Maritz had served as an officer with the Boer forces. After the peace of Vereeniging he refused to take the oath of allegiance and went into exile, operating various ventures in Madagascar before going to German South West Africa, where he adopted German citizenship and helped the German colonial troops to put down the Herero rebellion.

On his return to the Transvaal in 1906, he was deported, but came back after union in 1910 and, after a spell as a butcher in Braamfontein, Johannesburg, served with the South African Police. Then he joined the

UDF, took a course for staff officers and, at the behest of General Beyers, was appointed District Staff Officer in the north-western Cape, an isolated position far from his superiors' eyes and ideal for establishing contact with the Germans.

The report of the commission of inquiry into the rebellion described Maritz as 'a man of violent temper [who] appears to have been in the habit of frequently expressing anti-British feelings'. But Brigadier-General J J Collyer, in his account of the campaign in South West Africa, says that Maritz was not so much anti-English as resentful of the loss of his country's independence to the British.[10] Collyer describes him as 'a fine guerrilla fighter possessed of abundant courage and great physical strength [who] would brook no opposition to any scheme upon which he was bent.'

Maritz's physical strength was testified to by Deneys Reitz, who was with him in Madagascar. In his book *Trekking On* Reitz describes how he saw Maritz pick up a small Madagascan ox that had charged him and hurl it bodily away.[11]

Beyers may have regretted his part in the placing of Maritz in the north-western Cape, for there is some evidence that he started the rebellion prematurely. Pieter de Wet of the Vrij Korps is supposed to have said that Maritz had received a letter from Beyers in September instructing him to hold his hand until Beyers made the first move.

Lieutenant Cecil Freer of the Kaffrarian Rifles, who challenged Maritz to a duel when he went into rebellion at Vanrooisvlei. (Cory Library)

When he rose in rebellion at Vanrooisvlei, Maritz could not be sure of the support of all the men under his command, who were mostly members of the Active Citizen Force doing a training camp at Upington, so he used a subterfuge to disarm those who he thought might be loyal to the Government.

He was particularly worried about a machine-gun unit with four machine-guns. He had good cause, according to an account given later by the unit's commander, Lieutenant Cecil Freer, a King William's Town dentist serving with the Kaffrarian Rifles.

Freer said that Maritz paraded the men on the pretext of handing out their pay and, while they stood unarmed, some of his trusted men secretly seized the machine-guns. Maritz then declared his rebellion and

According to the Namibia Archives records, these are German soldiers posing beside a railway truck on which stands someone holding the Vierkleur flag of the old Transvaal Republic. They may in fact be Vrij Korps members, for the Korps fought under the vierkleur and not all of those in the picture are wearing full German uniform. (Namibia Archives)

told those who refused to join him to form up on the left, promising that they would be released, but without their weapons.

Freer, who appears to have been as naive as he was plucky, demanded the return of his machine-guns so that his men and the rebels could fight it out. When Maritz refused, Freer, who seems from his photograph to have been slightly-built, challenged him to settle the matter in a duel with swords, revolvers or even fists.[12]

Maritz spurned the challenge and seems not to have been amused by its ingenuousness. Either out of perfidy or anger, he reneged on his promise to free the loyalists and made prisoners of all those who refused to join him except 180 loyal burghers, who were released. The others were handed over to the Germans, a detachment of whom arrived at Vanrooisvlei the next day with De Wet's Vrij Korps – further evidence of Maritz's prior collaboration with the Germans.

With Maritz now openly siding with the Germans and rebellious talk swelling in the Union, the Government on October 12 declared martial law throughout South Africa.

Even Maritz's family were split by the rebellion. His uncle, Gert Maritz, assistant field cornet of the Delport's Hope Defence Rifle Association, wrote a letter to the English-language press expressing his sorrow and disgust at his nephew's 'traitorous conduct' and declaring: 'I would like publicly to disown him and to entirely disapprove of his shameful treachery.'

Maritz had agreed to a German request to attack Upington but he delayed doing so while he tried to find out what Beyers and De Wet were planning to do. He temporised by briefly occupying Keimoes, on

Records in the Cape Archives say this picture shows German forces identifying their dead after the action at Keimoes. The men in the centre certainly are wearing German uniforms, which means either that German troops took part in the action or that the men were members of the Vrij Korps wearing German uniforms. (Cape Archives)

the Orange River between Upington and Kakamas. Twice more he set out to attack Upington but each time turned back.

Instead he occupied Kakamas and declared a republic. Then he sent a force to occupy Kenhardt and other detachments south towards Calvinia and Carnarvon in the apparent hope that the people there would rise and join his rebellion. In fact, his emissaries received such a hostile reception from the local inhabitants that one detachment surrendered to the Government forces, which soon captured the other.

The loyal troops, under Brits, had meanwhile reached Keimoes, where Maritz attacked them on October 22. Maritz was wounded in the knee and his force retreated to Kakamas, where they were defeated by Brits two days later.

Unable to ride a horse, Maritz made a somewhat undignified exit from the battlefield at Keimoes in a motor car pulled by a team of mules and fled across the border to Jerusalem in German South West.

It would not be long, however, before Maritz would ride again.

References

1. *The Star,* September 26 1914.
2. Lucas, Sir Charles, *The Empire at War,* Oxford University Press; chapter entitled 'The South African Rebellion', p. 387.
3. *The Star,* September 28 1914.
4. *Ibid,* September 16 1914.
5. *Ibid,* September 19 1914.
6. *Ibid,* September 22 1914.
7. *Ibid,* September 29 1914.
8. *Ibid,* October 2 1914.
9. *Ibid,* October 3 1914.
10. Collyer, p. 33.
11. Reitz, Deneys, *Trekking On,* Faber & Faber, 1933; p. 29.
12. Burton, A W, unpublished diaries and manuscripts in Cory Library, Rhodes University, Grahamstown.

7

Heroes in Flight

The news of Maritz's uprising in the northern Cape only two weeks after the defeat of the Union forces at Sandfontein was enough to ignite rebellion in the Transvaal and the Free State. Within days De Wet, with Kemp at his side, had addressed another meeting at Kopjes to call his followers to arms, and the rebellion had begun in the Transvaal; not unexpectedly, at Lichtenburg.

There some of the commandos being assembled for service mutinied. It is not clear whether they were to have served within the borders of the Union or beyond, and perhaps it made no difference to them. They began holding up trains and commandeering supplies. Beyers, too, assembled a force in the Magaliesberg, disregarding a manifesto issued by the Dutch Reformed Church condemning rebellion as 'a faithless breach of the treaty signed at Vereeniging and a positive sin against God'.

Beyers's rebellion was short-lived, however. Little more than a week after setting out with his force it was attacked by Government troops at Kommissie Drift, near Rustenburg, and dispersed.

Now in flight, Beyers joined Kemp, whose force had already lost several men killed or captured by Government troops near Treurfontein.

From the joint force, now down to about 2 000 men, Beyers called for volunteers to ride with Kemp to South West to bring back rifles and ammunition obtained from the Germans by Maritz. With about 800 men, Kemp set out on November 2 on what was to be an heroic trek and one of the few achievements of great merit by the rebels.

Beyers then headed for the Free State with about 1 200 men in an attempt to join up with De Wet. Apprised *en route* of an offer of amnesty to rebels who laid down their arms and went home, he telegraphed acceptance to the Government on condition that none of the rebels would be prosecuted and that only volunteers would be used in the invasion of German South West.

This was in turn accepted by the government but Beyers insisted on first being given a safe conduct to meet De Wet to discuss the matter with him. While the government was trying to arrange the meeting his forces twice clashed with loyal troops, and lost several hundred men captured.

Then on November 16 the remainder of Beyers's force was scattered in a fight with troops near Bultfontein, and he ended up on the run with only a handful of followers.

After three weeks of being hunted through the Free State, Beyers and his band were trapped against the flooded Vaal River. All surrendered except Beyers and a companion, who rode their horses into the river and tried to swim across as their pursuers fired on them. Both were swept away by the swift waters and drowned. Beyers's body was pulled from the river, far downstream, several days later.

It was a brave but undignified ending for a man whose talents deserved better.

★ ★ ★ ★ ★

Kemp and his hard-riding commando had meanwhile struck deep into the Kalahari desert. After commandeering supplies at Schweizer-Reneke in the western Transvaal they headed for Kuruman, the little town built round an ever-flowing desert spring by the missionary and explorer Robert Moffatt, whose daughter was married there to David Livingstone.

Kemp's attempt to acquire more supplies and armaments was opposed at first by the small group of loyal commandos in the town

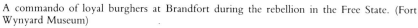

A commando of loyal burghers at Brandfort during the rebellion in the Free State. (Fort Wynyard Museum)

under the command of a lawyer named Frylinck. When the police and local officials surrendered the town anyway and allowed Kemp to help himself to horses and rifles, Frylinck withdrew into the desert with his little force of 80 men.

Then, when Kemp resumed his ride for the German border, Frylinck gave chase and harassed the rebels, like a terrier worrying a lion.

He was later joined by 300 more loyal Kuruman commandos who had been out on a patrol when Kemp entered the town. Either because he was forced to do so by the loyalists nipping at his heels or because he wanted to avoid the waterless stretch between Kuruman and the border, Kemp turned south towards the Orange River, despite the risk of being intercepted by loyal forces from Upington.

While his force was fighting with the Kuruman commando near Witsands a detachment of the Transvaal Scottish had to suffer the frustration of being prevented from joining in the fight.

'We could have gone to their assistance and smashed Kemp up and prevented him from going on to Upington and doing further damage,' Lieutenant S B Broome of the Transvaal Scottish recalled. 'All the men were straining at the leash and it required the utmost tact to stop open insubordination.'[1]

They were unaware then that Botha had ordered that the English-speaking regiments should as far as possible be kept out of action against the rebels.

The Imperial Light Horse had also been sent to the region but it too was held back at first from meeting Kemp's force. It did however capture a man considered to be a spy.

'Our pickets saw him coming over the sand dunes and as he came over each one he held up a white flag,' P W Hunter of the ILH wrote in his diary.[2] 'Three of our plain-clothes scouts went out to bring him in, and then all four were escorted in by six of the SAMR to our camp. The man, dressed in a sort of yellow corduroy, looked like an Italian but said he was a Frenchman.

'He said he had deserted from Kemp and wished to join us, saying he knew all Kemp's plans and would lead us to attack him. The man was suspected, searched and a despatch from Kemp to Maritz was found in his legging. He was sentenced to death and shot this morning.'

Three days later the ILH found itself in action against Kemp when it was sent out with the Natal Light Horse and loyal burgher commandos to intercept the rebels. Hunter was there to record it in his laconic style.

'We located Kemp with several hundreds of rebels at Rooidam, and the fun commenced. They were all over the show and the fight was awful. The rebels are deadly shots and are using dum–dum expanding

61

Captured rebels are marched off on foot by Union cavalrymen. (Cape Archives – AG)

bullets which, when they hit a man, make an awful mess. We lost five men killed (Ruxton, Oxenham, Sergeant-Major Grace, Lieutenant Froude and Whiteman), two died of wounds (Robinson and Galpin) and about 18 wounded.

'Our artillery put in some beauties and killed many rebels. The rebel casualties were much heavier than ours, though we don't know the exact number. The burghers also lost a few . . . Dozens of our horses were shot, including my own, so now there are several of us without horses until we get to Cape Town.'

Harassed almost all the way now by loyal forces, Kemp's commando fought as far as Swartmodder, only a few miles from the German border. But with refuge almost in sight, his fresher pursuers were fast catching up. Fate now presented him with a chance to shake them off and he seized and exploited it with brilliant audacity.

On his left were three sand-dune ridges lying parallel to his course. He swung into them and crossed over the first two lines of dunes, leaving a group of marksmen hidden behind the crest of the second dune. When the pursuers rode up they came under rapid fire at close range from the hidden marksmen and had to dismount hurriedly and take cover.

While they were thus distracted the main body of Kemp's force circled left and, crossing back over the dunes and across their own tracks, behind their pursuers, resumed their dash for the border.

Guarded by mounted loyalists, captured rebels sit beside a shed. The figure in white in the centre looks like a naval officer, but what a naval man would have been doing in this setting defies logical explanation. (Cape Archives)

Whether the marksmen were captured or escaped is not recorded, but the ruse enabled the rest of Kemp's force to get away.[3]

Soon afterwards they were met by a unit of the Vrij Korps that had come from South West to help them and which now escorted the tattered and tottering band into German territory.

It had taken Kemp nearly a month to complete his journey, trekking across long stretches of waterless desert and fighting off loyalist forces for a large part of the way. Only 500 men remained of the 800 with whom he had set out, and most of those had lost their horses and were marching and fighting on foot.

How hard the chase had been is indicated by a doctor serving with the government forces, who wrote: 'I had seen Kemp's pursuers pass through Prieska and, when they came back disappointed over his gallant escape, I saw their over-ridden, starving horses so desperately hungry that they devoured the guide ropes of a number of our tents.'

At Nakob on the German side of the border Kemp was met by Maritz, who immediately set about remounting and refitting the rebels while they recovered from their arduous trek.

Whatever the loyalists might have thought about the morality of Kemp's rebellious acts, none could question the courage, skill and fortitude with which he had led his men over more than 700 hostile miles.

★ ★ ★ ★ ★

In the Transvaal the rebellion petered out after Beyers's death. East of Pretoria a brief and ineffectual campaign was conducted by Christiaan Muller, a businessman of the city who had served with distinction as a commander during the Boer War. Muller's commando was surprised by a combined force of police and Carbineers early on the morning of November 6 while they were camped between two kopjes. The police dismounted and climbed one kopje while the Carbineers climbed the other.

'Suddenly a shot rang out, then another and another, after which it must have literally rained bullets on the men in the basin', wrote a member of the police detachment afterwards in the police magazine *Nongquai*. 'That they were taken by surprise was evident from the fact that only about three shots were fired by them in return. It was all over in a few minutes . . .'[4]

After the dispersal of Beyers's main force at Kommissie Drift scattered elements of it were chased northwards by loyal forces and captured one by one.

The most resolute of the Transvaal rebels was a soldier in the Union Defence Force, Jopie Fourie, who was reckoned to have caused more deaths than any other rebel before he was captured at Nooitgedacht on December 15 after a furious battle ending with a bayonet charge.

Cornered by a force of police and SAMR, Fourie's commando went to ground in a dry riverbed that gave them excellent cover. As the police force cantered up it came under 'a murderous flanking fire at phenomenally close range from an enemy totally concealed in the bush'. The rebels were ensconced behind the river banks and only their heads showed when they came up to fire.

The loyal forces worked their way closer to the river, 'bullets whining and spitting all around them as they moved from inadequate cover to inadequate cover'. With darkness now about to fall, the commanders decided that there was only one way to get the rebels out: with the bayonet.

The police, in an unaccustomed role, charged with the soldiers; in fact, the bayonet charge was led on one flank by Captain Fulton of the SAP. As the attackers leaped down into the river bed the rebels fired at them at point-blank range and there was merciless hand-to-hand fighting in the dusk. Sergeant Cullum of the SAP, hit in the right shoulder by a dum–dum bullet, drew his revolver with his left hand and tried to continue the fight, but collapsed. Sergeant Beart, with his right arm smashed above the elbow by a bullet, waded into the rebels with his left fist.

Several of the rebels were bayoneted before they had all surrendered. Only two of them were killed, however, and four wounded, while the SAP and SAMR lost 10 killed and 21 wounded.[5]

Because he was a serving soldier, had risen against his Governement without resigning his commission and had shot to kill at fellow soldiers, Jopie Fourie was court-martialled and shot by firing squad four days after being captured. As the only rebel to be executed Fourie inevitably became a martyr among supporters of the rebellion and his name has been honoured by some South Africans even among succeeding generations.

★ ★ ★ ★ ★

In the Free State the rebellion was more enterprising than in the Transvaal, with General de Wet and other rebel leaders rampaging spectacularly across half the province. Soon after the second meeting at Kopjes, De Wet began recruiting and on October 28 he entered the town of Vrede with 300 men.

There he made what became known as the 'five-bob speech', insulting the local magistrate, who had once fined him five shillings for striking a black man. He declared his intention to join up with Maritz and then march on Pretoria and proclaim South Africa an independent republic.

Continuing his recruiting march, he gathered men as he went and by the time he reached Lindley he had 1 200 mounted riflemen behind him. Looting shops for supplies, he went on, fighting a running skirmish with loyal forces from the Sand River to Winburg.

As the rebels approached Winburg, loyal commandos and a force of the SAP went out to intercept them, leaving a few civilians to defend the town. Deployed on a kopje at Doornberg, the loyal force watched the rebels approach in two lines of about 250 men each. Then a section charged the kopje. They were allowed to get to within 25 yards of the top of the kopje before the order to fire was given.

'The firing was sharp and from the front and side', recalled one of the policemen afterwards in *Nongquai*. 'The Excelsior and Thaba 'Nchu men who were in our troop behaved in a most gallant way and their fire was deadly. Not a shot was thrown away. The enemy were driven off in about seven minutes and they retreated to the positions we had previously occupied. White flags then began to pop up from behind various rocks and walls and the rebels were ordered to surrender. Eight were taken prisoners. We had three killed and six wounded. The enemy had 12 killed, 13 wounded and 11 captured in all.'

But the triumph of the loyal forces was brief. After leaving the kopje with their prisoners they ran into the main body of the rebels and came under heavy fire. Some distance away they could see the four troops of loyal commandos with whom they had left Winburg 'in full flight, no stand having been attempted'.

Abandoning their prisoners, the SAP troop made for a ridge and tried to make a stand but were outflanked and therefore retreated to Winburg.

'The enemy pursued us to within four miles of Winburg and were firing continuously, but there were no casualties on our side, their marksmanship being extremely poor.'

With the rebels apparently not intending to attack Winburg, the SAP contingent was pulled out and by November 9 was on guard outside Bloemfontein, where the government apparently feared an attack. But on that day De Wet entered Winburg and by now he was even more embittered than before, for his son had been killed in the fighting at Doornberg.

General Botha, on the trail of De Wet, rests on his campstool near Reitz in the Free State. On the right is a heliograph. (Cape Archives – AG)

He not only allowed his men to loot shops but also to rob private houses, to arrest the magistrate and assault the mayor. Then he headed east with a force now swollen to 4 000 men.

By now, however, General Botha himself was on De Wet's trail. Despairing of persuading Beyers and De Wet to abandon their uprising, he had come to the Free State to take charge of the Government forces.

Arriving in Winburg only a few hours after De Wet's departure on November 11, he found the place in disarray. 'Scarcely a thing could be got in the place,' recalled Moore Ritchie of Botha's bodyguard. 'Houses had been looted as well and in most of the stores the shutters were up and desolation abounded.'[6]

Botha left Winburg that night in pursuit of De Wet 'to the accompaniment of ringing cheers and shouts of encouragement' from the townsfolk and with the bodyguard whistling the tune of the latest popular song, 'It's a long way to Tipperary'.

'It was all quite stirring and enjoyable. But once clear of the town and engaged in one of General Botha's night marches, things rather ceased to be enjoyable,' Ritchie wrote later.

'During the all-night trek from Winburg . . . I had a first, thorough experience of the horrors of sleep fighting. It was bitterly cold – cold as the Free State night and veld knows how to be. And we could not smoke, could not talk above a faint murmur and nodded in our saddles.

'The clear stars danced fantastically in the sky ahead of us and the ground seemed to be falling away from us into vast hollows, then rising to our horses' noses ready to smash into us like an impalpable wall.'

Botha had failed in efforts to induce either Hertzog or former President Steyn of the Free State Republic to use their influence to dissuade De Wet from rebellion, Steyn taking the attitude that he could not do so without compromising his own opposition to the invasion of German South West. And it had proved impossible to bring Beyers and De Wet together to discuss the offer of amnesty.

Hard as it had been for Botha to send troops against the Boers with whom he had fought against the British in the South African War, it was even harder for him to take the field himself against his old wartime comrade, De Wet. A glimpse of Botha's distress is given by Ritchie, who describes how, while on guard in the grounds of the Prime Minister's residence in Pretoria, he would see, through a window, Botha sitting in the lamplight and talking with his aides and worrying late into the night about the cruel task facing him.[7]

As he pursued De Wet through the Free State, the usually cheerful Botha was grim and silent, Ritchie recalled.

'There was a sadness, there was a profound pathos about it. No wonder if it seemed to me that General Botha looked downcast, indeed, if stern as well, during the rebellion.'

Botha himself was later to say: 'For myself personally, the last three months have provided the most sad experiences of all my life. I can say the same for General Smuts . . . The war – our South African war – is but a thing of yesterday. You will understand my feelings and the feelings of loyal commandos when, among rebel dead and wounded we found, from to time, men who had fought in our ranks during the dark days of that campaign.'

From Winburg Botha headed south-east to Mushroom Valley, where his scouts had said that De Wet might halt for the night. Botha planned an encircling movement with forces under General Lukin, whom he had recalled from the invasion of South West to help to fight the rebels, and Coen Brits and a force under Colonel George Brand, son of the former President of the Free State, Sir John Brand.

Making only one brief stop in the march from Winburg, Botha's force reached Mushroom Valley just before dawn on November 12. Lukin, Brits and Brand were moving into position. It was still dark when Botha arrived in the big green Vauxhall open touring car that he used when not travelling on horseback. As the dawn light spilled into the valley Botha, sitting on his camp-stool, turned his binoculars on the tiny figures of De Wet's commando, 4 000 yards away.

The Cape Field Artillery rode up, unlimbered and trained their guns into the valley. Loyal commandos began galloping hell-for-leather on either flank. The rebels were beginning to stir round their cold campfires when Botha gave a curt order: 'Skiet!'[8]

The first shell bursting above the camp had a galvanising effect on the rebels.

'Move! I have never seen anything human break and scatter as those people did when the first 15-pounder shells dropped among them out of the still, sunlit morning,' Ritchie recalled.

Abandoning everything but their rifles, De Wet's men leaped on their horses and raced out of the valley – straight into the encircling loyal forces. After a short but hot fight, 3 000 of the rebels were captured and 22 lay dead. But the wily De Wet, as he had done so often against the British in the Boer War, slipped through the net and escaped with the rest of his force.

As the sun comes up over Mushroom Valley, Botha (left) trains his glasses on the attack that is to end effective action by De Wet in the rebellion. (Cape Archives)

But De Wet's rebellion was in effect broken, and Mushroom Valley became for him what Kommissie Drift had been for Beyers.

De Wet lost more men when he attacked Virginia Station four days later and was driven off by loyal forces. As he now fled westwards his force dwindled as rapidly as it had grown before Mushroom Valley. He crossed the main north-south railway line north of Vryburg and headed into the Kalahari with only about 100 men, making for German South West and a junction with Maritz and Kemp.

But hard on his heels was the determined and resourceful Coen Brits, who had declared rebellion a stain on his people's character. Switching from horses to cars, Brits's force picked off the stragglers from De Wet's shrinking band, then, when the cars outran petrol supplies, reverted to horses. The camels of the SAP post at Morokwen were commandeered to carry supplies over the desert.

Only once , near Morokwen, did the pursuers get near enough to open fire, wounding one of the rebels and killing three of their horses and getting their cars riddled with bullet holes in return.

Three weeks after the fight at Mushroom Valley, on December 2, the weary de Wet's pursuers caught up with him in Bechuanaland as he and his men stopped for a rest near the dry bed of the Molopo River. With two of his officers, De Wet made a break for freedom but his horse was too worn out to respond and he was headed off and captured.

De Wet told his captors that he had off-saddled only once, and then only briefly, in the past 50 miles. He confirmed that he was heading for South West, by way of Henning Vlei.[9]

Wessel Wessels and his lieutenants discuss surrender terms with troops of the Umvoti Mounted Rifles near Kestel in the Free State. (War Museum)

The hero of the Boer War, having been hunted and caught by his former comrades-in-arms, was taken back to his own country, a captive, to face trial for rebellion.

★ ★ ★ ★ ★

In the western Free State, where the uprising was led mainly by Rocco de Villiers, an attorney, the rebels did little apart from briefly occupying Parys, Vredefort and Kopjes.

In the east, however, they acted with greater vigour, led by a businessman from Reitz, Wessel Wessels , who openly proclaimed his support for Germany in its war against Britain. On October 24 a rebel force led by Niklaas Serfontein, the Member of Parliament for Frankfort, stormed and captured the town of Reitz. They held it for more than a month, with the support of most of the inhabitants, until Government forces reoccupied it on December 4.

Wessels had meanwhile seized Harrismith in an attack before dawn on November 2, in which his men stormed into the town hall, where the 200 men of the town guard lay sleeping, and captured them and their weapons. The rebels looted the town and sabotaged the railway to Natal by pulling up sections of the track.

The defenders of Bethlehem were not to be surprised so easily. They turned the Kaffrarian Mill into a fort, and the rebels were obliged to come into the town under a white flag on November 9 to demand its surrender. When that was refused they came back 600 strong in a mounted charge on the mill. But the fort held, and after three hours of ineffective shooting they gave up and departed.[10]

At the Haaksch railway bridge in the eastern Free State there was a contest of wills that sank to farce. After the rebels had blown up the bridge railway engineers went out with an escort in an armoured train and repaired it. That night the rebels blew it up again. Next day the railwaymen repaired it again. This went on for several days until the rebels changed tactics. After the railwaymen had passed by to repair the bridge yet again, the rebels pulled up a section of track behind them and lay in wait for the armoured train to return.

Detecting the sabotage on the way back, the railwaymen got out of the train to repair the track. As they lifted the first rail the hidden rebels opened fire. As one man, the railwaymen dropped the rail and ran for the sanctuary of the armoured train. But, being armoured, it had only one, very narrow, door. The ancient law of the survival of the fittest came immediately into effect and as bullets pinged off the armour beside them the 50 railwaymen fought each other for precedence.

Possibly because the rebels could not laugh and shoot simultaneously, only one of the railwaymen was wounded. He happened to be the last one in and he was hit in the last part of his body to pass through

With the rebellion broken in the Free State, Wessels's men come in to surrender at Kestell. (War Museum)

the door, which made it impossible for him to sit until the wound had healed.[11]

There was humour even in the act of looting shops for supplies. Deneys Reitz, who led a commando against the rebels in his native Free State, says in *Trekking On* that when the rebels commandeered supplies in Heilbron, most of their requisition notes were endorsed: 'Payable to bearer by the winning side.'

Rietz writes repeatedly about the lack of rancour among the rebel burghers, if not among their leaders. Describing how he accepted the surrender of a group of smiling rebels from his district, he says: 'To them, as to all the rebels I ever met, the rising was but a more acute phase of our original political differences, and I never came across one man who thought that he had committed an offence in taking up arms against the Government of his country.'

When a government commando from the Transvaal entered the Free State town of Reitz after chasing the rebels out, the inhabitants lining the streets were puzzled to see Boers instead of British troops coming in to occupy the dorp. An old woman rushed into the street and called out to the leading burgher: 'But where are the damned English?' He replied: 'Old woman, we *are* the damned English'.

Reitz (after whose forebears the town was named) tells this story in his book. But he also tells of the dejection on both sides, victors as well as vanquished, when David van Coller and his surrendering rebels rode past Reitz and his men as they sat their horses at the roadside.

'It was mournful to see the long files of sullen, dejected men ride past, many of them old friends, all of them our countrymen.'

On the day of the action at Mushroom Valley the Government offered an amnesty to all rebels who surrendered their arms and went home. Many rebels remained unaware of the offer, however, for some of their leaders kept it from them for fear that they might accept it and abandon the cause.

Even the rebel leaders in the east realised eventually that the defeat of Beyers and De Wet had made their cause hopeless. Wessels and his comrades surrendered, with 1 200 men, at Tiger River on December 8 and the rebellion in the Free State came to an end.

But in South West Africa Manie Maritz, in his sanctuary at Jerusalem, had nursed his grievances as well as his wound, and by December his knee was healed and he was ready to resume rebellion.

References

1. Juta, H C, *The History of the Transvaal Scottish,* Hortors, p. 86.
2. Hunter, P W, unpublished diary in library of National Museum of Military History, Johannesburg.
3. *Nongquai,* June 1914, p. 39.
4. *Ibid,* December 1914, p. 400.
5. *Ibid,* January 1915, p. 40.
6. *Ibid,* December 1914.
7. Ritchie, Moore, *With Botha in the Field,* Longmans Green, 1915.
8. Orpen, Neil, *Gunners of the Cape, the Story of the Cape Field Artillery,* p. 83.
9. *Nongquai,* January 1915.
10. *Ibid,* April 1915, p. 251.
11. *Ibid,* p. 252.

CHAPTER

8

End and Beginning

As Captain A W Burton of the South African Medical Corps drove by car towards Lutzeputz, with a red cross flag fluttering from the mudguard, he saw columns of smoke and dust rising in the distance.

Approaching Lutzeputz the doctor saw, scattered in all directions, boxes of bully beef and army biscuits, of prunes and raisins, bales of lucerne 'and other articles of our now retreating and disorganised forces.'

He stopped frequently to treat wounded men coming back from the fighting. Once he was stopped by a patrol of Maritz's rebels but was allowed to go on when they established that he was a doctor.

'Fighting was still going on and the whole scene was chaos and turmoil. Kit was scattered over the stones, broken waggons and dead animals littered the place,' Burton wrote in his diary.

Burton encountered Maritz amid the wreckage of the battlefield and it was his account of this meeting, in testimony at Maritz's trial, that helped to put him behind bars after the rebellion.

By the time Burton reached Lutzeputz the action was over and groups of rebels were roasting sheep over fires. Medical orderlies were attending to the wounded in three bell tents.

'Some of the wounded had no chance of recovery from extensive shell wounds which the ambulance orderlies had firmly bound up. All I could do was to ease their suffering with full doses of morphine before they died.'

While he was doing this he was called outside the tent and there found Maritz with three other men, one of them a German doctor. All four, including Maritz, were dressed in German uniforms.

Maritz went into the tents. A medical orderly who went in with him reported afterwards that he spoke to the wounded, told them he was sorry they had been wounded and said he hoped they would recover.

Back outside, Maritz spoke to Captain Burton.

'With his German whip in his hand, Maritz stroked his wounded knee and asked: "What food have you got here for these men?" '

When Burton said they had very little, Maritz promised that before he left the next day he would see that they got what they needed.

'The night was very long and the silence broken only by the groans of the wounded and the cries of night birds, and when day broke we had to dig another grave. In the afternoon, at about 4 o'clock, I saw a cloud of dust above the rebel and German army riding eastwards in the direction of Zwartmodder and Christiana, not very far from Upington.

'They left us without food at Lutzputz; maybe they forgot the promise, or, more likely, couldn't spare it,' Burton wrote.

From his travelling box of medicines and instruments Captain (later Major) A W Burton of the Medical Corps treated the wounded at Lutzeputz and at Upington. For this photograph he posed in front of a mule-drawn ambulance waggon with his orderlies and drivers. It is not certain whether the picture was taken during the rebellion or during the South West African campaign; probably the former. (Cory Library, Burton Collection)

Later he was to speak with some bitterness about the wounded being left hungry by the rebels, but at the time his main concern was obviously to provide for the present. The next day three mule-drawn ambulance waggons arrived from Upington, but without bringing any supplies.

Before departing the rebels had thrown a dead animal into the well to poison the water so that the government forces could not use it. Burton's resourceful medical orderlies dragged the rotting carcase out but then had to boil the stinking water several times over before giving it to the wounded or drinking it themselves.

They now had water, of a sort, but they were still without food. They were, in Burton's words, 'at our wits end' when a Bushman came to scavenge over the battlefield and told them he had goats some miles away which he would sell.

The doctor gave one of the orderlies, Sergeant Frank Orpen, a sovereign and told him to go with the Bushman and bring back two goats. When night came Orpen had not returned. Long after the full moon had appeared above the horizon Orpen returned, leading two goats. He tied them up and collapsed into exhausted sleep.

Next day he slaughtered one of the goats and minced the meat to make broth for the wounded. Then they set off for Upington, more than 50 miles away, with the 14 surviving wounded on the ambulance waggons and Burton and his medical orderlies walking all the way, his car having run out of petrol.

★ ★ ★ ★ ★

When Maritz encountered the Union forces at Lutzeputz he was on his way to attack Upington, largely at the behest of the Germans.[1] By inducing the rebels to attack the biggest town within easy striking distance of the border, the Germans hoped to force the South Africans to send back to the home front some of the troops who were advancing inland along the railway from Luderitzbucht. Tschaukaib had already fallen and the Germans knew that once the railway they had torn up as they retreated was rebuilt the South Africans would have overcome the element that had been relied on above all others to keep them at bay: the desert.

Von Heydebreck had first proposed an attack on Upington by Maritz's force on one side of the town and a German force on the other, but Maritz objected, arguing that Boers in South Africa who were still undecided about supporting the rebellion would be persuaded against it if the rebels were to be seen to be collaborating with the Germans in an assault on a South African town.

In the end Maritz agreed to accept a battery of German artillery, two pom-pom guns and two machine-guns to support his force in an attempt to seize Upington. A German force under Major Ritter would meanwhile attack Raman's Drift and Steinkopf.

Maritz's force had been joined late in December by Kemp's group, now recovered from its trek across the Kalahari and re-equipped by the Germans. (Soon after crossing into South West, Kemp had gone with Maritz to Keetmanshoop for a meeting with the German governor, Dr Seitz, to ask for arms and ammunition for pursuing the rebellion in South Africa.)

While Lutzeputz may have been an incidental military victory for Maritz, it was a psychological defeat, for on the battlefield there his men found newspapers that told them for the first time of the death of Beyers, the capture of De Wet and the virtual collapse of the rebellion. If Maritz and Kemp had known of these things, they had kept them from their men.

The morale of the rebels sank and on the night of Lutzeputz Maritz wrote a letter to Colonel Jacob van Deventer, commander of the Union forces at Upington, asking about surrender terms. But then, without waiting for the reply, he went ahead with the attack on Upington five days later, on January 24.

This puzzling behaviour is not explained by the delay in receiving Van Deventer's reply to Maritz's inquiry (which was still being considered in Pretoria). A likely reason appears to be that Maritz was forced into the attack by the Germans, to whom he was now deeply indebted and who were growing impatient with the lack of reward for their support for him.

From Lutzeputz, Maritz had taken his force to Christiana to prepare for the attack on Upington. While camped there, his men wounded a scout from the South African Mounted Rifles and a message was sent to Upington for a doctor to come and fetch him.

The ever-willing Captain Burton set out with an ambulance waggon at sunset on January 23, having first filled several water bottles with

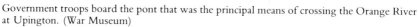

Government troops board the pont that was the principal means of crossing the Orange River at Upington. (War Museum)

lemon squash. Unknown to him, it had been made with contaminated water.

After being passed through the rebel outposts, the captain was received in the light of a lamp by a group that included the German doctor who had been at Lutzeputz.

The atmosphere was stiff and in an attempt to ease it Burton offered everyone a drink of his lemon squash. No sooner had the last man in the group taken a swig than Burton began to vomit, followed by all the others in the order in which they had drunk.

If the atmosphere had been tense before it was now angry. Burton was furiously accused of trying to poison the rebels – until he pointed out that he had been the first to drink and the first to vomit. Then it all became a joke.

In the album from which this photograph was taken it is captioned 'Changing the guard at Upington'. The unit is not identified but the album makes it clear the picture was taken during the rebellion. (War Museum)

'What an al fresco drama on an ill-lit, tragic stage,' he remarked in his diary.

Burton had brought a letter for Maritz from the South African commander in Upington but was not allowed to hand it over personally; the German doctor took it and said he would pass it on.

Burton left to return to Upington with the wounded scout under a bright moon.

'I was dozing when my sergeant nudged me and said, "Wake up, sir. I can see mounted and dismounted men coming along the road behind us in the moonlight." I used my binoculars and saw a man on a white horse leading a large column along the road, and a few minutes later saw him turn left and lead the way until they disappeared in the direction of Upington.'

The man on the white horse was obviously Maritz, setting off by a different route to attack the town. Burton ordered the ambulance driver to whip up the mules in an attempt to get there in time to give the alarm. But by the time the ambulance rattled at its best speed into town the defenders were already standing to their guns.

They had been warned by a man who had become a legend in the Kalahari: Scotty Smith, bandit, horse thief, illicit diamond dealer, occasional outlaw, expert escaper, bane of the police – and scout extraordinary.

Unlike the SAMR trooper whom Burton was bringing back, Smith had stayed out of rifle range of the rebels and watched them from a distance through binoculars. When Burton saw them setting out in the moonlight Scotty Smith was already galloping to Upington with the news.

Attracted perhaps more by the prospect of adventure than by financial gain, Smith served as a scout in both the campaigns against the rebels and in South West. He was one of the more romantic figures in both, a mysterious character surrounded by legends of uncertain truth. Supposedly of noble Scottish birth, he was said to have adopted the name Smith to hide his real name, George St Leger Gordon Lennox.

Before joining the Union forces as a scout he had led a band of freebooters in a life of real or suspected crime in Bechuanaland, the northern Cape and German South West. Horses were his friends and the desert his ally; when he wished to avoid being questioned about his recent activities, or apparently when he grew tired of what little civilisation there was in the region, he would disappear into the Kalahari for weeks with one or more of the horses with which he was so skilful.

He appears to have led a roving life before finding a spiritual home in the lonely Kalahari. He was reputed to have served as a soldier in Spain and on the Northern Frontier of India and to have been a 'pioneer' in Australia before becoming a policeman in the northern Cape and then, finding the discipline irksome but the environment congenial, he adopted a manner of life on the edge of civilisation and of the law.

One of the few descriptions of Smith that have been left for posterity is given by Burton, who saw him riding down a street in Upington. Although he was about 50, he had a thick, dark beard. He wore a deerstalker cap, with, as Burton puts it, 'a short peak fore and aft and with earflaps folded and tied on top of his head.

'A graceful rider he certainly was.'

Smith's warning may not have been necessary, however. According to one account,[2] Maritz had sent a message the day before the attack demanding the surrender of the town. When Colonel van Deventer refused, Maritz sent back a note boasting that he would have breakfast in Upington the next morning anyway.

At any rate, the townsfolk had time to take shelter in the church and the two hospitals before the rebels attacked at dawn on Sunday, January 24, with about 1 000 men, the German battery of four guns, two pom-pom guns and two machine-guns.

It began with rifle fire at the eastern end of town, recalls Burton.

'The rattling of rifle firing and booming of guns increased and our ambulance – divided into two parts – moved into action.'

The section under Burton went to two kopjes behind the church where the Cape Field Artillery and the burghers defending the town had taken up positions. At that end of town the action consisted largely of 'a long artillery duel between the Germans and the Cape Field Artillery, whose fire swept the flats over which the rebels advanced in extended order.'

While Burton seems to have had no doubt that the rebel artillery was manned by Germans, another account[3] suggests that the Germans provided only the guns and that they were manned by rebels who had formerly served with the Transvaal Republic Artillery.

The fighting was fiercer at the other side of town, where the attackers, under a rebel leader from Kakamas named Stadler, had approached along a dry river bed. Here the attackers were supported by the pom-poms, something like large machine-guns firing small shells from a belt.

'The noise made by the German pom-poms was like the barking of a pack of dogs and was most disconcerting,' Burton wrote.

From the river bed Stadler's force advanced to a stone cattle kraal but came under such heavy fire from the defenders – Boers who could shoot as well as Stadler's own Boers – that they were unable to advance into the town despite the covering fire of the pom-poms. The kraal was owned by a man called Pearson, who said afterwards that he had heard Stadler placing his men in it early in the morning after driving the cows out. Pearson asked Stadler to go away and make his attack elsewhere as his wife was ill and there were three children in the house. Stadler's response was to order Pearson and his family to leave the house immediately, an instruction that he was either unable or unwilling to obey, for soon afterwards the Pearsons found themselves in the middle of a raging battle.

As Pearson and his family huddled on the floor of the their house, bullets whipped through the mud-brick walls and whizzed over their heads.

'The rebels in the kraal were subjected to a cross-fire and dared not show their heads above the stone walls against which the bullets struck',

Burton says in his account. 'A rebel who scaled the wall of the kraal (presumably in an effort to advance rather to retreat) ran a few yards and was shot dead, and another who took refuge behind the house was killed.'

That the rebels were in fact able to shoot back is shown by the fact that thousands of cartridge cases were picked up in the kraal after the battle.

In an attempt to end the shooting, Pearson went to a window overlooking the kraal and shouted to Stadler to surrender. But after an hour of fruitless fighting Stadler decided to retreat and led his men away along the dry river bed, pursued for several miles by the loyal forces.

Over at the kopjes, Maritz and Kemp, unable to advance on foot against the sustained fire, tried a mounted charge, but that also was beaten back, with the Cape Field Artillery putting down a devastating fire at the close range of only 1 000 yards. After five hours of fruitless fighting the rebels gave up the attack and were chased out of town by Van Deventer's forces.

The defending artillery fired 243 shells during the battle and the Germans about 150 – most of which fell between the houses. No civilian casualties are recorded, although the occupants of one house escaped astonishingly without harm when, after four shells had exploded just outside, a fifth hit the house and blew away an entire wall, but on the opposite side from where the family were crouching.

After the attack on Upington had been beaten off Burton of the Medical Corps drew this map to illustrate the main features of the engagement. (Cory Library, Burton Collection)

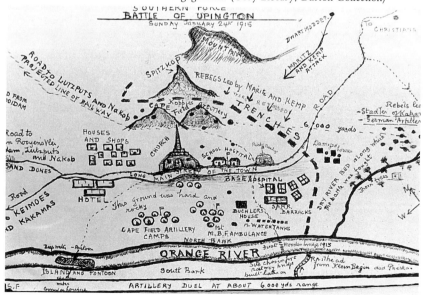

With bayonets fixed, soldiers of one of the Union infantry regiments guard rebels captured in the action at Upington. In the background is the Dutch Reformed Church. (Cape Archives)

For Burton's younger brother, a medical orderly with the First Mounted Brigade field ambulance, Upington was his baptism of fire.

'The rifle fire was terrific and the pom-poms gave us the creeps,' he said in a letter home. 'We moved along behind the firing line in our ambulance waggons and saw some gruesome sights. At first I could not bear to look at blood but afterwards I didn't care a bit. The majority of the killed and wounded are rebels and some of them I swear hadn't had a wash for a year.'

The rebels lost 12 men killed and 23 wounded in the attack, and 97 others were captured – most of them wearing German uniforms. Three of the defenders were killed and 22 wounded.

Burton counted 18 dead horses, 'some of them blown to pieces by shells'.

Before retreating the rebels buried their dead in shallow graves in the sand of the dry river bed but the wind soon uncovered them. They were reburied in deeper graves in the river by the defending troops. Several years later, when he was a Member of Parliament, Kemp obtained official permission to exhume them and carry back to their native Transvaal for reburial in his constituency of Wolmaransstad.

Upington was the end of the road for Maritz and Kemp. On the night of the battle, camped among his defeated force, Maritz wrote again to Van Deventer and proposed a meeting to discuss terms of surrender.

The conference was held on January 30 in a marquee pitched a few miles outside Upington. Kemp and most of the rebels surrendered there, and the rebellion effectively came to and end.

The Germans had made a last effort to revive the rebels' cause by attacking Kakamas, but it was too late. Von Heydebreck had sent Major Ritter with a mounted force to cross the border and attack Steinkopf, to which most of the South African invasion force had withdrawn. Hearing of Maritz's defeat at Upington, Ritter turned and headed there in the hope of being able to save the day, but he changed his mind and turned back.

The German commanders presumably decided to go for what they thought would be an easier target – Kakamas, about 50 miles downstream from Upington on the Orange.[4] Major Ritter received his orders to attack Kakamas on January 27. He was told not to remain in South Africa for more than 14 days.

His force of 205 mounted riflemen, four artillery pieces and four machine-guns approached the unsuspecting town in the early hours of January 31. A patrol was sent ahead to cut the telephone lines to Upington. At dawn the German artillery opened up at 1 000 yards on the South Africans guarding the ferry landing on the north bank while the riflemen approached the landing on two flanks.

The South Africans immediately tried to send reinforcements across the river but were foiled by heavy artillery fire on the ferry pontoons.

Pressing forward along the north bank, the Germans captured a South African outpost. A cavalry charge on the ferry landing was frustrated when it ran into wire fences and the attack was pressed forward on foot. With artillery support the Germans seized the ferry landing and captured 11 members of the Calvinia Commando who had been defending it.

Now they realised that the pontoons were on the south bank and that they had no means of crossing the deep, swift river to get to Kakamas. In the meantime other South African troops got between the two German flanks and Ritter decided to abandon the attack. The South Africans seized the opportunity to push reinforcements across the river, and the retreating Germans came under heavy fire. They swung their guns round and opened up a brisk artillery fire, which covered the retreat but was unable to save the rearguard from being captured.

By nightfall the artillery and one wing of the German force had struggled back to the rendezvous at Biessiespoort, but the other wing was still fighting off a strong attack by South African infantry and artillery. Not until 11 p.m. were they able to break away and make for Biessiespoort, where they arrived shortly before dawn in a desperate condition. They had been fighting for much of the day and all night without water, and some were delirious when they reached Biessies-poort.

As they headed back to the border the Germans counted their losses: seven officers and men killed, six wounded and 16 captured.

The German account of the action notes that the South Africans cleverly exploited the terrain and that 'their marksmanship, even at far distances, was good, resulting in heavy losses of horses and mules'.

This ill-planned attack on Kakamas was the only German attack in any strength across the South African border during the First World War, and it entailed the deepest penetration of the Union.

On March 1 and again on the 19th German forces attacked the South African Police station at Rietfontein, on the western border of South Africa and a little south of the Bechuanaland border.It was another pointless and costly exercise, for the attacks were beaten off and the Germans lost 26 men killed, wounded or captured. That was the last cross-border attack made by the Germans; from then on they were strained to their utmost to fight off the growing South African onslaught, which by March was coming at them from four sides.

References

1. Goldblatt, I, *History of South West Africa,* Juta, 1971; p. 204.
2. Rayner, p. 123.
3. Lucas, p. 419.
4. Pamphlet in Cory Library giving German account of the action.

CHAPTER

9

Punishment

The energetic Botha did not wait for the rebellion to wind down to its anticlimactic conclusion; while the last of the rebels were still being rounded up he set off for German South West to take personal command of the campaign. But from the battlefront he sent to Parliament an appeal to 'put aside . . . all feelings of revenge or reprisal' and to exercise forbearance in the treatment of the rebels, especially the rank and file.

His plea was accepted and reflected in a special Act passed by Parliament establishing maximum penalties for convicted rebels. Taking their cue from that, the courts imposed sentences that were considered absurdly light by some South Africans, especially English-speakers who had lost kinsmen in the fighting.

On the government side, 131 were killed fighting the rebels and 272 wounded. The rebel casualties were never precisely established, but 190 are thought to have been killed. Smuts told Parliament the casualties on both sides were about 1 000, which would put the number of rebel wounded at about 400.

Kemp, perhaps the most heroic figure in the whole affair, was given the heaviest penalty because he had held an army commission shortly before rebelling and had then collaborated with the armed forces of an enemy. He was sentenced to seven years' imprisonment and a fine of 1 000 pounds.

De Wet got six years and a fine of 2 000 pounds; Wessels five years and 1 000 pounds, De Villiers four years and 500 pounds; Serfontein four years and others to shorter terms.

The prosecution of some of the Anglo-Boer War heroes in the courts of their own land for doing what many of their countrymen thought was right increased the bitterness felt by some Dutch-speakers over the loss of their republics in the Anglo-Boer War and left wounds that were to erupt again years later in the Second World War, when South Africans were again called to fight against Germany.

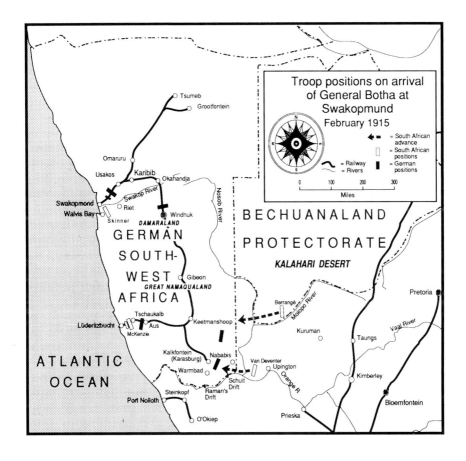

Troop positions on arrival of General Botha at Swakopmund February 1915

◄ ■ = South African advance
☐ = South African positions
▬ = Railway
∿ = Rivers
■ = German positions

0   100   200   300
Miles

The prophet Van Rensburg, who had surrendered with Kemp at Upington, was sentenced to 18 months' imprisonment.

Light though they were, the sentences did not run their full course. Under continuing pressure from Hertzog, the Government freed De Wet and most of the 289 jailed rebels before Christmas of 1915 and the rest were released within the next year.

Kemp spent only 21 months in the Old Fort Prison in Johannesburg before being freed. He was elected to Parliament in 1920 and became Minister of Agriculture in Hertzog's cabinet in 1924. When Hertzog and Smuts united in 1933 he retained the portfolio and in 1935 he became Minister of Lands.

Maritz was not among those tried with De Wet and Kemp. From Upington he fled with a few followers into German South West. Despite the undertaking by the Germans to give the rebels sanctuary if their revolt failed, he seems not to have felt welcome and went to Angola, and from there to Europe. He returned to South Africa in 1923, driven presumably by homesickness, and was promptly tried for treason and sentenced to three years' imprisonment, a sentence that seems extraordinarily lenient compared with Kemp's. Even that term he did not serve out; he was released by Hertzog when he came to power in 1924 and went farming in the same South West Africa whose conquest he had plotted to prevent.

One of the ironies of Maritz's close association with the Germans was that he was unable to win their respect. They were disappointed with his military failures in the rebellion. They felt that if he had agreed to von Heydebreck's early proposal for a joint attack on Upington, Botha might have had to divert forces from the Transvaal and the Free State, giving both Beyers and De Wet a better chance of success.[1]

Maritz was seen as 'less of a general than the situation called for', a commander whose 'lack of resolution in battle and frequent contradictory actions were mainly to blame [for the lack of success].'[2]

That the Germans had hoped for a successful rebellion in the Union and were ready to give it every support is clear from the vast quantities of weapons that were stockpiled in South West Africa before the outbreak of war and the readiness with which these were fed to the rebels.

While sailing to South West Africa to take command of the Union forces in the north, Botha plays a game of deck quoits on the ship, probably the *Galway Castle*. It would be a long time before he would be able to enjoy such relaxation again. (Cape Archives)

But it is far less credible that the Germans ever contemplated an invasion of South Africa, as many there believed. Some military and historical analysts have argued that the intention to attack and conquer South Africa is clear from the construction of a railway reaching as near to the border of the Union as Kalkfontein (Karasburg), much further south than economic realities required, and from the establishment of a large military base at Kalkfontein, where there was no other logical reason to have one.[3]

Certainly the building of an extraordinary length of 1 320 miles of railway was hardly in accordance with the economic strength of the colony or with the money spent on other development.

In a debate in the Reichstag a certain Herr Lattmann was reported to have said openly that the railway was built 'to facilitate considerably an attack on the Cape Colony', and a few years before that a German publication had said that 'the next piece of African territory to belong to the Fatherland will be the Transvaal'.[4]

While these pre-war sentiments may have proved useful for Allied wartime propaganda they hardly represented official German policy. Berlin had actually reduced the number of troops in South West before the war, and with fewer than 3 000 regular soldiers in the colony at the outbreak of war the Germans clearly were in no position to take on the

There was a strong military influence in German South West Africa at the outbreak of the war, even though the number of troops had been cut back after the crushing of the Herero revolt. Here Governor Seitz talks to bemedalled officers after a formal parade. (Namibia Archives)

In one of their regular exercises in the colony, German troops stand with guns at the ready for an imaginary enemy. (Namibia Archives)

Riflemen and machine-gunners of the *Schutztruppe* in a pre-war exercise in the South West African bush. (Namibia Archives)

overwhelmingly stronger South Afican forces without reinforcements from Germany.[5]

When war was declared the German forces were under orders not to cross the border with South Africa, and Governor Seitz rescinded the order only after the British auxiliary cruiser *Armadale Castle* had shelled Swakopmund on September 14.

The Germans' eagerness to attack Upington was not due to any immediate ambitions of conquest but strictly in the interests of encouraging Boer rebellion in the Union. By fomenting rebellion they may have hoped to increase their influence in an independent South Africa divorced from the British Empire and dominated by Afrikaners, who were considered to have strong Germanic roots.

An ultimate German take-over of South Africa may well have been envisaged by some in Berlin.[6] But at first ambitions were much more limited.

In the treaty that Seitz signed with Maritz the Germans agreed to recognise and protect the independence of a republic in South Africa and to support its attempts to acquire Delagoa Bay (Lourenço Marques in Portuguese East Africa). The intention apparently was that this would give the republic its own seaport, which in turn suggests that Maritz envisaged a state comprising only the old Transvaal and Free State republics. But how they thought that Portugal could be induced to part with the best harbour in Mozambique was not clear.

Nearly all the German troops in SouthWest were mounted infantry, such as these men being viewed by an officer. (Namibia Archives)

In return for all that the Boer republic would support a German claim to Walvis Bay, the former British possession that had become part of South Africa with the creation of the Union in 1910. The agreement was made conditional on Maritz raising a rebellion in time to prevent a South African invasion of South West.[7]

This condition was confirmed in a telegram from the Kaiser himself which was published in Windhuk in October 1914.[8]

While the Germans were clearly plotting rebellion with Maritz before the outbreak of war, it has been suggested that this was a form of insurance, and that what they most wanted was to have South Africa stay neutral and not have South West dragged into the war at all.[9]

But they could hardly have expected the British to allow German warships to use the South West African ports or the Windhuk wireless station to continue keeping the German fleet in communication with Berlin.

So the possibility of an invasion by South Africa, especially if the rebellion failed, was taken seriously. But it was expected to come overland, across the Orange. What was not taken with equal seriousness was the possibility of an invasion from the sea, for between the coast and the heartland of the territory were deserts that the Germans considered impassable by large armed forces.

The South Africans were of a different opinion.

References

1. Ungleich, T R, *The Defence of German South West Africa during World War I,* MA thesis, University of Miami, 1974; p. 82.
2. *Ibid.*
3. Dane, Edmund, *British Campaigns in Africa and the Pacific.*
4. Rayner.
5. Von Oelhafen, Hans, *Der Feldzug in Südwest, 1914-15.*
6. Dane, p. 27.
7. Lucas, p. 421.
8. *Ibid.*
9. *Ibid,* p. 422.

CHAPTER
10

Seaborne Landing

All the street lights were on when Captain C K de Meillon and his small landing party cautiously entered Luderitzbucht, rifles at the ready, on the night of September 18. But the town was curiously deserted.

Some of the houses seemed empty and the front door of one was open. De Meillon went inside and found a pot of hot coffee on the dining room table and in a bedroom a bed still warm from a recently departed occupant. He sat down and drank the coffee. Both the hot coffee and warm bed made it evident to him that the town had hastily been abandoned by the Germans, civilians as well as soldiers.

He was certain that the alarm had been given by a German patrol that his party had encountered soon after landing on the beach from a ship's boat. The Germans had retreated in haste after a brisk exchange of shots.

De Meillon was unhappily aware that he had failed in his primary task, which had been to take his party inland and cut the railway to trap the Germans in the town. But he was not one to waste time with futile regrets. He finished the coffee, took off his boots, got into the warm bed and went to sleep.

It had been a rough landing in which nothing had gone right, and De Meillon and his men were exhausted. They had been sent ashore by the commanding officer of the invasion force, Colonel P S Beves, when the fleet had arrived off Luderitzbucht to find heavy seas making a large-scale landing in small boats inadvisable.

Colonel Beves had been expecting the Germans to oppose the landing and to defend the harbour and the town. He had nevertheless to consider the possibility that they would not make a fight of but withdraw along the railway line to defensive positions inland. He might not be able to stop them from destroying the harbour installations, the wireless station and the seawater desalinating plant but he could try to trap them in the town.

He planned a landing south of the town by a small force that would then march inland and try to cut the railway, which was the only way out across the desert for the Germans.

To lead this mission he chose his chief intelligence officer, Captain de Meillon. One of the most colourful personalities in the South West African campaign, De Meillon had been born in Holland and had emigrated to South Africa. During the Anglo–Boer War he had fought on the Boer side, and won a reputation for bravery and audacity. He had been captured three times, had escaped twice and then been sent to a prisoner of war camp in Ceylon, which had held him until the war ended.

He had refused to live under British rule in South Africa and had gone to German South West but had returned to South Africa after losing a court action over disputed mining rights. His military experience and knowledge of South West Africa made him invaluable to the South Africans when war broke out, and he had acepted a commission with Colonel Beves's invasion force. De Meillon and his party had sailed to Luderitzbucht on the *Galway Castle*, a Union Castle liner converted into a troopship for the war. After being taken close inshore by a motor whaler, the *Magnet*, the party were to be shuttled ashore in groups in a small rowing boat.

Skilfully handled by an Australian named Wearen, the dinghy had got safely through the surf and deposited De Meillon and the first boatload of his party on the beach. But on the way back to the whaler

A Salvation Army girl is there to wave goodbye to men of the 1st Battalion of the Transvaal Scottish as the *Galway Castle* leaves Cape Town for Luderitzbucht. (SADF Archives)

92

the dinghy had overturned in the surf and Wearen, rather than try to swim to land through the breakers, had swum back to the *Magnet*, half a mile offshore. There was now no way of getting the rest of De Meillon's landing party ashore.

With the few men who had got ashore, he had set out in an attempt to complete the mission, only to find that they landed far from the town – about 15 miles, he estimated afterwards – and the railway. When they had stumbled on the German patrol he had realised that the element of surprise had gone and he had decided to reconnoitre towards the town. It had been a long, cold march along the beach, with sand continually flung in their faces by the howling wind.[1]

Now De Meillon was asleep in a German's bed while his superior officers paced the decks of the storm-tossed invasion fleet out in the cold Atlantic and wondered what had happened to him.

They soon found out in the morning when, the seas having abated and the white flag of surrender having been seen flying from the town hall, the invasion force landed on the jetties of Luderitz harbour.

There to meet them was a large crowd of German citizens whom De Meillon and his men had rounded up to form an unwilling reception committee. They included the editor of the local *Zeitung*, the chief customs officer and the burgomaster, Herr Kreplin, who formally surrendered the town.

As the first boatloads of troops entered the harbour it was noticed that 'from one or two of the houses white flags that looked like tablecloths were hysterically waving'.[2] This eagerness to surrender may have resulted from the fact that the British cruiser *Astraea* was steaming close inshore, with her guns trained on the town.

The British flag was now hoisted by a party of the Transvaal Scottish under Lieutenant-Colonel Dawson Squibb in what the Reuters news agency correspondent with the invasion force, W S Rayner, described as 'a quiet but impressive ceremony'.

Rayner found himself 'wishing that someone would desecrate the whole scene by starting the strains of the national anthem and raising lusty cheers for His Majesty the King. It was very different, for instance, from the manner in which the Transvaal Scottish installed their head-quarters at Kapp's Hotel an hour later.

'The Scottish flag was hoisted in anything but silence. The bagpipes played and there was great and unrestrained rejoicing all round.'

The German civilians treated their conquerors with appropriate coolness.

'The few inhabitants who were to be seen about tried to look as if they hadn't noticed us, although we rather more than filled Luderitz-bucht and the Transvaal Scottish are a little obtrusive at times,' observed J P Kay Robinson of the ILH, who brought a dry humour to his published recollections of the campaign.[3]

'There were a lot of ladies, however – ladies who did not look like ordinary inhabitants and who stood on the verandahs of the houses and smiled kindly at us. We blushed by battalions and passed on.'

For the seizure of Luderitz Beves had a relatively small force consisting of the 1st Transvaal Scottish, the Witwatersrand Rifles, one squadron of the Imperial Light Horse, and six guns of the 7th Citizen Force Battery – altogether only 1 824 men or 1 200 rifles.

Beves's force was one of the three with which the South African defence chiefs had decided to invade South West at the meeting in Pretoria on August 21. The combined strength of the three forces was 4 000 rifles and 14 guns, against which the Germans were estimated to be able to throw between 7 000 and 8 000 riflemen and a vastly superior number of guns.

The plan also envisaged a naval bombardment to destroy the wireless station and the port landing facilities at Swakopmund to deny these to German naval vessels.

Colonel PS Beves, Commander of the first South African force to invade South West Africa from the sea. (Cory Library)

Swakopmund was duly shelled on September 14 by the former Union Castle Liner *Kinfauns Castle*, which had been converted into an auxiliary cruiser, and the wireless station was put out of action.

Ten days later the *Kinfauns Castle* again shelled Swakopmund, and destroyed some dockside cranes. The Germans protested against what they said was an attack on a non-military target, a seaside resort. It was in retaliation for that, they said, that German warships shelled the English seaside town of Scarborough. The British Admiralty explained that the second shelling of Swakopmund was in retaliation for a German attack on Walvis Bay, in which the pier and a steam tug were blown up with explosives.

German records confirm this story but give it a twist unflattering to the Royal Navy.[4] The German version is that a force led by Lieutenant Scultetus attacked the police station at Walvis Bay on September 23. The port facilities and tug were blown up and the 'English' personnel captured (all South African forces were referred to by the Germans as English or British) were taken back to Swakopmund for interrogation.

No sweat in this landing. South African soldiers file down from a troopship off Luderitzbucht to board a tug that will carry them ashore. (Cape Archives)

All this took place under the noses of the British, for the *Kinfauns Castle* was anchored in the bay at the time, presumably to discourage the very thing that was now taking place.

When her commander, Captain Crampton, saw the pier and tug going up in smoke and realised what was happening he steamed up and began firing on the German raiders as they rode back to Swakopmund along the beach. He failed to inflict casualties on either the Germans or their 'English' captives.

Captain Crampton then sailed to Swakopmund and by signal demanded an undertaking that Walvis Bay would not be attacked again. Receiving no reply, he opened fire on Swakopmund. According to the German accounts, 57 shells hit the town, demolishing a bridge, the customs house and several other buildings.

In Luderitz the South Africans were settling in. The hospital on Shark Island in the bay was taken over and other hospitals were set up in the drill hall and the Europaischer Hof hotel.

The local brothel became the headquarters of the transport section of the invasion force. What became of the bordello's former occupants is not recorded, but Robinson's account suggests that business was somehow continued elsewhere, as it always has in this sort of situation.

The other German civilians continued to be unfriendly, however, and when it was found that they were signalling information to the German troops a few miles outside the town most of them were bundled onto a returning troopship and taken to Cape Town to be interned.

The German troops had in fact retreated no further than Kolmanskuppe (Kolmanskop), the diamond mining village on the outskirts of Luderitz. Kolmanskuppe got its municipal services from Luderitzbucht and for a while the South African engineers were puzzled about why there was such a heavy demand on the port's power station. When they discovered that they were still supplying Kolmanskuppe they lost no time in cutting off the enemy's light and water.

While there was little looting, the invaders appear to have had a good look into the vacated homes. Rayner came to the conclusion that 'they must have been a pretty Bohemian lot', for few houses were without pornographic pictures or literature.

Despite the prohibition of looting a number of South African soldiers were seen to have gramophones and a selection of German records. During one parade the strains of 'Deutschland Uber alles' suddenly rang out across the parade-ground. An investigation ordered immediately by a scandalised sergeant-major traced the music to a gramophone among the belongings of one of the soldiers on parade, who explained sheepishly that it had a tendency to start playing of its own accord.[5]

A British warship provides protection as South African soldiers are carried ashore from the troopship that brought them from Cape Town. The Germans' decision not to oppose the landings was no doubt influenced by the presence of the big guns of the Royal Naval cruisers. (Fort Wynyard Museum)

Since many of the German civilians either could not or would not speak English, the South Africans frequently had problems of communication. None had a bigger problem than the member of the South African Police contingent who was ordered to go out and buy a blowlamp to melt the sealing wax used to seal stores.

At the local hardware shop his request in English evoked only uncomprehending shrugs from the shopkeeper. He had no more success with Fanagalo, the pidgin compound of African languages that serves as a lingua franca in South Africa. In desperation he tried sign language and the account in *Nongquai* of the incident records that 'his efforts to illustrate a lamp in a gale speedily attracted quite a respectable crowd. A spasmodic movement of the arms, intended to depict the pumping that is necessary to get a blowlamp lit, produced first a bicycle pump, then a garden spray and finally an enema pump.

'A hissing noise near the paint-work of the shop door and a movement supposed to illustrate the act of scraping the burnt paint only brought forth a hand fire-extinguisher.'

The shopkeeper's wife was now summoned to see whether she could divine the SAP man's need, but when he tried to imitate a blowlamp with his mouth the *hausfrau* misinterpreted his meaning entirely, became indignant and walked out in dudgeon. The fact that nobody in the crowd of onlookers could understand what the South African wanted only increased their enjoyment of the impromptu street theatre. Now red-faced, dishevelled and dismayed, the SAP man gave up and stormed out of the shop. As he did so his eye was caught by a glass display case near the doorway, prominently displayed in which was – a blowlamp. *Nongquai* says he was 'so carried away by his feelings that he fell upon the neck of the storekeeper.'[5]

Army officialdom seemed to consider itself excused from the prohibition of looting when it came to beer, as some ILH troopers discovered when they found a store of German beer – 'dozens upon dozens of cases of it, large , beautifully long bottles of pale, cool-looking Pilsener'.[7] Before the troopers were able to make the most of their find word of it reached higher ears. Headquarters sent waggons to collect the beer – and then sold it to the ranks at ninepence a bottle.

With the rebellion in South Africa preoccupying the Government and the UDF, the invasion force at Luderitz largely marked time after coming ashore. There were only minor actions as the South Africans pushed the Germans out of Kolmanskuppe and further back along the railway.

As they got further from the relative comforts of Luderitz and deeper into the desert the invaders began to experience the miseries of sand. As De Meillon had discovered within minutes of landing in the colony, the wind blew often on the coast and when it blew the sand moved, in fine clouds that filled tents and penetrated every crack, orifice and aperture. Goggles and veils were issued to the troops but proved of little avail.

'I have seen men rip the veils from their faces because it's necessary to breathe,' Rayner reported.

The sand was everywhere; in bedding, clothing, even food.

'We breathed sand, we chewed it, we took it in our food, literally – there was sand in the sugar; we thought sand, we dreamed it.'

The sand clogged the breeches of the rifles, sticking to the 'Russian petroleum' that was the standard issue for lubricating them until the Transvaal Scottish learned that the Germans had overcome the problem

The South Africans must have had mixed feelings about the Royal Navy when they landed at Swakopmund and found that this dockside crane, which would have been very useful to the invasion force, had been smashed by naval gunfire. (Cape Archives – AG)

by using graphite. Until they could get 'graphite, rifles, for the lubrication of' from army stores the Scottish used ground-up leads from pencils.

A particularly unpleasant effect of the ever-present sand was that it became lodged in the salivary glands under the tongues of some soldiers and caused great pain when they ate. The sand had to be removed surgically.[8]

Even burials had sometimes to take place amid wind-whipped sand, leading someone in the ILH to refer to one such funeral, at which a Transvaal Scottish piper was playing a lament, as 'a sandstorm with a stomach ache'.

Performing one's toilet after sleeping on the sand during an extended patrol was a matter of 'shaking as many pounds of sand out of your clothing as was possible without disrobing'.[9]

In all this sandy discomfort a certain young subaltern of unworldly mien became something of a trial to many, including the Brigade Major of the Transvaal Scottish, Major 'Fatty' Jones. Once, when a sand-plagued soldier gave an impolite response to an order from the subaltern, the scandalised young officer picked up the field telephone, called up the major and said: 'Sir, one of the men has just told me to go to hell! What should I do?'

There was a longish pause at the other end before the weary response: 'Don't go, old boy. Don't go'.[10]

One of the first skirmishes fought by Beves's troops came when units of the Imperial Light Horse and the Rand Light Infantry tried to intercept the German retreat from Kolmanskuppe. Trooper Gruman of the ILH was wounded but insisted on going back into the action after having his wound dressed. He was hit again and killed.

Robinson was in that action and described a poignant scene.

'At the edge of the granite [outcrop] lay a man – one of our men – shot through the heart. Another man was kneeling over him, his head down to the other's breast as if listening for sound of life. With one hand he had commenced to loosen the other's collar; in the other he held, loosely, the strap of a water bottle. They were brothers, these two, and they were both dead.'

The brothers were both prominent South African sportsmen, Rex and Wilfred Winslow. One had seen his brother fall and had rushed to his help, only to be shot dead himself.

They were buried at Luderitz, and over their grave someone, a relative perhaps, has taken it upon himself to have inscribed: 'Tell England, ye that pass this monument, that we who rest here died content.'

De Meillon was also in the same action and was shot through the thigh. Robinson recalls him, 'dark moustached, debonair, lying propped up against a rock, blood all over his breeches . . . smiling cheerfully and airily waving a cigarette to illustrate some point or other to the man bandaging him'.

On October 3 Brigadier-General Sir Duncan McKenzie arrived with reinforcements, and C Force became Central Force with a strength of about 6 000 men under his command.

McKenzie, a member of a pioneer Natal family, was a farmer who sought adventure beyond his own pastures and beyond the provincial polo fields. He had joined the Natal Carbineers as a trooper at the age of 21, and had operated as a transport rider among other things. During the Boer War he served with distinction with the British forces, command-

Officers converse beside a sentry outside the Luderitzbucht jail, which was taken over by the Transvaal Scottish as their headquarters – and was the scene of a memorable St Andrew's Nicht celebration. (SADF Archives)

ing a unit of the ILH and taking part in the relief of Ladysmith, the battle of Spioenkop and other actions. He went on to command the field forces in the Zulu rebellion in 1906.

He is said to have had a despotic reputation among the troops under his command and this earned him the nickname of Shaka, after the Zulu king.

McKenzie's force included a keen diarist, Frederick Addison, to whom posterity owes a debt for having recorded his impressions of the campaign in diaries and later in an unpublished manuscript titled *Horse, Foot and Gun – 1914-18*.

Addison was one of several members of his family who signed up with the Natal Carbineers at the outbreak of war.

'In those days it was a privilege to be a member of a local volunteer regiment,' he writes, 'and I was lucky to be accepted by such a famous unit. One arrived complete with horse and saddlery, which counted as a sort of entrance fee.'

'We were all bursting with patriotic fervour, consequently it was easy to persuade my sister, Cicely, to hand over her horse, Ashton, to King and country . . .'

Addison had a cavalryman's view of things, and it is worth repeating in a chronicle of a campaign in which the horse was as vital as the soldier himself.

'When mechanisation came into the army life, something beautiful and noble went out of it with the horse. Those who have never seen a mounted regiment or battery of horse artillery on parade or in action have missed one of the glories of the military spectacle.

'All the same I am glad this lovable animal has been taken out of our quarrels and no longer suffers mutilation and agony while mankind is practising man's inhumanity to man. One can look at a a lorry or a tank knocked out by shellfire with curiosity, but a gun team of horses killed in this way is quite a different picture.

'And when six hundred of us, with our manly chests gleaming wih freshly-issued ball ammunition in crossed bandoliers, our felt smasher hats jauntily turned up on the left hand side, with spur chains deliberately slacked off to make a jingle when we walked, our knee-high black riding boots and all the other war equipment hung on ourselves and our unfortunate horses, we certainly did have a martial appearance.'

Addison confirms that he and his fellow troopers did not know for which theatre of the war they were making until after the regiment had entrained for Cape Town. There it spent some weeks camped at Rondebosch.

'The only bright interlude I can recollect is when the whole regiment rode to Muizenberg beach, where we undressed, off-saddled and rode naked and bareback into the surf in squadron line. No doubt that delectable seaside resort has seen some strange sights, but I doubt if it has [ever again] seen six hundred men stark naked, gambolling in the breakers on horseback.'

Addison's pride in his regiment is expressed unashamedly: 'The mounted regiments of Natal were as fine a body of horsemen as one could find anywhere in the world; a great proportion of them were off the farms and belonged to the Natal polo clubs. They were magnificent material and nearly all fit to hold commissions in any regiment. This quality was also to be found in the infantry regiments and artillery units of South Africa.'

At first the regiment was commanded by Lieutenant Colonel D W K Mackay, 'a farmer boy from Estcourt, who had been shot through the jaw during the Boer War, so his commands were sometimes a bit vague'.

All the members of Addison's C Squadron were from Howick, Boston and Nottingham Road, and he and six others (including two other Addisons) had been educated at one of the best private schools in the country, Hilton College.

The Carbineers sailed from Cape Town in the *Galway Castle* with no one to see them off except three women, whose remarks to the troops made it clear that 'they were trying to collect payment on promissory notes for professional services rendered'.

At Luderitzbucht the Carbineers were taken ashore in lighters towed by tugs. But not their horses: 'the horses we simply hoisted overboard in slings and dumped in the sea and they swam to land and seemed to enjoy it,' says Addison.

If McKenzie's troops were expecting to be thrown into action against the Germans they were disappointed. McKenzie had a reputation for dash and daring but there was little he could do in that line from Luderitz, where the military options were limited by two factors: water and transport; in a word, the desert.

Luderitz itself was supplied by desalinated seawater and wells and its resources were not enough for the invading army, which had to bring along much of its own water. The largest transport vessel in the invasion fleet, the SS *Monarch*, carried – in addition to 4 000 horses, tons of fodder and other supplies – 750 000 gallons of fresh water from the Table Mountain reservoirs in Cape Town. Every time it sailed thereafter from Cape Town with fresh supplies it brought more Table Mountain water for the men in the desert.

Inland the only water was at isolated wells, few of them providing enough to supply large numbers of men, horses and mules. So an invading army had either to rely on capturing an adequate well at the end of a day or two of marching or it had to carry sufficient water with it.

When it marched the army had to cross deep sand, often stacked in high dunes that moved and changed swiftly with the wind, or long stretches thickly set with jagged rocks that cut through boots and lamed horses and made fast progress impossible.

The best means of penetrating the interior was therefore along the railway, which meant rebuilding it at one end as fast as the retreating Germans destroyed it at the other.

Their own experience had convinced the Germans that the desert was impassable to an army and they considered it their strongest defence. Their attention was therefore concentrated on defending or destroying the railway.

What they had not bargained for was the speed with which the South Africans were able to rebuild it and their ability to march troops alongside it, using the line mainly for carrying water and supplies.

On the line from Luderitz and elsewhere in the South West campaign the remarkable achievements of the invasion force in relaying torn-up lines and building new railways were due largely to the use of engineers, operating staff, locomotives and rolling stock from the South African Railways and Harbours.

The General Manager of the SAR & H, William Hoy, was made Director of Military Railways, with the rank of Colonel. He was knighted for his services by the grateful British in 1916.

Besides calling on the railwaymen to help them to fight the war, the UDF brought in one of the captains of South African industry, Sir George Farrar, chairman of one of the largest gold mines, East Rand Proprietary Mines.

Farrar had been a member of the Reform Committee which was implicated in Jameson's raid into the Transvaal Republic from the Cape colony. He had served with the British in the Anglo-Boer War and had afterwards been knighted for his services in helping to bring about union in 1910.

Soon after the campaign began in South West this mining magnate volunteered for service, was given the rank of Colonel and made Assistant Quartermaster-General of McKenzie's force. He turned his organisational talents largely to helping to rebuild the line from Luderitz through the desert and keep supplies moving along it.

Farrar believed in 'hands-on' management, and that was how he died, lying crushed and ripped in the sand beside the track after the light trolley that he was riding on the line had collided with a moving train during a dust storm (some accounts say it was a fog).

Rebuilding the railway was in one sense the easiest part; after that it had be kept clear of the sand that drifted continually over it and over everything else in the desert that did not move.

A rifle laid down on the sand could disappear within minutes.

Some soldiers discovered that, in the absence of water for laundry, a shirt could be cleaned by lying it on a dune and letting the sand scour it – but if it was not watched closely it would soon disappear. Waggons are said to have vanished overnight, swallowed by the windblown march of the dunes.

The Germans had spent a large proportion of their transport budget on the unending task of clearing the sand from the line from Luderitz across the desert to Keetmanshoop. The invasion force faced the same problem. Fighting the enemy was a rare event; most of the time the soldiers spent shovelling sand; and that could be heartbreaking when the wind was blowing.

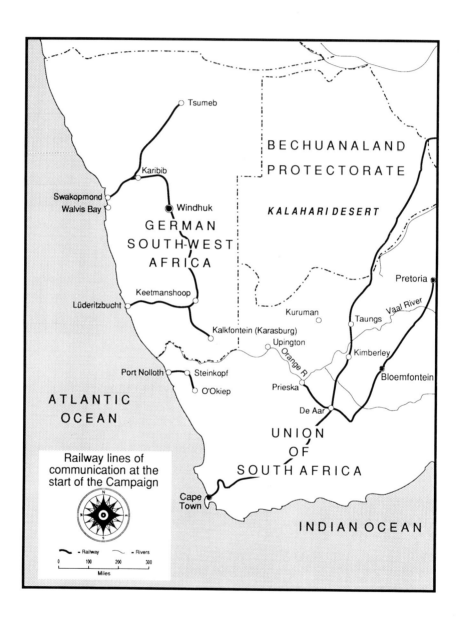

Tsumeb

BECHUANALAND
PROTECTORATE

Karibib

KALAHARI DESERT

Swakopmond
Walvis Bay

Windhuk

GERMAN
SOUTH-WEST
AFRICA

Pretoria

Keetmanshoop

Vaal River

Lüderitzbucht

Kuruman

Taungs

Kalkfontein (Karasburg)

Upington

Orange R.

Kimberley

Port Nolloth

Steinkopf

Prieska

Bloemfontein

O'Okiep

ATLANTIC
OCEAN

De Aar

UNION
OF
SOUTH AFRICA

Railway lines of
communication at the
start of the Campaign

N

W   E

S

Cape
Town

INDIAN OCEAN

— Railway   — Rivers

0   100   200   300

Miles

One traveller on the line recalled that it took five and a half hours to travel 22 miles. When the train was stopped by sand on the line, soldiers wearing veils and goggles shovelled it away. But by the time they had finished, the sand had built up round the back wheels and immobilised them. While that was being cleared away the sand accumulated again before the front wheels. Only by shovelling everywhere at once and removing the sand faster than it blew in could they get the train moving.

Sometimes a work party would toil for hours to clear the sand off a section of track only to see it the next morning under six feet of sand.[11]

Not surprisingly, soldiers found ingenious ways to escape work on the sand-shovelling details. A Solomonically simple method of selection was devised by Sergeant-Major Paget of the Kaffrarian Rifles, commonly known as 'Pullthrough' Paget because his tall, thin frame was considered to look like the length of cord used to clean rifle barrels. He decreed that the last 20 men on parade each morning would form the shovelling party, while the rest provided pickets to guard them against German attack. After that the Kaffrarian Rifles were always on parade long before time, and some men formed up hours before the bugle call.[12]

It took only four weeks from the landing at Luderitz for the first train to steam out of the port. It consisted of only one locomotive and seven trucks, but it represented a considerable logistical feat, for both engine and rolling stock had been shipped from Cape Town and unloaded at Luderitzbucht with primitive rigging.

Working round the clock, using floodlights and military search-lights to illuminate the track at night, the railway regiment restored 200 miles of track in the first two months.

While the Luderitz line was being rebuilt the South African line that had ended at Prieska in the northern Cape was being extended urgently towards the German South West border to provide transport for the invasion across the Orange River. Starting on September 7, the engineers built 142 miles of track to Upington by November 20 – an average of about three miles a day, which was a record for railway construction in South Africa.

Later the line was to be pushed on a further 172 miles to Kalkfontein to join the German South West system at the end of June 1915 and give the invasion force a direct rail link to the southern front. But some fighting had to be done first.

References

1. Rayner, p. 28.
2. Robinson, J P Kay, *With Botha's Army*, George Allen and Unwin, 1916; p. 15.
3. *Ibid.*

4. Ungleich, p. 60.
5. Robinson, p. 18.
6. *Nongquai,* October 1914, p. 326.
7. Robinson, p. 16.
8. Coleman, F L, *The Kaffrarian Rifles,* published by Kaffrarian Rifles Association, East London.
9. Robinson, p. 51.
10. Juta, p. 79.
11. Rayner, p. 70.
12. Coleman.

CHAPTER
11

Sand and Sweat

As had become their custom in the desert, where temperatures as high as 137 degrees Fahrenheit had been registered inside a tent, most of the men were walking about the camp near Tschaukaib wearing only boots and pith helmets. That was standard, if unofficial, dress for days when there was no strong wind to blast the skin with sand.

It made every sense for just such a calm day to have been chosen for a visit to the front line by a group of nurses from the military hospital in Luderitz. It is not known who made the arrangement for the visit and why; perhaps it was thought that the sight of pretty nurses would relieve the monotony of life in the desert for the troops. It did.

When their parasols appeared over the top of the sand dunes there was at first incomprehension, then disbelief. As the parasols were followed by increasingly clear evidence of who were approaching, disbelief turned to certitude, then to panic.

'It seemed for all the world as if we were being routed by the Germans,' recalled one who was there.

'Someone set up a cry of "Women!" The next minute, naked and semi-naked forms shrieking the fateful word were careering all over the place in a mad scramble for cover.'[1]

There was another cause of panic in the desert. Camels, it was found, had as dramatic an effect on the horses of the ILH as the nurses had had on its unclothed men.

Three camels were captured from the German Camel Corps, which had about 500 of them. They ended up in the care of the ILH, apparently on the theory that as camels were vaguely similar to horses in that they, too, had four legs and could be ridden, they should be given to the cavalry. Robinson speculated that it happened like this:

Brigade Major to Brigadier: 'Ahem! Sir! Three camels have just turned up . . .'

Brigadier (absently): 'Ah. Just ask them to step in, will you?'

B M: 'Camels, I said, sir.'

B: 'What? The devil!'

B M: 'No, sir. Camels, sir.'

B: 'Camels? Good God! Where from?'

B M: 'They didn't say, sir. What are we to do with them, sir?'

B: 'Do with them? Um! Well, er, let me see. Um. Er. Oh, confound it! Give 'em to the ILH.'

Robinson, who was one of those who ended up riding the beasts, recalled that 'there was nothing very lovable about them. They bit us and they sneered at us, they frightened our horses and they smelt abominably. But they aroused the envy and the admiring interest of all the other regiments, and the nurses used to come up from the hospital to take photographs of them so . . . we kept them.'

The man given direct responsibility for the care of the camels was Corporal Owen Letcher, FRGS,[2] who appears to have been chosen mainly because of some vague connection in some military mind between geography and deserts. The powerful odour emitted by the camels was something new and frightening to the horses of the ILH, and they never got used to it, especially when it came to them out of the night. Stories are told of troopers clinging to their mounts and trying desperately but unsuccessfully to stop them as they bolted in terror through the darkness from the alien smell. Not always did the riders

These waterless, shifting desert sands presented a formidable barrier to the South Africans and in some ways were a more difficult enemy than the German troops. (Cape Archives)

To conquer the sands of the Namib desert the Germans brought in camels. In this picture are members of the 500-strong Camel Corps, which was used mainly for patrolling. (Namibia Archives)

manage to stay on their horses, either in nocturnal or daytime encounters .

'The smell sent horses crazy,' Rayner wrote. 'Riderless horses were not infrequently seen.'

Corporal Letcher was a Fellow of the Royal Geographical Society by virtue of his wide travels in and knowledge of Africa. Besides being an explorer he was also a journalist, an author, a big-game hunter and a mining engineer, a Member of the Institute of Mining and Metallurgy, London.

He was not the only member of the invasion force who might be considered to be serving below his social station. Botha's pledge to use only volunteers in the South West Africa campaign was easy to fulfil; there was a rush to join the invasion army, and some able-bodied men had to be turned away. Professional men signed on as privates and even former officers joined the ranks rather than be left out.

Only 12 years after the Boer War, this eagerness by South Africans to join the army was extraordinary and can be explained only partly by patriotism and admiration for Botha. To some degree it was attributable to economic recession in the Union, but it seems also to have arisen from the simple desire for adventure.

Most of the infantry and departmental units were drawn from the Active Citizen Force, which was filled by volunteers in the first year of its operation, 1913, and, according to Collyer, 'contained the pick of the experienced volunteers and young manhood of the country'.

The gaps left by ACF men who were turned down on medical grounds were filled by men who 'literally tumbled over each other to get enlisted. Men in good positions as employers of labour and magistrates clamoured to be taken on, if only in the ranks'.

Rayner recalls walking with a colonel down King George Street (the invaders had renamed it) in Luderitz when a relatively elderly sergeant passed and saluted. The colonel stopped to talk amiably to him. He explained afterwards that they had been captains together in the same regiment in the Boer War. Not being in the UDF, his friend had been unable to get a commission when recruiting opened for South West and so had joined as a private.

After the occupation of Swakopmund, Ritchie went for a swim in the sea and there met, as privates and corporals in one regiment, 'six wealthy farmers, a handful of solicitors, bank clerks, a sub-native commissioner or two and the no-longer-youthful secretary of one of the most eminent semi-public companies in Africa'.

At the beginning of the campaign Botha is said to have called together 35 officers who had served under him in the Boer War and told them to choose 15 from among them to join his staff. He left them alone for a while to make their choice, and when he returned he was told: 'You choose the 15 you would like; the rest of us will serve as privates'.[3]

Many men got into the army as members of special regiments raised by former officers. Hartigan's Horse, for example, was formed by Lieutenant-Colonel M M Hartigan, who was then serving in the SAP as Deputy Commissioner, Eastern Division, Cape Province. Recruiting for the regiment opened on January 17 1915 in Grahamstown, and within a week more applications had been received than could be accommodated. Most of the recruits had previous military experience. More than a hundred applications received by mail from other parts of the country had to be refused. By January 30 Hartigan was able to wire the Minister of Defence that he had a regiment ready to leave for any destination at a moment's notice.[4]

Privates in the UDF were paid three shillings a day, warrant officers six shillings, junior officers 10 shillings while lieutenant-colonels and regimental commanders got 20 shillings. In the ranks there was an additional allowance for specialists such as cooks, machine-gunners and signallers. Married men got an extra two shillings a day on condition that half their pay was given by stop order to their wives. A widower received one shilling a day for his first child and and sixpence a day for each other dependant child.

Rations, calculated to give each man 5 000 calories a day, were good when the food could be got to the men. When conditions permitted they

Swarms of flies added to the discomfort suffered by the invasion troops in the desert, as the cover of this contemporary booklet shows. One account tells of huge piles of dead flies being swept up by the sanitation teams; another says it was 'no exaggeration to say you could not put a finger on the canvas (of a tent) without touching a fly'. (Transvaal Scottish Museum)

A HYMN OF HATE.

Deutscher or Turk they matter not—
A blow for a blow and a shot for a shot.
We love them not, we hate them not—
We hold old Seitz in his narrow gate—
We have but one and only hate,
   We grouse as one, we hate as one,
   But not our wily foe the Hun—
   We do not care, we do not care
   If Hans and Fritz have lost their hair—
   For Kultur we've no hate to spare,
   But hark to the Sergeant-major's gloat !
   This is the stunt that gets our goat—
      It's Camp Fatigue !

It is known to you all, it is known to you all,
In every spot where the bugles call
Where the sand is hot or the ditch is damp,
And they pitch their blasted standing camp,
And the hate it swells to a raucous roar
Of thirty millions less or more,
Of thirty million blokes in arms
All thoroughly used to war's alarms,
With veld-sores on their blooming mits,
From polishing spurs and cleaning kits,
Who tote the dirt, and pitch the tents
On half-a-dozen continents—
Who do the regimental chores,
Who put up lines and draw the stores,
From Kolmanskop to the Dardanelles,
Amid the music of busted shells—
From Suez sand to Walfish Bay
They sweat and sweat and sweat all day,
With rage and curse and grunt and groan—
The Frank, the Russ, and Botha's Own,
They have one Hate, and one alone—
      It's Camp Fatigue !

The South African soldiers found themselves doing more camp fatigue than fighting the Germans. One poured out his lament in this poem published in *Ballads of Botha's Army,* with an accompanying cartoon. (Transvaal Scottish Museum)

IT'S CAMP FATIGUE!

"From polishing spurs and cleaning kit"

"The stores"

could supplement their rations and other official issues with cigarettes, soap, writing paper and other purchases from the South African Garrison Institute (Sagi). Once they headed into the interior, however, they were often on short rations, sometimes doing forced marches for days on half and even quarter rations. The staples in the field were bully beef and the hard army biscuit.

One man tried to mail a biscuit home to the Union with the address on one side and a facetious message on the other; the army censored it, biscuit and all.

In the manner of censors in all armies, the UDF censors used their black ink without discrimination. A Labour Party MP complained in Parliament that 14 texts from the Bible had been censored from a letter he had received from the front in South West.[5]

The Germans, whose rations always included large quantities of beer, found that the South African commissariat 'differed from the German rations mainly in the vast consumption of jam and biscuits'.[6]

The jam was invariably apricot and some soldiers found it difficult to face apricot jam for years after they returned to civilian life. But when the troops were on short rations the humble apricot was relished and prized in its preserve form.

When the Durban Light Infantry were travelling by train to Cape Town to embark for South West after two months of short rations during the rebellion, they found special significance in passing through the two fruit-producing areas from which their jam had come.

'The Wellington variety had not measured up to that of Paarl and the troops let each centre know their views . . . Paarl was cheered to the echo,' wrote Colonel A C Martin in his history of the regiment.[7] When moving fast in the field, far from army cooks, the troops usually mixed their bully beef and biscuits in a kind of stew. Invariably the stew had a bit of sand in it and sometimes it had other things too. A soldier from Ireland serving with the Natal Horse Artillery was once seen to be eating a form of stew with distaste. Spitting out a mouthful, he exclaimed: 'Praise the saints! Thim ants have no bones in thim!'[8]

While they were still in and near Luderitz the South African troops enjoyed occasional concerts, a *divertissement* that was soon to become a dimly remembered luxury for most of them. Some remarkably fine musical talent had been acquired by Central Force incidental to the recruitment of fighting men, and the troops heard some excellent piano and vocal performances on stages built from planks and crates.

The Engineers were the envy of the camps for through their supply line connections they were able to get films brought out from Cape Town by the master of the *Clan McMillan* whenever the ship brought fresh stores.

'But nothing could be compared to the Transvaal Scottish St

Andrew's Nicht celebration,' Rayner noted. 'It opened with a dinner party in a cell of the gaol at which the general (McKenzie) was the principal guest. Haggis specially sent from the Rand was piped in. Then followed a concert on a stage with pot plants and electric lighting, with music provided by a piano and the bagpipes.'[9]

There was friendly rivalry between the units, and the exchange of nicknames was not always flattering. The ILH, for instance, were referred to as the Illicit Liquor Hunters by the Natal Carbineers, who were in turn named the Cherry Blossom Brigade, a nomenclature drawn from a well-known brand of boot polish and the Natal troopers' pride in their shining riding boots.

Once the South Africans had chased the Germans out of Kolmans-kuppe every soldier who could find an excuse to be there went looking for diamonds; surreptitiously, because of an official prohibition on diamond prospecting by the troops. 'Once a diamond was seen then that particular spot came to be searched with tooth-comb effectiveness, prohibition or no prohibition,' Rayner wrote.

But very few stones of any value were picked up, not even by the men of the Kimberley Regiment, who were assumed to have a special expertise.

As the restored railway line crept steadily inland patrols probed deeper into enemy territory and the general officer commanding was sometimes out with them, for General McKenzie believed in being up in front with his troops; a characteristic frowned on by some in the UDF who believed it was not the function of a GOC to risk his person in minor engagements.

The general's son, Gordon, who was then serving as a lieutenant with the Natal Carbineers, described a patrol in which the GOC and his orderly captured a German. Three of the enemy out on their own patrol were surprised by the general and his patrol, lying in wait just before dawn behind a hill near Garub. The general shouted 'Hands up!' but the Germans turned and galloped off. The South Africans opened fire and killed one of the Germans and wounded and captured the other two.

For several more hours the general waited with his force in hiding, until another six Germans approached and 'more or less rode into us'. An ILH patrol had been sent under cover to try to cut off their retreat, but the attempt failed. As they raced off, however, the general and his orderly galloped after one of them and captured him. The orderly was a diminutive boy of only 15 who had turned up in Cape Town and begged so persistently and persuasively to be allowed to join the Carbineers that he had been signed on, with his parents' permission. The general had taken him on as his orderly.

Back at the camp, the little orderly, hearing someone ask who had caught the German, replied: 'Me and the general'.[10]

References

1. Rayner, p. 79.
2. *Ibid,* p. 70.
3. Rayner.
4. *Nongquai.*
5. Rayner, p. 25.
6. Von Oelhafen, p. 21.
7. Martin, A C, *The Durban Light Infantry,* published by the Regimental Association; p. 164.
8. Robinson, p. 64.
9. Rayner, p. 52.
10. McKenzie, A G, *Delayed Action,* published privately.

12

The Flying Machines

The cold Atlantic air whipped into his cockpit as Lieutenant Alexander von Scheele banked his double-decker Aviatik P14 over Luderitzbucht and looked down at the South African ships in the harbour and the roadstead.

He counted the vessels as well as he could and then, flying over the town, noted the dispositions of the South African troops. Then he turned and flew back inland towards his own lines.

Over Rotkuppe, about 20 miles from the coast, he swooped down over the South African camp and, flying as low as he dared, heaved propaganda leaflets over the side of the open cockpit, a hundred of them containing an appeal to the Boers with the South African forces to join the rebels back home in fighting against England.

As the leaflets fluttered down in a cloud, von Scheele turned and flew over the camp again. Now he dropped improvised bombs, with hope but no certainty that any would hit their target.

He could see little figures aiming rifles at him and then artillery shells began bursting in the sky, throwing out shrapnel. Now von Scheele could see holes appearing in the fabric on his wings. He turned and headed home to the airfield at Aus, 70 miles back along the railway line.

He landed there 'with much damage to his wings' from the South African ground fire.[1]

And so aerial warfare came to Southern Africa – and perhaps for the first time to all Africa. Von Scheele's flight on November 21, 1914, only three months after the outbreak of the First World War, appears to be the first recorded use of an aircraft for an offensive military purpose as distinct from reconnaissance in the sub-continent. It was to be followed by more bombing attacks by German aircraft on the South African positions and later, when the South Africans got aircraft of their own, by similar raids on German positions

There were no aerial dogfights in the campaign, however, for by the time the South African planes took to the air the campaign was in its later stages and the Germans, forced constantly to retreat by Botha's outflanking movements, had been unable to build new airstrips. Their aircraft had all crashed and they had lost their capacity for aerial operations.

On both sides the aircraft were used primarily for reconnaissance and communication by message-dropping, for their aggressive capacity was still limited; machine-guns had not yet been mounted on aircraft and even on the Western Front in Europe military aviators were still shooting at each other in the air with rifles and revolvers. The aerial bomb was still being developed and had not reached South West Africa.

German accounts tell of von Scheele tossing out hand grenades at Rotkuppe but they may well have been artillery shells. These were certainly the main form of aerial bomb dropped by the Germans in South West. At first they were probably thrown over the side of the cockpit, perhaps falling end-over-end and with it being a matter of sheer luck if one hit the ground nose first and exploded. But the Germans

'Fritz and his machine' is what the handwritten caption says in the album from which this photograph was taken, confirming that it was one of the German aeroplanes used against the South Africans but not identifying either the aircraft or the men in front of it. The civilian dress of the man on the left suggests he might be Willy Truck. (Fort Wynyard Museum)

immediately overcame that snag by fixing a strip of canvas to the base of the shell to cause drag to keep it nose-down.

Once a German with a sense of humour substituted a pair of ladies' bloomers for the canvas strip.

The South Africans soon learned when to dive for cover when a German aircraft was overhead, for the canvas tail, fluttering violently behind the falling shell, made a loud crackling noise, 'like a giant stuttering in wrath' as one trooper described it.[2]

For aerial bombing the Germans used four-inch artillery shells weighing more than 30 pounds. Two primitive forms of bomb-bay were used. One was nothing more than a couple of canvas nose-bags, of the kind used for feeding horses, slung underneath the aircraft. The shells were placed in the nose-bags and when the pilot wanted to drop them he pulled a cord, which turned the bags upside down, causing the shells to fall out.

A more sophisticated contrivance was made by fixing a metal tube of a diameter slightly larger than the shell to each side of the fuselage. Each tube was closed at the bottom by a spring-loaded lid, to which was fastened a cord leading to the cockpit. To release a bomb the pilot pulled one of the cords and opened the lid, allowing the shell to drop out.[3]

When war broke out there were only three German pilots in South West: von Scheele, Lieutenant Paul Fiedler and Willy Truck. Another, Bruno Bruchner, had made the first flight in the colony earlier in the year. He had also made the first flight carrying air mail, from Swakopmund to Karibib, shortly after he had disembarked at the port.

The flight was not uneventful. Soon after he had taken off, his bowels, which were not yet accustomed to the local water, began making urgent demands. He was not the first newcomer to the colony to experience this phenomenon, but he was the first to do so a thousand feet up in the air. He was forced to land in the desert to attend to the problem. Fortunately, he was able to take off again without mishap but soon afterwards he ran out of petrol and had to make another unscheduled landing, at Aukas.

After obtaining fuel he flew on to Usakos, where he landed in the main street outside the hotel and became an instant celebrity among the townsfolk, who had never seen an aeroplane before. By the time he got to Karibib he had made more emergency landings than most modern-day pilots make in a lifetime and had taken off on terrain most would refuse even to contemplate.

Fiedler and Truck were brought out to South West by Governor Seitz with the idea of forming an air reconnaissance unit in the *Schutztruppe*. War broke out only a few months afterwards and they were pressed into military service, together with Truck's Aviatik. Von Scheele became its pilot and Truck the mechanic.[4]

The old meets the new in the Namib desert. From his horse, a *Schutztruppe* soldier watches a German aeroplane soar in the sky. (War Museum)

120

The plane was a two-seater but the 130 hp engine was not powerful enough to keep two people airborne and von Scheele invariably flew alone, although they did fly together on a reconnaissance flight to the Orange River on September 23 1914 to observe the movements of Lukin's force.

Fiedler was a pioneer not only of bombing but also of aerial photography in South West and his pictures of the Union troop dispositions were immensely useful to the Germans in planning their tactics against the South Africans.

Only once did he and von Scheele take their aircraft out together on a joint offensive mission: on April 15 1915 they made a bombing raid on Arandis, von Scheele in the Aviatik and Fiedler in his Roland Taube.

Because of the inadequate power of their engines, they could never take off with more than four bombs; mostly they carried only two. The South Africans could therefore be fairly certain that after the second bomb had fallen they were safe from aerial attack for the rest of the day, for the Germans flew only one mission on any given day. It was always flown soon after sunrise, presumably because it was more difficult for their planes to take off with a load in the heat of the day.

One account speaks of three shells being dropped. Lieutenant (later Colonel) C G Nettleton of the Kaffrarian Rifles related that when the alarm sounded 'I got down beside the railway embankment between two half-buried water tanks. I felt sure the first two bombs would miss us, but the third was coming straight for my hollow until a few hundred feet from the ground . It is hard to judge time and direction in times like this, but I would say the shell took half a minute to drop 1 000 feet.

'I got down flat when the bomb was near the ground, and then with a terrific bang it burst and a cloud of flame and dust and smoke rose outside my barrier of water-tanks and sandbags. Bits of shell went whistling overhead, and three telegraph wires were cut and dropped near me.

'A fellow of the Pretoria Regiment made a bolt for a trench but did not have time to reach it so fell flat where he was and waited for the first shell to burst and as he was getting up a second shell burst, and a splinter got him between the shoulder blades. He died later in the day.'[5]

After the first attack on the South African camps a bugler was posted every morning on the highest point, the top of the water tower, which meant that after sounding the alarm on sighting the plane he had to scramble down quickly to take cover. Later the South Africans evacuated their camps every morning between reveille and 7 a.m. and held their parades after 'Fritz', as the raider was known, had paid his call.

For many of the Union troops, the first sight of Fritz was more exhilarating than frightening, as Addison wrote in his diary at Tschaukaib.

'None of us will ever forget November 29,' he says. 'While we were drinking our early coffee Cherry Sutton made a classical pun by saying "There comes the Aus fly," and sure enough there was an aeroplane approaching camp. None of us had ever seen an aeroplane, and we were just spell-bound and lost in admiration at the novel sight.

'We grabbed our horses off the horse lines and scattered with them while the Rand Light Infantry lay on their backs and let fly with every rifle they had. A battalion of infantry firing as hard as the bolt could be worked has to be heard to be believed.

'This flying crate circled the camp and dropped a bomb made up by using an artillery shell tied to a long streamer of cloth. It went off with a real bang but no one was hit. The pilot just heaved it overboard. Thus we saw our first aeroplane, saw the first aerial bomb ever dropped in Africa and thousands of rounds fired and not a thing hit. While this unique bird of prey was flying round the camp we all bolted in every direction trying to keep up with our horses . . . while we gazed into heaven.'

Fritz, whether he was von Scheele or Fiedler, might not have been pleased to know that his visits came to be welcomed by the South Africans as a diversion from the boring routine of camp life in the desert. Blazing away with rifles and machine-guns at the German planes became a form of sport, not unlike duck-shooting, except that the duck could shoot back, or bomb back, and there were casualties on the ground.

Central Force had no proper anti-aircraft guns to use against the Germans; all it had in this line was a 15-pounder artillery piece that had been converted in the army ordnance workshops at Fort Knokke, Cape Town, to give it an elevation of more than 60 degrees. Because of its singular appearance this weapon was nicknamed 'Skinny Liz' by the troops.[6]

Whether it ever scored a hit is unknown; it certainly never brought an aeroplane down. Its most effective performance seems to have been when it was used as a straightforward artillery piece, firing horizontally, in an action later in the campaign.

For lack of anything but Skinny Liz the South Africans also fired shrapnel at the German planes from ordinary four-inch and 4,7-inch guns. Despite their lack of elevation, these guns were thought to have inconvenienced the German airmen somewhat. Certainly something was hitting their planes: the Windhuk newspaper, *Sudwest,* reported that two aircraft were hit by shrapnel at 6 000 feet, one of them in 150 places.

'Our aviators have discovered that the British artillery can shoot very well,' the newspaper said.[7]

That it was not a one-way affair is confirmed by a report in *Nongquai* from a contributor serving with the SAP Artillery.

'On 18th January, at 5.40 a.m., the alarm was given and the plane was observed just above the camp. It was a misty morning and we could only see the machine from time to time, as it kept at a great height. After circling for some minutes over the camp, the plane dropped two bombs. The first fell about 100 yards to the south of one of the 12th Battery's guns and did no damage; the second just near to the gun.

'Corporal Keeping was injured in the head and died about noon, and the whole of the detachment were injured.'

The despatch reported that 'our friend the airman paid us another visit at 5.45 on the 20th January but we were better prepared, and when he was about 4 000 yards away and well up, the four-inch guns got off a couple of rounds and the plane altered its course.

'The 7th Battery got off some rounds also and the firing caused the aeroplane to clear off rapidly, but not before about 20 rounds had narrowly missed him. With the guns we have here at present it is difficult to get sufficient elevation to bring the 'plane down. Anyhow,

How the bombs looked from the other end. This remarkable picture, one of the first aerial photographs made in wartime, was taken over Tschaukaib, probably by Fiedler, during a bombing raid. At left is the railway line and Tschaukaib station. The South African tents and trenches are clearly visible. *Nongquai* of November 1915, from which the picture was copied, says it was taken from an altitude of 6 000 feet. The two large clouds of smoke are from bombs and in the top right hand corner a smaller puff of smoke can be seen as a 4,7-inch gun fires at the aeroplane. (SA Police Museum)

the beggar had to clear off without getting a chance to drop his bombs on this occasion and he will have to have more respect for our camp in the future.'[8]

Mules and horses are said to have trembled with fear during the air raids, but the goat that was the mascot of the Pretoria Regiment soon got into the habit of walking into the officers' mess tent when the alarm was sounded, according to the Reuters correspondent. It stayed there until the raid was over, even on an occasion when shell splinters slashed through the tent.[9]

In common with soldiers in other wars, many of the South Africans found on their first experience of aerial bombing that it felt as though the pilot was aiming the bomb specially at them personally. After Fritz had dropped a couple of bombs at Garub, a young Afrikaner freshly arrived at the front leaped from the trench in which he had been crouching and, shaking his fist at the departing aircraft, shouted: 'You damned skelm – you aimed that at me'.

Familiarity bred contempt, however, and after that when the Germans raided, the young man would pop his head out of his trench after each bomb and cheerfully call out: 'Any more for any more?'

Fritz and Company were no respecters of Sundays; they bombed without compunction on the Sabbath. Robinson records that when a German plane came over his camp one Sunday morning during a church service the padre looked up at it as it circled overhead. Then he looked down at his Bible. Then he looked up again, and down again. The men sat still and silent, waiting for a cue from him. The padre looked up once more at the plane . . . then he lifted up the skirts of his surplice 'with an almost indescribably feminine grace of action' – and ran for a trench.

His congregation were so convulsed with laughter that some were slow to get into trenches themselves but either by good luck or divine intervention none was hit by the bombs.[10]

In addition to bombs the Germans are reported to have also dropped metal darts, although there is some dispute about whether this happened only in Europe or in South West Africa too. The 'flechettes', each about a foot long, are said to have been dropped six at a time. Each was probably capable of going right through a man but this was never established as there is no record of anyone ever having been hit by one.

There are many stories of lucky escapes from bombs. At Tschau-kaib the commanding officer of the Rand Light Infantry escaped unhurt, but two men between whom he was standing were wounded by a shell dropped by Fritz. The second shell dropped in this raid fell four feet from another RLI man but failed to explode. It weighed 34½ pounds, was 15 inches long and four inches in diameter.[11]

Fiedler and von Scheele had more than one crash each in their under-powered machines. Von Scheele crashed for the last time on May

While her crew stand stiffly at attention for the camera, Skinny Liz points her blunt snout to the sky, ready to fire at German aeroplanes. (Fort Wynyard Museum)

15 1915 while based at Kalkfeld. He was seriously injured and his plane was wrecked. It was taken to Tsumeb and thrown into the Osikoto lake to prevent it falling into the hands of the advancing South Africans. After the war von Scheele flew again, in Argentina. He was killed in 1939 in a crash while flying in Spain.

Fiedler was injured when he crashed in a high wind near Karibib in April 1915, and did not fly again in South West. His Roland Taube, damaged in the crash, was taken to Tsumeb, where it was set alight and destroyed by the Germans as the South Africans advanced on the town. They had served their country well, those two brave Germans, taking their frail and under-powered craft again and again into the heat, dust and sudden winds of South West to give the Germans a psychological and reconnaissance advantage that ended only when the South Africans got aircraft of their own.

No official record seems to have been kept of the number of raids made by the German planes. Rayner counted at least 16 raids on Central Force, at Rotkuppe, Haalenburg, Tschaukaib, Garub and Aus. He recorded three soldiers killed and 19 wounded in the raids. Other raids were made on the Northern Army at Arandis, Trekkoppies and over the Swakop River valley.

Like the other casualties in the South West campaign, these were paltry figures in relation to the terrible slaughter in other theatres of the war. But this was a different kind of campaign. It was not enemy firepower that had to be contended with so much as hostile terrain, not entrenched defences so much as vast distances, not huge armies so much as heat, cold, sand, disease, hunger and thirst – above all, thirst.

References

1. Von Oelhafen, p. 67.
2. Robinson.
3. Von Schumann, G, Radio Namibia, April 9 1990.
4. *Ibid*
5. Coleman, p. 29.
6. Rayner, p. 82.
7. *Ibid,* p. 8d2.
8. *Nongquai.*
9. Rayner, p. 84.
10. Robinson, p. 157.
11. Simpkins, B G, *The Rand Light Infantry,* Howard Timmins.

CHAPTER

13

The Thirstland

The men were covered with fine dust as they marched into Garub and through cracked lips they shouted: 'Water, water!'

Then they broke ranks and ran for the water carts and 'it was only the straight talking of their officers and the armed sentries who had been placed over the carts that prevented the small supply of water being rushed by them', a *Nongquai* correspondent reported.[1]

Like so many other marches in the campaign, the 40-mile march from Tschaukaib had for that particular unit been a tortured journey that only the fittest and most determined finished on their feet. Even with careful husbanding their water bottles had soon been drained as they marched, sweating profusely through deep sand, thick dust and temperatures that had risen in daylight above 137 degrees Fahrenheit. Many men had fallen out from exhaustion and thirst.

In their advance inland from Luderitz along the line of the railway the main preoccupation of the South Africans was water rather then the enemy, who had relied on the desert rather than force of arms to block the advance. Even the relatively small force of about 6 000 men, and a much larger number of horses and mules, required more water than the wells, the desalination plants and the transport ships could provide. Every man and animal had to go short. At Tschaukaib, where the conditions demanded a much greater consumption than a man would normally need, the ration in camp was one-and-a-half gallons a day for drinking and washing. But sometimes there was not enough for that.

It was harder when the men marched, for then they were carrying webbing equipment with bayonet and 150 rounds of ammunition; a mess-tin with two pounds of bully beef; a haversack with one pound of bully beef, 18 biscuits, two pounds of jam and shaving kit; a tunic, a greatcoat, a water bottle and a rifle weighing nine-and-a-quarter pounds – the whole lot weighing about 42 pounds.[2]

The Kaffrarian Rifles found a 23-mile march from Grasplatz 'one of the most exhausting undertaken by the regiment while in South West

Africa'.[3] It followed a track that resembled a very sandy beach, into which the men's feet sank deep and on which there was a tendency to slide backwards with each step. Some men could not keep going unaided and had to be helped by stronger comrades.

The men had left Grasplatz with no regrets; for, despite its name, meaning 'grassy square', it was not a place where anyone would choose to linger, least of all the wag who, in the sea of sand where no blade of grass grew, had stuck a sign reading: 'Protection of Meadows Act. Anyone found damaging a blade of grass in the vicinity of Grasplatz will be fined five pounds. By Order'.[4]

While the infantry as they footslogged through the sand might have envied the cavalry, the march inland was no pleasure-jaunt for the mounted regiments either. The horses sank knee-deep in the sand, and often their riders had to dismount and lead them. And it was the cavalry who had to make the patrols out into the desert to watch for German attacks on the flanks. Away from the railway, the dunes were sometimes like high hills, for in this region are the highest sand-dunes in the world.

Horses would sometimes refuse to descend a particularly high and steep dune and for that eventuality the ILH developed a special technique: the horse would be stood facing the edge of the dune, a

Long experience of the desert had taught the Germans to take water wherever they could find it. Here *Schutztruppe* use their drinking mugs to scoop water into canvas bags after a fall of rain. (Namibia Archives)

trooper would stand on either side of the animal's hindquarters and they would link hands behind it. On the count of three they would heave with all their might, sending the horse sliding, and perhaps sometimes rolling, down the dune. In the soft sand at the bottom the horse would regain its feet, its dignity and its rider.

The Germans did not rely entirely on their ally, the desert, to stop the invaders; they gave it some help by poisoning the wells and waterholes as they retreated to deny the water to the South Africans.

Often they threw a dead animal or the entrails of a slaughtered beast into the water and unless the South Aficans were able to get them out before they reached an advanced stage of decomposition the water was made unusable until the well had time to purge itself. Carbolic acid and sheep dip were widely used as well poisons. One method was to punch holes in a can of carbolic acid and throw it into a well, which would be kept poisoned for some time by the acid seeping slowly out of the holes. Here again the contaminated water had to be drawn off, and it often took several days before the the water became at all potable.

South African troops were forbidden to draw water from a newly captured well or water hole until it had been tested for poison.

When the practice first came to the attention of the South Africans, General Botha sent a strong protest to the commander-in-chief of the German forces, saying it was a violation of civilised standards and warning him that if the poisoning was not stopped he would be held personally responsible and dealt with appropriately at the end of the campaign. The German denied that there was anything unethical about it, as warning notices were always posted at poisoned water.

According to South African accounts a few such notices were found at spoiled wells, but more often than not they were absent, either because they had not been put up or because they had been blown away by the wind.

While the practice infuriated some of the South Africans there is no record of reprisals – except in the case of a captured doctor who defended it, saying that as the water belonged to the Germans they were entitled to put whatever they liked in it. When he then demanded beef tea, his captors gave him a vile-tasting brew that made him complain angrily. He was told that as the beef tea belonged to the South Africans they were entitled to put whatever they liked in it.[5]

No one is known to have died from drinking poisoned water, (although some were made ill) but that was not the Germans' main intention. Their purpose was to reduce the military effectiveness of the South Africans and hamper their advance through lack of water. Besides poisoning wells, the Germans made widespread use of land mines and sometimes used both in combination. Most were contact mines, set off by the weight of the victim, but sometimes remote-detonation mines were used, with the charge set off electrically by a soldier hidden some distance away at the end of a pair of wires connected to a galvanic plunger.

Compared with modern mines, those used by the Germans in South West were simple but potentially highly lethal. The contact mine consisted of a wooden box containing about 20 sticks of dynamite on top of which were stacked old horse-shoes, nuts and bolts, pieces of artillery shrapnel and any other scrap iron available. Above the lid of this box a second lid was held by wooden pegs. Linking the second lid to the fuse of the dynamite was a friction tube. The top lid was lightly covered with soil. When a soldier stepped on it his weight broke the wooden pegs and the top lid was depressed, activating the friction tube, which ignited the dynamite.

Another simple detonator used in the German mines consisted of the T-joint of ordinary quarter-inch plumber's piping, in the cross-section of which were two glass phials, one containing an acid and the other a combination of chemicals that would react with the acid. The chemicals and the acid were brought together when the phials were broken by a steel rod in the other section of the T-joint being forced down by the intended victim stepping on it. Small wonder that some mines went off after the intended victim had departed – or failed to go off at all.

The Germans had huge quantities of explosives in their stores and used them liberally in their mines. As a result, when a mule, for instance, detonated one it 'came down as a rain of flesh'.[6] When a man was blown up by a mine the effect was similar. However, the unreliability of the German mines left many South Africans able to tell stories of escaping unharmed after riding or walking over one.

Soon after the South Africans began rebuilding the railway from Luderitz, German saboteurs infiltrated behind the UDF lines, tore up a length of rail and laid a mine under the track in front of the gap. Sir George Farrar drove out on his motor trolley to inspect the damage and rode over the mine, which failed to explode. Only then was it detected by the South African engineers, who found that it had not gone off because the flanges on the wheels of the trolley, which were supposed to detonate the mine, were not long enough to reach the detonators.

Farrar inspected the device and said: 'I would have made a better job of it than that'.[7]

Because they were difficult to detect, the mines were a serious nuisance to the South Africans. The best they could do was to introduce an early form of mine detector that was even cruder than the German mines: an agricultural harrow drawn by a team of mules. The theory was that if the mules did not detonate the mine the harrow would, or would at least rake up its top lid. It could have proved an expensive

130

technique, as all the mules of Central Force had to be brought by ship from Cape Town.

Booby traps were used by the Germans almost as liberally as mines. Invariably when the South Africans occupied a settlement they would find that doors, windows, water pumps and other fittings requiring the use of leverage had been linked by strings to detonators attached to hidden sticks of dynamite.

When the thirsty South Africans entered Tschaukaib one of the first things they made for was a water trough inside a shed. But none of them could open the tap supplying the trough. Neither brute force nor a delicate touch would budge it. So somebody used the tap as a convenient hitching post to tether the Brigadier's horse.

Victims of thirst, two horses lie dead in the desert, while the living ride on. (War Museum)

Soon afterwards there was a huge explosion and the horse was blown through the roof.[8] Either its greater weight on the mine buried under floor or the way in which it had pulled on the tap had been enough to set off the charge.

After the occupation of Aus, a unit of the SAP Artillery made a diversion to Klein Aus and bivouacked for the night in a small square in which they had been delighted to find horse lines with chains and everything ready for a camp. Unlimbering their guns in the square, the gunners tethered their horses to the lines and went to sleep nearby. In the morning engineers found four large mines buried in the square. They traced the detonation wires from the mines all the way back to Aus and concluded that the Germans had expected the South Africans to occupy

131

Klein Aus first, whereupon those in the square would have been blown up from Aus.[9]

Later, after Kalkfontein had been captured, a South African soldier tried to enter a building there and, finding the door difficult to open, gave it a hard tug. Something snapped and the door flew open to reveal what it was: a wire connected to a mine buried in front of the door, directly beneath where the soldier had been standing.[10]

Orders were issued to the South African troops not to march through narrow passes or restricted pathways until they had made sure that no mines had been buried there. They were forbidden to enter any building or drinking area until it had been searched for mines. According to one account,[11] any captured Germans were to be told to drink first any water they were suspected of having poisoned.

During the advance from Garub to Aus, De Meillon's confidence in his knowledge of the German psychology proved his undoing. In Luderitz, after he had slept in a strange bed on the night of his landing, someone had remarked to him: 'You had a nerve!' De Meillon replied: 'It's not that – I know the Germans.'

Approaching Aus, De Meillon saw dust in the distance and, thinking it was the enemy in retreat, he cantered forward, saying: 'I knew the Germans would not fight.' Then a volley of shots rang out from a hidden German force. De Meillon began firing back but then was hit and fell dead.

The Germans buried him where he died. One account says that they put up a cross bearing his name and the date of his death and laid one of his spurs on top of the grave.[12] Another account says they then planted mines beside the grave, which was next to the road from Garub to Aus.

'Later when we advanced on Aus we . . . found they had laid land mines in close proximity to the grave, knowing that we would be interested and go and inspect it. A mule waggon with ten mules was moving up the sandy road past the grave, probably swinging on the upward incline, when they exploded a land mine. The pair of mules in front of the wheelers were blown in half.'[13]

The engineers later built a masonry topping to the grave and erected a cross of teak. A memorial service was then held and was attended by several hundred officers and men, attesting to the respect in which De Meillon was widely held. They had to travel from distant camps, the nearest being seven miles away. The Last Post was sounded by massed buglers and the firing party was a hundred strong.

★ ★ ★ ★ ★

As in other wars, the troops of McKenzie's force had to contend more with boredom than with enemy action. Even when there was cause for celebration, such as at Christmas, the physical materials for celebration

The problem of how to wash with very little water was humorously exaggerated by cartoonist Walter Houx Kirby, a trooper with the Natal Light Horse who was wounded and captured at Gibeon. He published his cartoons privately in a booklet titled 'Hunting the Hun in German South West Africa'. Kirby was wounded again while serving with the South African Scottish at Delville Wood in France. In the Second World War, as a Lieutenant-Colonel, he commanded the 3rd Battalion, Transvaal Scottish and was killed leading it into action at Sidi Rezegh. (Transvaal Scottish Museum)

were scarce. Addison records that Christmas Day was marked by the cancellation of parades and the issuing of extra rations and a few bottles of light German beer.

The force found a way to see in the New Year with traditional noise, however. At midnight the first blockhouse on the railway line at Luderitzbucht fired a volley, and immediately afterwards the next blockhouse followed suit. And so the volleys rippled in succession from blockhouse to blockhouse all the way along the railway line to Tschaukaib, 80 miles away.

'It was most impressive', says Addison.

On occasions the celebration was impromptu and unexpected. Addison writes that among the gifts from home that arrived too late for the festive season there was one for Major Park Gray: 'a huge home-grown ham from his farm.

'While he and his officers were washing down the dust in their throats with whisky, Fawcett Sclanders, the gallant major's first cousin, slipped under the [mess] tent flap and pinched the ham.

'Had the army pay chest been stolen a bigger turmoil could not have been created, but Fawcett's pals ate every scrap of that beautiful ham and no one was shot for the crime.'

References

1. *Nongquai*, April 1914, p. 225.
2. Simpkins.
3. Coleman, p. 130.
4. Rayner.
5. Rayner, p. 113.
6. *Ibid*, p. 113.
7. *Ibid*, p. 105.
8. Coleman, p. 132.
9. *Nongquai*, May 1915, p. 297.
10. *Ibid*, June 1915, p. 352.
11. McKenzie, A G.
12. Rayner.
13. McKenzie.

CHAPTER
14

The Battle at Sea

On a clear day in December, Admiral Maximilian Graf von Spee's German fleet and the powerful British fleet that had been hunting him through the southern oceans met by bizarre chance in the wide reaches of the South Atlantic, and one of the great sea battles of the First World War erupted.

That thundering encounter in the cold seas off the Falkland Islands was to have an important consequence many miles away in the scorching deserts of German South West Africa.

In both London and Pretoria there was an acute awareness of the vulnerability of the supply lines of the South African force that had invaded the German colony. The only way of supplying the invasion force was by sea along the 450-mile route from Cape Town to Luderitzbucht, which was vulnerable to attack by German warships.

There was particular concern about the threat presented by von Spee's East Asiatic Squadron, which had had not been affected by the Allied efforts to bottle up the German fleets in the North Sea and was marauding at large in the south.

Anxiety was heightened when on November 1 von Spee's ships sank a British flotilla in the Battle of Coronel off the Chilean coast. In that engagement the older and slower British ships had simply been no match for von Spee's fast armoured cruisers, the *Scharnhorst* and the *Gneisenau*, with armour plating six inches thick and formidable fire-power of eight 8,2-inch guns and six 5,9-inch guns each. The two armoured cruisers were supported by three light cruisers.

It was clear to the South Africans that they would have to make a second landing in the north, not only to ensure that the Germans did not rebuild the bombarded wireless station at Swakopmund but also to take possession of the port facilities there and at Walvis Bay. Through these would have to pass the supplies for a thrust inland to capture the capital and cut the north-south railway that was the spine of the German defensive system.

Both British and South African strategists were agreed that a northern landing would be risky while von Spee continued to lurk in the southern seas and with the Royal Navy unable to spare enough warships to protect the supply lines to Walvis Bay and Swakopmund as well as to Luderitz.

The commander of the British fleet at Simon's Town, Vice-Admiral Herbert King-Hall, was blunt about it in a cable to the Admiralty in London:

'As regards conveying expedition and protecting communications, I am unable to do this until whereabouts of German squadron are definitely known or they are dealt with.'

The British considered it imperative that von Spee's fleet should be destroyed, not only to remove the threat it posed to Allied operations but to restore the prestige that had been sunk at Coronel. Other German warships were operating in the Indian Ocean; the *Emden* had sunk British merchant shipping and the *Konigsberg* had sunk HMS *Pegasus* off Zanzibar. But those were lone raiders that might be taken care of by the Simon's Town fleet if they rounded the Cape to threaten the invasion of South West. Von Spee's powerful group was another matter.

Vice-Admiral F Doveton Sturdee was sent out with a fleet strong enough to tackle Von Spee. The difficulty was to find him. For weeks Sturdee searched without success; the elusive German seemed to be lying low, perhaps guessing that the Admiralty would have sent a powerful fleet to hunt him after Coronel.

Then the British had a remarkable stroke of luck.

Sturdee was no doubt feeling in need of some luck when he led his fleet into the British naval base at Port Stanley in the Falkland Islands to refuel so that he could continue the hunt for von Spee.

On December 8 Sturdee had no idea where von Spee was. But by one of history's strangest accidents von Spee, thinking that Sturdee was hundreds of miles away, was in fact steaming up to Port Stanley with the intention of shelling the British base.

Alerted by a lookout to the approach of the Germans, the astonished British abandoned their coaling and hastily got up steam. Von Spee sailed on, completely unaware of what awaited him on the other side of the headland that hid Port Stanley from his sight.

He found out with a shock when a shell from a twelve-inch naval gun came screaming over the headland. He could have no doubt where it had come from. As the realisation burst sickeningly upon him he must have known that he had made a blunder that would be fatal.

He put about and tried to run for it, knowing that the eight-inch guns of the *Scharnhorst* and the *Gneisenau* could not match the twelve-inch guns of Sturdee's two battle cruisers or their superior speed. But it was too late.

136

In the running battle that followed, von Spee tried to give his smaller ships, the light cruisers *Nurnberg*, *Dresden* and *Leipzig*, a chance to get away. But Sturdee sent his own three cruisers, the *Carnarvon*, *Cornwall* and *Kent*, and his light cruiser, the *Glasgow*, in pursuit while he engaged the *Scharnhorst* and *Gneisenau* with his battle cruisers, the *Inflexible* and the *Invincible*.

Von Spee knew that his only hope lay in getting close enough to the British ships to bring them within range of his guns. But Sturdee used his superior speed to stay out of range, while keeping the Germans within the eight-mile range of his own guns.

Even when the German shells did reach the British warships few penetrated their thick armour.

Meanwhile, shell after giant shell exploded into the *Scharnhorst* and the *Gneisenau* until there was little left but tangled steel, raging fires and dead men. Von Spee refused to surrender while he still had a gun working, and the last shot from the sinking *Scharnhorst* came as the water closed over the one remaining gun and its crew. Then it closed over von Spee and his surviving officers on the bridge and then over the battle flag still flying at the masthead

On the *Gneisenau* they had no more battle flags to hoist after having had three shot away in succession and they fought on without one. The *Gneisenau*'s officers were now fighting not to win or to survive but for honour. A battle-parched sailor who left his gun to get a drink of water was shot dead by his officer. As the cruiser sank her captain ordered the survivors to abandon ship and then he went down with it.

By the time the last shots were fired in the battle, 150 miles from where it had begun, all but one of the fleeing light cruisers in von Spee's fleet had been overtaken by the British cruisers and sunk. Only the *Dresden* escaped, slipping into a fog bank that mercifully appeared.[1]

Seventeen days after the battle of the Falklands the South Africans landed at Walvis Bay to set the other jaw of the vice that was soon to begin closing on the German forces in South West Africa.

References
1. Bruce, George, *Sea Battles of the Twentieth Century*, Hamlyn.

CHAPTER
15

The Northern Landing

Daylight was just beginning to give form to the waves that they had been hearing all night when the reconnaissance force under Colonel P C B Skinner rounded a bend in the beach and saw Swakopmund ahead of them.

Skinner's main force, the third wave of the South African seaborne invasion of German South West, had landed at Walvis Bay 18 days earlier, on Christmas Day. His next target was Swakopmund, the port and seaside resort 23 miles up the coast. He had decided on a reconnaissance in force to find out how strongly the town was defended and what sort of reception the invaders could expect. He was about to find out that it would be spectacular.

The 350-strong reconnaissance force had ridden all night along the beach from Walvis Bay, with one stop to rest and to feed and water the horses.

'It was bitterly cold and we were all very sleepy', Trooper Hunter of the ILH recalls in his unpublished diary. 'When we were about two miles from Swakopmund and could just see the town in the dim light of breaking day we turned into a bend in the beach and halted.

'We drew up in troop formation and were just preparing to advance on the town when an enormous explosion shook the ground under our feet and a huge column of iron, rocks and debris shot into the air.

'Horses reared up and many of the fellows were thrown from their horses and these stampeded madly away.

'At first we thought that the cruiser *Astraea*, which had come round from Walfisch Bay to support us, had opened fire on us, mistaking us for Germans, and we decided to rush forward on the town, when just a few yards in front of us another explosion rent the air and a huge black column shot up into the air.

'Then it was that we saw that the Germans had planted landmines for us, about the most awful form of destruction known in warfare. Our major shouted "Make for the dunes!" and well we did, as just behind us

138

a third mine exploded. Unfortunately, this mine killed two signallers.

'We crossed the dunes and advanced on the town in skirmishing order and saw a patrol of Germans, about 100 strong, galloping off. Number 3 Troop and B Squadron chased them and caught two prisoners, but Frank Boag got a rifle bullet in his shoulder, a severe but not serious wound.'

Skinner's detachment carried on towards Swakopmund and, meeting no further opposition, occupied the town. Hunter's squadron returned to Walvis Bay the next day, but a few days later it was posted to Swakopmund and again rode along the beach.

'This time,' he wrote in his diary, 'we saw the huge holes torn in the ground by the mines, which had been electrically fired, and portions of the horses scattered over a wide area by the [third] mine, a head in one part, a hind leg in another, and the graves of the signallers who were also killed.'

A few days after Skinner's entry a note addressed to the South Africans was found in the desert outside the town.

'Trust you enjoyed your reception,' it read, 'and desire to inform you that warmer ones are in store for you. [Signed] Swakopmund Entertainment Committee'.[1]

Soldiers line the railings and crowd into the rigging as a troopship prepares to sail from Cape Town. The mounted riflemen in the foreground are unintentionally showing the variety of hats worn in the Union forces. (Cape Archives – E)

A search of the area where the mines had been detonated had meanwhile disclosed the hiding-place from which they had been triggered. It consisted of a large packing case sunk into the sand just above the high water mark, with only enough above ground to allow for air and peep holes. The top and entrance were skilfully camouflaged with seaweed. Inside it the searchers found evidence that the brave German who had hidden there to detonate the mines, one by one, had had a long wait before his enemy came riding along the beach, as his commanders had known they eventually would. In the dugout were found the electrical device used to set off the mines, a mattress, a candle, some reading matter and half a bottle of peppermint liqueur.[2]

Skinner's landing at Walvis Bay had been unopposed, apart from a skirmish between the Germans and a detachment of the Rand Rifles.

His invasion force of two infantry brigades, one mounted regiment and seven guns of field artillery, was the first part of a larger force the despatch of which represented a radical change from the original plan of campaign. That had envisaged a seaborne landing only at Luderitzbucht and thrusts overland across the Orange. Having entered the colony at those points, the South Africans would of necessity have had to advance north by land.

This was how the horses and mules were lowered from the transport ships on to the pontoons that carried them to the beach at Walvis Bay. (Fort Wynyard Museum)

The advantage of this plan was that it would give the invasion force safe lines of communication across the Orange, with only the supply lines of the Luderitz force vulnerable to attack by von Spee's fleet. But it had serious disadvantages.

The first was that it meant fighting the campaign on the enemy's terms and allowing him largely to dictate strategy and to take maximum advantage of the natural geographical defences. He could not easily be outflanked or otherwise manoeuvred out of position.

From the South African perspective, South West Africa was a formidable natural fortress. Almost as large as the Union itself, the territory was surrounded by daunting obstacles. On the west was the Atlantic Ocean, enabling the German navy, unless driven from the high seas, not only to attack the seaborne supply lines of an invader but also to bring troop reinforcements and fresh supplies from Germany or its other colonies.

On the east the Kalahari Desert presented a waterless barrier to an invading army. To the south was another desert, in Namaqualand, and a river, the Orange, flowing strongly in season and with few easy crossings. To the north was Angola, a colony of neutral Portugal.

All these barriers could be defended with relative ease by the Germans because of the railway system, which made it possible to move troops swiftly from one end of the territory to the other. From Tsumeb in the north one line ran like a spine down the middle of the colony to Kalkfontein in the south, only about 50 miles from the South African border. From that railhead troops could be deployed quickly to any Orange River crossing.

Two other lines ran from the central line to the coast, one to Luderitzbucht and the other to Swakopmund, which enabled the defenders to move troops rapidly to defend those key ports.

The best way to neutralise those defences was obviously to land at Walvis Bay or Swakopmund and to strike inland to capture Windhuk, the capital, or Karibib, where the lines joined. In that way a wedge could be driven between the enemy forces in the south and those in the north. Each would then be made more vulnerable to defeat by the superior South African forces that could be brought against them.

As long as von Spee's fleet was lurking in the Atlantic, however, the South African command could not undertake a landing on the centre of the coast unless it were assured of adequate protection by the Royal Navy, since the Union had no navy of its own. This the British fleet was unable to guarantee, for it did not have enough ships to escort supply convoys shuttling continually over the more than 700 miles between Cape Town and Walvis Bay.

When von Spee's fleet was destroyed at the Falklands, the situation changed overnight; a landing at Walvis Bay or Swakopmund became not only feasible but urgently necessary. As with the landing at Luderitzbucht, there would still be the problem of getting the invading army across a waterless desert. But to the strategists at military headquarters in Pretoria that seemed preferable to the invasion forces fighting their way up the length of the colony from the Orange River and Luderitzbucht.

A new plan of campaign was put into effect, which required the deployment of four separate forces.

McKenzie's Central Force, operating from Luderitzbucht, would occupy Aus and then push on east along the railway towards Keetman-shoop. It would have in the field two mounted brigades of two regiments each (later increased to three, totalling 1 800 men) and two six-gun batteries of field artillery. To garrison Luderitzbucht and protect the lines of communication there would be seven infantry battalions, in two brigades, and two four-gun batteries of heavy artillery.

Striking across the Orange River from Upington would be Southern Force, under Colonel van Deventer, with 29 burgher commandos, totalling 5 000 men, and one four-gun battery of field artillery. Operating in four columns, the force would thrust north towards Keetmanshoop, roughly along the line of the railway from Kalkfontein.

Eastern Force under Colonel C A L Berrange would march on Keetmanshoop from Kuruman, crossing the Kalahari desert. It would have four regiments of mounted riflemen (1 200 in all) and one section of heavy artillery.

Northern Force would march east from Swakopmund to Windhuk, to cut the central railway spine. The first force that had landed under Skinner's command would be strengthened and come under the command of General Botha himself, with Skinner commanding an infantry brigade. The force would consist of two mounted brigades totalling 4 700 burgher commandos, with each brigade supported by a four-gun battery of field artillery. To protect the field force's lines of communication and the railway construction crews and to garrison Swakopmund there would be two infantry brigades, two unbrigaded infantry battalions, a mounted regiment and a battery and a section (six guns in all) of heavy artillery.

Each of these forces would have its own complement of administrative, medical and engineer units.[3]

The spearhead of the South African offensive was the cavalry, an effective force of 13 000 mounted riflemen supported by artillery. In fact the campaign is seen by some authorities as the last great cavalry operation in military history. While cavalry was used in other theatres of the First World War, nowhere else was its function so crucial, nowhere else in the war were there the wide-ranging movements by horsemen, extending over hundreds of miles and nowhere else did strategy hinge on the mounted soldier as it did in South West.

Of the 13 000 mounted riflemen, 8 000 were deployed in the south and 5 000 with Northern Force. Most of the latter were burgher commandos.[4]

While the mounted units operated more spectacularly, the infantry regiments did more than mere guard duty. They were the anchor on which the cavalry movements swung and they also covered a lot of ground, making forced marches that are recorded in military history as among the longest and fastest ever made anywhere.

With the four invasion forces operating far from one another, each was theoretically vulnerable to attack by a concentrated enemy force, but only in the unlikely event of the Germans abandoning one or more of the fronts. The Germans were in fact now compelled to spread their forces wide and, after Sandfontein, were seldom the stronger numerically in any battle.

To keep central and northern forces supplied, an armada of ships, numbering more than 25 at one point, had to be assembled.

For many of the men, especially the burghers, the trip to Luderitzbucht or Swakopmund was not only their first ocean voyage but also their first sight of the sea.

One of the medical officers of Northern Force, Dr H F B Walker, overheard two burghers arguing, as they leaned over the stern of the troopship, about how it maintained course. One was sure that the vessel was steered by a rope that was trailing in the water behind it. But the other, pointing to the wake left by the ship in the calm sea, said: 'No. Look, there's the road'.[5]

Another interested medical spectator on a voyage to Walvis Bay was Burton, now a major, who travelled on the *Galway Castle*. An outbreak of measles and whooping cough affected more than 20 per cent of the burghers on the boat.

'In the dense fog and murky weather, for five days and nights the victims sneezed, coughed, spat and vomited, to give the fatigue squads some hard work in cleaning up the ship to the satisfaction of the ship's doctor, who, I could see, was more amused than disgusted,' Burton wrote in his diary.

Even the steeple of a little church is prominent in the monotonous flatness of Walvis Bay. This picture shows the Engineers' park as it begins to fill with stores brought ashore from the invasion fleet. (Cape Archives)

Men, horses and equipment as heavy as railway locomotives and armoured cars came ashore on pontoons like this, which were built from a design found in a German office. (Cape Archives)

The first wave of the Walvis Bay invasion force sailed in six cargo vessels, escorted by the Royal Navy cuisers *Hyacinth* (flagship of Admiral King-Hall) and *Astraea*, and the former Table Bay tug *Ludwig Weiner*, renamed HMS Afrikander and armed with a 13-pounder gun and a three-pounder. Already waiting off Walvis Bay was another British warship, HMS *Albion*, the *Armadale Castle* and a hospital ship, the *Ebani*.

The *Galway Castle* carried the lst Infantry Brigade, composed of the South African Irish regiment, the Rand Rifles and the South African Engineer Corps. On board the *Gaika* were the 3rd Infantry Brigade: the 2nd Transvaal Scottish, the 2nd Kimberley Regiment, two batteries of heavy artillery, two machine-gun batteries, the crew of the anti-aircraft gun 'Skinny Liz', and a motorised contingent.

The *Monarch* carried the Imperial Light Horse, the 1st Rhodesians and the Intelligence Scouts. The *Rufidji* carried 170 black members of the Military Post and Telegraph Administration, 400 stevedores and 50 men described, in the extraordinary fashion of the day, as 'sanitary natives'! Their function presumably was the highly unsanitary one of tending the army's latrines. On the *Den of Glamis* were another 500 'natives', not 'sanitary' in this case but railway construction workers. Troops and non-combatants totalled 6 000 men. The fleet also carried 888 horses, 683 mules and 200 draught oxen.

In addition to the guns of the artillery batteries the ships carried in their holds large quantities of ammunition, several railway locomotives and trucks, rails and sleepers for building the railways, motor vehicles, mule-waggons, motor boats, rowing-boats, pontoons, borehole drilling rigs, electric-lighting plants, seawater condensing plants, water-tanks, steam-cranes and winches, timber, firewood, coal, petrol, building materials, tons of food for the men and animals and thousands of gallons of drinking water from the Table Mountain reservoir.

When all that had been unloaded the ships sailed back to Cape Town to fetch more. But unloading at Walvis Bay, and later at Swakopmund, was not as easy as loading at Cape Town. Since the facilities at the South West African ports were rudimentary, the engineers had virtually to build two new ports. The bigger vessels could not tie up in harbour and had to anchor two miles out at sea. From there the men, the animals, the locomotives, the waggons and all rest of the cargo had to be brought to shore on lighters and pontoons.

To get the animals ashore the engineers built rafts of empty barrels and oil drums, based on a German pattern found at Luderitzbucht, on to which the animals were lowered in slings, sometimes bucking and kicking. The rafts, each carrying up to 40 horses or mules, were towed close inshore and from there were hauled in through the surf by gangs on the beach, pulling on long cables. When the raft touched bottom a ramp was run

Rev William Meara in his army chaplain's uniform. For him the fogbound sand dunes of Walvis Bay became like 'God's own rose garden'. (Methodist Archives/Cory Library)

out to it and naked black men plunged into the surf to lead – and sometimes wrestle – the animals on to the beach.[6]

Once a group of panicky horses broke free on the beach and galloped off into the dunes. Soon afterwards a patrol found, attached to a pole stuck into the sand on the outskirts of town, a note from the Germans thanking the 'English' for the fine horses.

With 24 rafts in operation, as many as 1 500 animals could be landed in a single day, although the average was about 1 000 a day. Unloading operations were frequently hampered by rough seas and by fog that prevented essential ship-to-shore signalling. Despite that, no men and only a few animals and pieces of cargo were lost. The mood of most of the troops on arriving at Walvis Bay was one of dismay as they gazed out from the ship (fog permitting) at a panorama of sand and nothing but sand.

'But oh, what a wild, barren, cheerless waste the country seems to be,' Captain William Meara, army chaplain, wrote in his diary on arriving at Walvis Bay. 'Right from the shore away inland as far as the eye can reach there is nothing but sand, sand, sand; a wild, seemingly useless desert waste. Sand dunes reaching from skyline to skyline'.[7] But not even Walvis Bay could depress the chaplain; it seems only to have strengthened his faith.

'I am sleeping in the open . . . on a sailcloth . . .,' he wrote later. 'The men and officers are asleep in a position ready for action and all to stand to arms. I have had a very gracious consciousness of the presence of the Lord with me these latter days. And so today, with a wild, bleak, barren desert, a cheerless waste, all around me, I have felt as though I was in God's own rose garden.'

Captain Meara, an Irish-born Methodist minister, served as a chaplain with the South African forces in France as well as in South West Africa. He was subsequently minister at the Methodist Central Hall in Johannesburg for 16 years.

In the sands of Walvis Bay he found an appreciative flock. An entry in his diary for Sunday, January 10 1915, reads: 'It was really fine. I sat on a box outside my tent and the men and non-coms sat on a sand dune in front and we sang hymn after hymn until the darkness fell.'

The chaplain's entry into the rough life among the sand dunes appears either to have had a profound influence on the men or to have provided some light amusement. Shortly after his arrival he wrote: 'I find the swearing has perceptibly lessened and in the tent beside mine from which very bad language used to come they were singing hymns last night.'

If the men were mocking him it was wasted, for he took it quite differently. And if they were, it was not for long, for the chaplain marched and suffered alongside the soldiers in the heat, dust and thirst for the rest of the campaign.

Life became considerably more pleasant for the troops when they moved from Walvis Bay to Swakopmund where, according to O'Shaughnessy, the journalist, there were many hotels, beer gardens, movie theatres and a music hall.[8]

O'Shaughnessy does not say whether all these establishments remained in business but they presumably did, for no record seems to exist of their having shut down and the German civilians, unlike those in Luderitz, did not have to be shipped south for internment. In addition to the emporia mentioned by O'Shaughnessy there was an even larger

After the bleakness of Walvis Bay the South Africans enjoyed being in Swakopmund, the colony's holiday resort. This aerial view was taken during the campaign. (Cape Archives)

brothel than the one in Luderitz, housed in a fine building in the centre of town.

Captain Meara was incensed by the bountiful evidence of immorality that he found in the seaside resort, which apparently included as much pornography as the South Africans had found in Luderitzbucht.

'I find that Swakopmund, like Luderitzbucht, seems to have been characterised by immorality, at least in some parts of the town,' he wrote. 'The low, disgraceful and obscene pictures found in some of the places were bestial and reveal the baseness of those who either lived or frequented the houses and beer halls.'

Some soldiers of the Rhodesia Regiment were also disappointed in Swakopmund, but for a different reason. They built themselves a dugout and, to keep the sand from falling in, they lined the walls with barrels containing an unknown liquid. For reasons unexplained, they never tried to find out what the liquid was. When their unit was moved on and another regiment took over the dugout a soldier with an inquiring mind stuck a bayonet into one of the barrels and discovered that they were filled with good German beer. The new occupants took much pleasure in informing the Rhodesians of their discovery.[9]

As they confronted each other at fairly short range across the sand

147

dunes the South Africans and the Germans had exchanges that sometimes verged on the bizarre.

Near Swakopmund the Imperial Light Horse maintained a cossack post on a hilltop during the day. When they left it in the evening and returned to camp the Germans would move in and occupy the position, making way at dawn for the ILH After this silly situation had prevailed for some time the ILH one morning found several bottles of beer at the position, with a note asking for cigarettes in exchange.

The South Africans, who had plenty of cigarettes but very little beer, were happy to oblige. It soon became clear that the Germans had plenty of beer but not many cigarettes and a regular trade developed. Every morning the ILH men would pick up beer and leave cigarettes and both sides seemed very happy with the arrangement.

One morning one of the ILH noticed the end of a steel rod sticking out of an area of freshly disturbed ground at the cossack post. It looked too much like a mine for the South Africans' liking, so they sent for the sappers and, sure enough, buried under the cossack post the engineers found a mine big enough to have blown the entire ILH detachment to pieces. After that the only trade was in bullets.

References

1. O'Shaugnessy, W W, *The Northern Campaign,* second half of joint account with Rayner of the campaign.
2. *Ibid,* p. 174.
3. Collyer, p. 54-55.
4. *Ibid,* p. 5.
5. Walker, H F B, *A Doctor's Diary in Damaraland,* Edward Arnold, 1917.
6. O'Shaughnessy, p. 246.
7. Meara, William, unpublished diary in Cory Library, Rhodes University, Grahamstown.
8. O'Shaughnessy, p. 175.
9. O'Shaughnessy, p. 178.

CHAPTER
16

Uppercut and Right Hook

Puffing through the desert came a locomotive, pushing an open truck. Sitting in a wicker chair in the truck was General Louis Botha, Prime Minister of South Africa and Commander-in-Chief of its armed forces.

Behind the locomotive was a kitchen van, a water truck and another open truck carying 40 picked riflemen. General Botha was on his way from Luderitzbucht to the front at Tschaukaib to inspect the troops and to talk to the commander of the Central Force, General McKenzie.

He had stopped at Luderitz while sailing to Walvis Bay to take direct command of the Northern Force. Apart from discussing strategy with McKenzie, the commander-in-chief wanted to see the troops and raise their morale, for he knew they had been through a trying time, suffering from heat, dust, disease and discomfort, enduring painful marches but getting little chance to do what they had signed up to do: fight the enemy.

His concern was appreciated by one of those travelling with him in the open truck, Roderick Jones, general manager of Reuters news agency. The country in which the troops were living struck Jones as 'a blinding desolation as far as the eye can reach, with sand dunes and lone kopjes here and there to break the demoniac monotony of the place'.

The monotony was broken in another small way by the signs that the men had put up to designate their temporary places of residence, with names such as Fort Has Beans, Dryazell Halt and Fort Botha.

The commander-in-chief had little need to worry about the men's morale, however. At Tschaukaib he took the salute as the troops marched in review before him and, acording to Jones's account, they were anything but despondent.

'It was an event to be remembered, this review, in the heart of the desert, in sight of the enemy outposts, under a blazing African sun and amid an apparently unfathomable expanse of sand . . . . There was something unique in such a setting, in the stirring skirl of the pipes as the Highlanders, men of magnificent physique, swung by, and in the drums

General Botha, standing under the Union Jack, takes the salute as the infantry of Central Force marches past at Tschaukaib. (War Museum)

and fifes and bugles playing the other units past this Dutch commander-in-chief who, attended by a mixed Dutch and English staff, stood under a great Union Jack, the only splash of colour in this drab patchwork of sand and khaki, taking the salute and, when all was over, doffing his helmet and lustily calling for "three cheers for His Majesty the King".'

Then, according to Rayner, 'the desert literally trembled from the cheering.' McKenzie then called for three cheers for Botha.

'Cheers! The very hills rang with them. I have never seen such enthusiasm before, seen nothing quite so emotional at any time.'

Rayner recorded that a Dutch-speaking officer (who had been a Cambridge blue) said as he watched the scene: 'Only in the British Empire could this thing have come to pass.'

Addressing the troops after the march past, Botha thanked them for putting up with the waiting and boredom and the hardship while the rebellion at home was put down. He said he took the blame for it all.

As Botha rode back to Luderitz in his open truck, troops from the English-speaking regiments that composed Central Force lined the railway.

'The cheering started at Tschaukaib, it died down 40 miles away', Rayner wrote. 'Helmets were doffed at the front and a long, rolling, wave set in motion all the way to Luderitzbucht.'

There, Botha went back on board the *Galway Castle* and sailed on to Walvis Bay to begin the offensive that was to end the campaign.

★ ★ ★ ★ ★

Six months had passed since the start of the war and, with the rebellion at home all but over and the invasion forces all in place, the South African army was ready to begin closing the net on the Germans in South West Africa.

Northern Force was about to move east from Swakopmund. Central Force was well into the desert in its advance from Luderitzbucht. Van Deventer's Southern Force now headed north across the border.

The Union Castle liner *Galway Castle* became the principal troopship of the fleet that shuttled between Cape Town and South West Africa to keep the invasion forces supplied and reinforced. She reverted to her normal role as a passenger liner after the campaign. There was much sadness among South Africans when they heard that the *Galway Castle* had been torpedoed by a German submarine on September 12 1918, 48 hours out of Plymouth. She sank with the loss of 154 passengers. (Cape Archives)

And Berrange started Eastern Force on its prodigious trek across the Kalahari. By successfully leading his force of more than 2 000 men on a march of 147 miles from Kimberley to Kuruman, and then through 250 miles of deep sand to the South West African border, Berrange accomplished what one historian has called 'one of the most adventurous single feats in the whole record of the war'[1] and another has described as 'one of the most romantic and adventurous movements in the war'.[2]

In some ways Berrange's march was perhaps no more noteworthy an achievement than Kemp's ride across the Kalahari. Berrange had elaborate logistical support and his only enemy was time, whereas Kemp and his men had to live off the land and were harrassed all the way to the South West border by loyal forces. Kemp did, however, swing south to more congenial territory in the later stages of his journey, whereas Berrange turned north and cut straight through the inhospitable heart of the Kalahari. By any measure, however, Berrange's march was a remarkable feat, both logistically and in physical endurance. If it did

151

nothing else, it clearly demonstrated the value of the motor vehicle in desert warfare.

Berrange left Kuruman on March 16 with his mounted column, consisting of the 15th South African Mounted Rifles, the Kalahari Horse, Cullinan's Horse and the Bechuanaland Rifles, with three guns and several machine-guns. Two weeks later, on March 31, he crossed into South West Africa near Rietfontein. His men were enabled to keep marching by an elaborate system of advance water points established ahead of the column by motor vehicles carrying the water in drums.

And to keep the motor vehicles running, mechanical workshops were set up along the route, in the wilderness, by an engineering unit.

As Berrange's column approached the border the German force that had been occupying the former South African Police border post at Rietfontein abandoned it and retreated to the post at Schaapkolk on the German side. Berrange brought up his guns, shot down the walls of the German blockhouse and captured the surviving defenders.

Then Eastern Force marched on Hasur, whose fortified positions the outnumbered Germans abandoned.

Advancing to Kieriis West, the force found the way blocked by another fort, a strongly defended structure in a mountain pass. That, also, was stormed and the 300 German defenders put to flight.

And there Eastern Force linked up with Van Deventer's Southern Force, an achievement that was to present a serious threat to the Germans on their south-eastern flank, and which may have been what persuaded them to abandon the strongly fortified positions at Aus on the railway line from Luderitz without a fight.

A captured German officer, when asked why the fortifications at Aus had been abandoned, replied: 'What could we do, with that column [Berrange's] making such a lightning-like dash all the time to our rear?'

Together the two Union forces went on to attack Kabus and overwhelm the 300-strong German garrison and its two guns.

★ ★ ★ ★ ★

Van Deventer began his march from Upington at the end of February, with his first objectives Schuit Drift on the Orange and Nabas, north-west of Nakob and Ukamas. Elements of the Kenhardt-Calvinia Commando, the Murraysburg Commando, the Namaqualand Commando, the Karroo Schuiters and Naude's Scouts advanced along the north bank of the Orange and attacked Schuit Drift. The terrain was too rugged for horses, and the attack had to proceed forward on foot. One German position was stormed and captured by Major Naude, leader of the Scouts, and one of his men, even though both were wounded. In the meantime the German positions were being shelled from across the river by a section of the Cape Field Artillery.

Raman's Drift, which had been abandoned by Lukin in the withdrawal after the battle of Sandfontein and the outbreak of rebellion in the Union, was retaken in January. By the middle of March all crossings on the Orange were in South African hands and Central Force was heading into the German colony, making for Keetmanshoop.

While his left wing advanced from Raman's Drift, Van Deventer led the right column from Schuit Drift to Nabas. The well-entrenched German forces there resisted for nearly five hours before Van Deventer's men, having worked their way close despite the lack of cover, charged the enemy positions. After close fighting the surviving Germans fled towards Kalkfontein.

Advancing north, Southern Force captured Ukamas, one of the more important German military bases in the south-eastern part of the colony – and from which Major Ritter had launched his attack on Kakamas in January – and then Hudab.

Van Deventer captured Kalkfontein, the southern rail terminus and an important German military base in the south, on April 5. The left wing of his force, under Colonel Bouwer, arrived there two days later. On its way north from Raman's Drift it had cap tured Warmbad, whose hot springs had in peacetime drawn Germans from all over the colony.

The South Africans now had access to the German railway system, which was the same gauge as that being pushed towards the border from

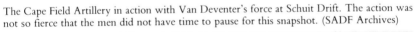

The Cape Field Artillery in action with Van Deventer's force at Schuit Drift. The action was not so fierce that the men did not have time to pause for this snapshot. (SADF Archives)

Prieska. By closing the gap between the two railheads they would soon give themselves a direct rail link to the battlefront.

The next objectives were Keetmanshoop and Seeheim, where the southern railway joined the line from Luderitzbucht. But the advance was threatened by relatively strong German forces ensconced in the Karas mountains, east of the railway from Kalkfontein to Seeheim. Van Deventer decided to make a three-pronged advance.

The signallers at work in the desert. Before the advent of the transistor radio, setting up a field wireless station was an elaborate business requiring the erection of a tall mast held by guy ropes for the aerial. (Cape Archives – E)

He sent one force west of the mountains, along the railway line, another round the east of the range to try to link up with Berrange and a third straight through the mountains.

The eastern flanking force was opposed all the way and encountered strong resistance at Davignab and Platbeen, where it fought a brisk action against about 200 enemy on March 27. The Germans were determined to prevent their force in the mountains from being outflanked and forced to retreat.

But on the western flank their determination crumbled dismally at the first sight of the Union advance. The commander of the western force, Colonel Celliers, sent a scouting party far in advance to test the strength and disposition of the enemy forces. South of Seeheim, they made contact with the enemy, and in a short fight they killed one, wounded four and captured 14 without loss to themselves.

The Germans, thinking that the scouts were the main body of Celliers's column, evacuated Seeheim, and in such haste that they omitted to destroy the railway bridge over the Great Fish River, so that it was left intact for the South African railway traffic that was soon to begin moving along the line.

With both flanks of the Karas mountain position turned, the Germans abandoned it and retreated to Keetmanshoop. And even this

154

important town was abandoned when Berrange made a bold attempt to put part of his force astride the railway and cut off the enemy's retreat. His attempt was frustrated when the Germans made a determined stand at Garuchab, 40 miles east of Keetmanshoop.

The advances in the south were highly satisfying to General Smuts, who had been exercising indirect control over the operations from his office in Pretoria.

'The distance from Kalkfontein to Keetmanshoop is 130 miles over a country of the most difficult character, and the endurance of the troops and the rapidity of movement, considering the nature of the route and the destruction of all means of watering animals, deserve very high commendation,' he commented.

Smuts had been left in charge of the government when Botha had hurried off to lead the troops in South West as soon as the rebellion had been broken. Never a man to stay out of the main action, Smuts chafed at being deskbound in Pretoria while Botha was in the field. He seized the first opportunity to get into the war himself, and on April 14 he arrived in Kalkfontein to take direct charge in the south.

With the loss of Seeheim and Keetmanshoop and the southern railways and the landing of a Union force at Walvis Bay, matters were beginning to look desperate for the Germans.

References

1. Saxon Mills, J, *The Campaign in German South West Africa*, chapter three in *The Empire at War*.
2. Dane.

CHAPTER
17

The Other Side

Colonel von Heydebreck had always been a respected figure in German South West, especially among the soldiers he commanded. After his victory at Sandfontein he was a hero.

Six weeks after Sandfontein he died; not a heroic death, but still a soldierly one. He died on November 12 1914 in a hospital bed, with his stomach ripped by fragments from a rifle grenade.

The grenade, a new type recently brought out from Germany, was being tested at the military base at Kalkfontein on November 9. The commander-in-chief, always interested in new weaponry, had been watching closely. Six grenades had successfully been fired, seemingly confirming the assurance from Berlin that the grenades could not possibly explode prematurely while being fitted to the rifle barrel.

But the seventh grenade did just that, hurling splinters of steel into the group standing around it. One trooper was killed and three wounded. Von Heydebreck was hit in the stomach and Surgeon-General Berg in the thigh.[1] Von Heydebreck underwent an operation but he knew he was going to die and he dictated a farewell message: 'I send to all members of the Imperial Army my best farewell wishes and I confidently hope that the Imperial Army will continue to march to victory. His Majesty the Kaiser, hurrah!'[2]

The colony went into mourning.

Colonel Grant, the South African commander whom von Heydebreck had defeated at Sandfontein, was a prisoner in the hospital at Keetmanshoop being treated for his leg wound when he heard of the accident to von Heydebreck.

'I called at the commandant's office today to inquire after Colonel von Heydebreck and was told that he is in a dangerous condition,' Grant wrote in his diary on November 11.[3]

His entry the next day reads: 'The news today is that Col von Heydebreck died this morning. All flags are at half-mast. I called on the commandant to express my condolences.'

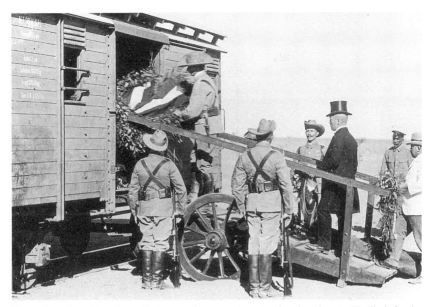

Colonel von Heydebreck's coffin is carried into a railway truck to be taken to Windhuk for the state funeral. (Namibia Archives)

Next day Grant went to the railway station to pay his respects in person to his dead enemy as a special train carrying the body of the German commander-in-chief passed through Keetmanshoop on its way to Windhuk for the funeral.

'The whole garrison paraded at the station, also all the towns-people,' Grant wrote. 'I attended also. The body was in a truck, the coffin covered with wreaths and guarded by soldiers.'

Von Heydebreck's death was one of the greatest misfortunes suffered by the Germans in their defence of South West. He had served in the colony for 17 years and knew it intimately. Besides that he was a bold and imaginative soldier and an effective leader.

His natural successor was Major Victor Franke; but Franke could not immediately take over the command as he was leading a punitive expedition against the Portuguese in Angola when von Heydebreck died. For the time being, Major Ritter was given overall command of all forces in the south.[4] Franke, who was then aged 48, was highly professional but a soldier of a different kind from his predecessor. He appears not to have had the imagination that had inspired von Heydebreck's trap at Sandfontein, none of the boldness of the plan for a German assault on Upington, none of the aggressiveness behind the attack on Kakamas. He struck the South African military leaders as a

157

cautious commander. Yet he was one of the few German officers in the
territory to hold the illustrious 'Blue Max' decoration, awarded for his
service in the Herero rebellion.

Not that a less cautious attitude by Franke would have made much
difference to the final outcome, except perhaps to leave more graves on
the battlefields and more widows at home. For von Heydebreck and
Franke were agreed that the forces available to them could not hope to
defeat the South Africans on the battlefield. In numbers alone, they were
vastly inferior. Against the 50 000 troops South Africa had put into the
field by the the time the campaign was over, the Germans could muster
no more than 7 000. That is the estimate given by Collyer. German
sources put the figure somewhat lower. The highest estimates are no
more than 2 000 regular *Schutztruppe* and slightly more than 4 000
reservists in the *Landswehr*, with about 480 policemen capable of
military service.

The disparity in numbers was to a large extent offset, however, by
logistical and territorial factors. The South Africans had to move their
troops long distances by land or sea (much longer than in any European
theatre of the war) to get them to the German border and, having done
that, they had to get them across formidable deserts. That entailed
bringing large quantities of supplies, including even water, over the
same long lines of communication and to keep the supplies moving as

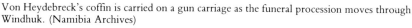

Von Heydebreck's coffin is carried on a gun carriage as the funeral procession moves through
Windhuk. (Namibia Archives)

Colonel Franke, Von Heydebreck's successor as commander-in-chief, was an able if less adventurous soldier. (Namibia Archives)

the lines became ever longer with the advance of the Union forces to the north of the vast territory.

The defenders of the colony, on the other hand, could use their railway system, which included two lines across the otherwise impenetrable desert as well as the central line, to move troops rapidly from one front to another and to keep them supplied. That gave them the effect of a considerably larger force than they actually had. And that is why the South Africans, whose forces were of necessity spread comparatively thinly over the various fronts, considered it necessary to commit as many troops to the campaign as they did.

However, von Heydebreck and Franke and Governor Seitz were all influenced by the belief prevalent in Windhuk and Berlin that the future of all the German colonies would be decided not in those territories but in Europe and the North Sea, and especially the latter. So the defence of South West Africa was seen essentially as a holding action; even if the South Africans conquered the territory they would ultimately be thrown out when Germany had defeated Britain and her allies in Europe and on the ocean.

And there was little doubt in anyone's mind in Windhuk at the end of 1914 that Germany would win in the end; did not its troops already stand victorious on French and Belgian soil?

Savouring the pleasures of the colonial life, Franke (at right with tame cheetah on chain) and a fellow officer are served wine by servants on the verandah. (Namibia Archives)

In August of that year few in Windhuk were certain that South Africa would enter the war on Britain's side and invade South West. It was considered more likely that Afrikaner opposition to fighting for Britain would keep South Africa out of the war, even if it did not lead to a successful Boer rebellion. The last thing that any German would have believed was that the territory would not only be conquered by a largely Afrikaans-speaking South African army but that South Africa would still be in occupation of the territory half a century later.

So both von Heydebreck and Franke shared the same view of what strategy should be followed in defending South West. Von Heydebreck's plan was to concentrate his defences in the south, from where the invasion was expected. The coast would be only lightly defended, for the South Africans were unlikely to launch a seaborne invasion; and if they they did, they would find it either impossible or extremely difficult to move an army across the deserts. If, however, the unexpected happened and the South Africans did reach the interior of the colony, von Heydebreck would fight a defensive retreat and make a last stand in the mining areas of the north.[5]

Wherever they attacked the invaders would find a terrain made unusable by a scorched earth policy of tearing up the railway lines, mining the roads, blowing up the bridges, poisoning the water supplies, abandoning the farms and destroying food supplies.[6]

When Franke took over the command of the German forces with the elevated rank of Lieutenant-Colonel he adopted a similar policy, with the approval of Governor Seitz. Both men hoped that von Spee's fleet would not only discourage a seaborne landing but would make it possible for South West to receive supplies and reinforcements from Germany. The battle of the Falklands dashed those hopes but it did not destroy their belief in a final German victory. That belief appears to have been maintained right up to the final surrender and to have been responsible for their reluctance to destroy anything that could not easily be rebuilt when the South Africans were eventually thrown out or withdrew under a peace agreement.

★ ★ ★ ★ ★

Thoughts of giving up South West Africa were not lightly entertained in either Windhuk or Berlin. The colony was one of the jewels in the German imperial crown, whose other components in Africa were German East Africa (Tanganyika), Togo and Kamerun in Africa; and in the Pacific, German Samoa, the Bismarck Archipelago and New Guinea. South West Africa was Germany's largest foreign possession (322 000 square miles), with the largest population of Germans (about 14 000 civilians in 1914) and the best climate and potential for settlement. Before the First World War it was regarded by many Germans as their country's 'place in the sun'.

German links with the territory went back to 1842, when the first Rhenish Mission station was established. The missionaries were followed inevitably by traders and later by settlers. Despite frequent appeals from British interests the British Government refused to annex the territory and attach it to the Cape Colony and only went as far as annexing Walvis Bay in 1878. The view in London then, according to some historians, was that as long as Britain had the only good harbour on the coast the Germans or anyone else could have the rest, which was mostly desert.

Not even when diamonds were found in the northern Cape colony in 1868 could interest be aroused in London in the possibility that they might exist also north of the Orange River. In 1883 a Bremen merchant, Herr Luderitz, obtained a cession of 215 square miles at the place that had been named Angra Pequena by the early Portuguese navigators and was soon to become Luderitzbucht. The following year a German protectorate was established over Great Namaqualand, and in 1885 that was extended to include Damaraland. Thus a great military power in Europe was able to establish a colony on the border of what was to become the Union of South Africa, a country strategically placed astride one of the main sea routes and rich in minerals.

Berlin immediately appointed an Imperial Commissioner, Dr Ernst

Goring, father of the man who was to become one of the pillars of Nazi Germany a generation later, Field Marshall Hermann Goring. The Germans exercised a firm authority over their new possession and when the Hereros rose in revolt in 1904 Berlin sent out 15 000 troops with artillery and machine-guns to suppress them.

The exercise was put under the command of Lieutenant-General Lothar von Trotha, who had led operations in the Boxer rebellion in China. So firmly did the Germans act against the Hereros that they left little doubt in the outside world that their intention was nothing less than genocide; the extermination of the Hereros and the acquisition of their grazing lands for German settlement.

The Hereros fought vigorously and killed more than 2 300 German soldiers; but they lost vastly more of their own people. After crushing the rebellion, von Trotha issued his notorious 'Extermination Order' of October 2

With upswept moustache and hat brim and Iron Cross on his chest, Lieutenant-General Lothar von Trotha is the epitome of the German militarist of his day. His suppression of the Herero uprising was ruthless. (Namibia Archives)

1904, declaring that the Hereros were no longer German subjects and any who did not leave the territory would be shot. Many of the surviving Hereros were rounded up and driven to the Bechuanaland border, and those who lagged or fell out were bayoneted or shot. The order was revoked by Chancellor von Bulow when news of it reached Berlin, but by then it was too late for the victims. Some of the remaining Hereros were herded on to Shark Island off Luderitzbucht and left there to die, which they did with cries that are said to have at times disturbed the sleep of the residents of Luderitzbucht.

Of the 50 000 Hereros in the territory at the beginning of the uprising, only 15 000 were left alive at its end.

German South West Africa assumed its final form in 1890 when the Caprivi Zipfel, the incongruous finger of land reaching from the north-eastern corner deep into central Africa, was added in the pie-slicing process by which the great European powers divided up Africa among themselves in the scramble for colonies at the end of the century. Under an Anglo-German convention Germany, in exchange for Zanzibar, was given Heligoland and the strip of land stretching from South

West Africa to the Zambezi, which the Germans named after the then chancellor, Count Caprivi.[7]

Why Germany wanted this geographic oddity is a matter of conjecture. Some historians believe the intention was to gain access to the Zambezi River in the belief that it was navigable to the Indian Ocean – which makes little sense since the Victoria Falls had already been 'discovered' by European explorers. A more likely theory is that Berlin wanted to throw the Zipfel like a boom across the path of the British in their plans for uninterrupted possession of territory stretching from the Cape to Cairo. Cecil Rhodes, the chief proponent of the Cape-to-Cairo notion, is known to have been furious at the deal that gave the Zipfel to the Germans.

An extension of this theory is that the Germans saw the Zipfel as a stage in the acquisition of territory linking South West Africa with German East Africa, which would have had the German flag flying across the continent from the Atlantic to the Indian Ocean.

★ ★ ★ ★ ★

When the war broke out there was grave unease in South West Africa. The Germans there saw themselves in an insecure situation, with a British Dominion (South Africa) to the south, British protectorates (Bechuanaland and the Rhodesias) to the east, the Royal Navy to the west and to the north a colony of Portugal, which, while ostensibly neutral, was an old ally of the British. Under the Act of Berlin of 1885, signed by Germany, Britain, France, Belgium, Spain, Portugal and the United States, the territories of the Congo basin were supposed to be kept out of any war between any of the signatories. But when war broke out in 1914 the British Government said it could not adopt a neutral posture in Africa.[8]

It lost no time in sending a detachment of the British South African Police from Rhodesia to seize the administrative centre of the Caprivi Strip, Schuckmannsburg.

The Germans had no strong forces there, and the seizure was unopposed; in fact the whole business was very civilised and polite. One section of the BSAP force set out by train from Salisbury on September 10 and at Hartley found that 'the ladies of that sporting little township had come to the station and provided a most excellent tea for us'.[9] In Hartley they, too, were doing their bit for the war effort.

At Victoria Falls a contingent from Bulawayo and '40 armed native police' joined the force. They dug trenches to defend the Victoria Falls bridge, more as an exercise than in any serious expectation of a German attack. Then they trekked into the Caprivi on what was to be perhaps the first British conquest of the war.

At Sesheke they drew lots to see who would ask the Germans to surrender to avoid bloodshed. Lieutenant Stephens won and, accompanied by two corporals, one black and one white, crossed the river by boat. On the other side they were met by a black sentry who was obviously expecting them and who led them to the cluster of modest buildings that was Schuckmannsburg. The German Resident, Herr von Frankenberg, was waiting for them on his verandah.

After some formal discussion he agreed to surrender and the parlementaire group returned to the river to fetch the rest of the BSAP force. Reaching Schuckmannsburg at dusk, the BSAP formed up on the square, Herr von Frankenberg formally surrendered and he and his white police sergeant were arrested and immediately released on parole. It was too late to raise the Union Jack, so the BSAP contented themselves with lowering the German flag. First thing next morning they hoisted the British flag, with the men drawn up on the square and giving three cheers for His Majesty the King.

Von Frankenburg's native police force was told to disband and go home and, leaving a detachment of its own black police to occupy Schuckmannsburg, the BSAP took the German resident and his sergeant off to be interned in Livingstone.

And that was all there was to what was perhaps the most amicable confrontation of the whole war.

★ ★ ★ ★ ★

Ready though they might have been to give up the Caprivi Strip without a fight, the Germans were not going to surrender the rest of the territory so easily. But von Heydebreck and Franke were painfully aware that the armed forces had been allowed to decline far below the strength that had been thrown against the Hereros.

Chroniclers of the period differ, however, over how badly run-down the German defences were. Von Oelhafen paints a picture not of a heroic group of hardy pioneers but of a community consisting largely of riff-raff.

'In Germany there was a general belief that the farmers must be particularly useful soldiering material, since riding, shooting and resourcefulness . . . was to some extent their daily bread. That may have been true of the old settler countries, such as that of the Boers, where a class of farmers based essentially on the land had come into being, whose roots were there and most of whose sons were capable of military service.

'But the population of South West Africa consisted predominantly of immigrants; few of the farmers were familiar with agriculture, and they were satisfied to wrest a bare living from their few acres with much labour and disappointment. Neither the townsmen nor the countrymen had ever soldiered, nor could they ride or shoot, while those who were

White ducks for the gentlemen and veiled bonnets for the ladies are the order of the day as Governor Seitz, with binoculars hanging from his neck, goes to the races at Windhuk. It seemed then that the sun would never set on the German empire. (Namibia Archives)

already fit and willing were sent back by the civil authorities to look after the crops . . .

'South West Africa harboured the all-too-motley populaton of a very young settlers' colony; some of them had left Germany only reluctantly, there were adventurers from all sorts of countries, rootless, with no allegiance, from across the borders, most of them morally beneath contempt. Their physical condition also left much to be desired. New to the country, they were inadequately protected against tropical diseases and much given to the vices of the tropics; they were prematurely burned out.

'Many of them, with extraordinary ailments and aged before their time, donned the soldier's tunic, and it was obvious at a glance that they were totally incapable of any useful military service.'[10]

According to von Oelhafen, these men were sent into action before they had received adequate training, and that made them more of an impediment than a help to the hard core of professional soldiers defending the territory.

Against this force, according to von Oelhafen, the South Africans were able to put a better class of soldier.

'The careful selection of the enemy fighting men was apparent from the first transport of enemy prisoners after the battle of Sandfon-

It was not all horse racing at the Windhuk racecourse. For variety the Camel Corps showed that it could do a steeplechase with the best of them. (Namibia Archives)

tein . . . most of them in hard, fit physical condition. The human material was very good. Even in the later days one saw very few elderly men; unfit men, never.

'Although quite unused to German standards of discipline, it was obvious that they were perfectly controlled by their leaders, and even though looting, theft and other irregularities were the order of the day, there were no atrocities committed against non-combatant whites.'

Von Oelhafen's view of the quality of the German soldiers available to Franke is supported by chaplain Meara, for what his unprofessional opinion is worth. At the end of the campaign, after Botha had addressed the assembled Union troops, Meara wrote in his diary: 'It was a great contrast to see our men, smart, alert and soldierly, and compare them to the heavy, slovenly, unsoldierly appearance of the Germans.'

Von Oelhafen found that 'the soldierly qualities of the citizens of the Union were good. Even though there was a good deal of riff-raff among the English, to whom the campaign was opportune for a while, nevertheless that had no adverse effect on the development of the national characteristics: toughness, intelligence, dash, self-confidence, commercial talents, patriotism.'

His view of the German soldiers was not shared by the British historian, Saxon Mills, who wrote that 'the German population consisted largely of well-trained reservists, ready to hand for the time when the German forces would invade South Africa and be welcomed everywhere by the insurgent Dutch.'

According to Saxon Mills, 'the Germans were hopelessly outnumbered but the personnel they had available reached a high standard of efficiency, and if, as in East Africa, they had been led by a resolute and skilful commander, the defence of German South West Africa might have been greatly prolonged. As it was, they showed to little advantage in the fighting.'

This view is supported by others, who have found the South West Africa campaign noteworthy in that the Germans held out against enormous odds for nearly a year without drafting combat soldiers from the native population, as was done in East Africa, where von Lettow Vorbeck's askaris were still fighting on the Mozambique border when the armistice was signed in 1918.[11]

Von Oelhafen's views about looting by the South Africans are contradicted by a report published in a Windhuk newspaper as the Union troops approached the capital. As it was the same newspaper that had earlier described the Union troops as 'rabble' and 'fat-bellied sluggards' its objectivity may perhaps be questioned. Nevertheless it told its readers that 'we may rely with complete assurance that not a hair on the head of a single citizen will be harmed by the enemy. General Botha's troops are neither Russians nor undisciplined French but are men of a kindred race, of the same Teutonic extraction as ourselves, whose leader would never countenance any improper conduct against members of a fellow-cultured nation.

'Wherever the enemy have thus far occupied any portion of our territory they have behaved themselves as becomes civilised soldiers. Men, women and children have been treated by them with the utmost respect and consideration . . . News reaches us from Keetmanshoop that our womenfolk left behind there have been treated with every possible respect, with great courtesy, and similar reports come from farms of the north.'

References

1. Von Oelhafen, p. 55.
2. Rayner.
3. Grant, R C, unpublished diaries in Cory Library.
4. Von Oelhafen, p. 55.
5. Ungleich, p. 50.
6. *Ibid*.
7. Walker, Eric A, *A History of Southern Africa,* Longmans.
8. Ungleich, p. 40.
9. *Nongquai*.
10. Von Oelhafen, p. 14.
11. Ungleich.

CHAPTER

18

Death in Angola

The Germans were uneasy as they stood in the Portuguese fort at Naulila in southern Angola. It was beginning to look as though they had ridden into a trap.

They had been been suspicious when the Portuguese had invited them into the fort, but they had agreed to enter when they were assured that they could bring their weapons with them. Now the leader of the German party, Dr Schultze-Jena, noticed that the fort's garrison had quietly taken up their own weapons.

His unease turned to concern when the commander of the fort, Lieutenant Sereno, announced that his orders were to take the Germans to his superior officer at Cuamato to discuss the problem that had brought the German party to Angola. Schultze-Jena gave orders for his party's horses to be got ready. Portuguese soldiers tried to prevent them from being saddled but were brushed aside by the now alarmed Germans.

Schultze-Jena told the lieutenant that he would return to his camp and wait for a message from Cuamato. Lieutenant Sereno was adamant: the Germans would not be allowed to leave the fort except to go to Cuamato.

Shouting to his men to ride, Schultze-Jena leaped on his horse and galloped for the gate. The Portuguese opened fire and the doctor and one of his men fell, fatally wounded. Lieutenant Loesch and Trooper Jensen made it out of the gate but they had ridden only a few yards when Loesch toppled from his horse, dead, and Jensen fell, wounded.

He crawled through the bush to the bank of the Cunene River. Before he could make any attempt to cross the river he was found and captured by the Portuguese. One of the three black policemen in the German party had been killed in the shooting, and his body was thrown into the river. The other two, both wounded, were imprisoned, but managed to escape a few days later and take the news of the incident to the German authorities.

Within a short time Lisbon and Berlin found themselves contemplating, with some alarm on either side, the possibility of going to war over the incident.

Governor Seitz in Windhuk in fact took it for granted that a state of war now existed between the two countries. On October 25 1914, six days after the shooting, he and Colonel von Heydebreck decided to send a punitive expedition to Fort Naulila to avenge the death of the Germans.[1]

Dr Schultze-Jena had gone to Naulila on a mission of war, but not against the Portuguese. He was trying to secure supplies for the war against the South Africans.

Despite the close ties between Portugal and Britain, the Germans looked to Angola as a vital outlet to the outside world and as a source of supplies once the South Africans declared war.[2] Soon after the outbreak of the war Windhuk had asked the German consul in Luanda to buy as much food as possible and send it overland to avoid the risk of interception by British warships. At the same time a merchant in Luderitz, Herr Busch, was sent to Mocamedes on a similar mission.

When no further word was heard from Luanda, a German merchant marine officer, Lieutenant Brauer of the Woermann Line, was sent in a motor fishing vessel to Mocamedes to try to make contact with the German vice-consul there. Brauer safely reached Mocamedes, but found

The Germans used the machine-gun with a special skill on the battlefield, and nobody appreciated this more than the South Africans. But in the action against the Portuguese who were ensconced in Fort Naulila they had to resort to hand grenades and bayonets to win the day. (Namibia Archives)

The *Schutztruppe* were essentially mounted riflemen but they were trained to fight on foot as well. (Namibia Archives)

himself caught up in a contest between the German and British vice-consuls. The British representative was trying to stop any supplies going to German South West from the Portuguese territory.

Brauer learned that despite the British representative's efforts a convoy of waggons carrying food had set out for South West from Lubango, a town south-east of Mocamedes and 150 miles from the border. It was travelling under the protection of a German 'railway studies commission'.[3] Brauer was told that the attitude of the Portuguese had hardened, and it would be impossible to get any further supplies in Angola.

He also learned that in August the Portuguese had sent 1 250 troops from Lisbon and about 800 black askaris to the border with German South West. Ostensibly these forces were intended to deal with rebellious tribes on Angola's southern border but the Germans suspected that their real purpose might be to block the movement of German supplies.

The energetic British vice-consul had not been idle while Brauer had been making his inquiries; he had been trying to get a British auxiliary cruiser (probably the *Kinfauns Castle*) to take up a position to intercept Brauer's vessel on his return with further supplies. Learning of this, Brauer hastily put to sea.

Brauer was not lacking in initiative himself. Despite the risk of interception by the British warship, he paused in his voyage back to

170

German South West and tried to fish up the undersea telegraph cable from Cape Town to Britain and cut it. He failed and sailed on, and safely reached Cape Cross, 130 miles north of Swakopmund, where it was possible for a small boat to anchor and offload.

Cape Cross appears to have been used on more than one occasion by the Germans to land supplies and in an attempt to put a stop to this the British warship HMS *Albion* shelled the place, destroying buildings used by a company taking guano off the rocks. The customs building and a condensor for obtaining fresh water from seawater were damaged.[4]

Even after losing the big wireless stations at Swakopmund, Aus and Windhoek, the Germans operated a radio station at Fort Sessfontein near the coast in the north of the territory and this was used to maintain contact with ships running the British blockade to bring supplies from Germany.

Brauer's report of the departure of the food convoy from Lubango was confirmed by an emissary sent by the German vice-consul there. It was then that the authorities in Windhuk decided to send Dr Schultze-Jena, who was the district officer at Outjo, to Angola to meet and escort the convoy across the border into South West Africa.

Schultze-Jena left Outjo with an armed escort of 13, including the four black policemen, and arrived at Erickson's Drift on the Cunene on October 16.

When using their modern guns the German artillerists were effective. But many of their guns were obsolete and much of their ammunition was old and relatively often failed to explode. (Namibia Archives)

A member of the railway study commission, a geologist named Vageler, had been camped nearby in Angola and two days earlier he had learned that the food convoy had been seized by the Portuguese. When he became aware of the presence in the vicinity of Schultze-Jena's party he rode south to find them and warn them of the hostile attitude of the Portuguese. Before he could find the other Germans he was seized by the Portuguese and taken to Fort Naulila and then to Humbe.[5]

From his camp on the river Schultze-Jena sent a messenger to Fort Donguena with a letter to the district administrator at Humbe informing the Portuguese of his arrival at the border. The next day Lieutenant Sereno arrived at the camp with 30 soldiers and, according to von Oelhafen's account, disputed the Germans' right to be there, as they were trespassing across the border. The Germans produced their own map to dispute that, and Sereno said the matter should be referred to the senior officer of the Cuamato military district, who was at Fort Naulila.

Sereno and his patrol nevertheless spent the night at the Germans' camp and surprised them by taking elaborate security precautions. During the night some of the Portuguese tried to approach the Germans' horses and had to be kept away by the sentries.

The next morning Sereno invited the Germans to accompany him to Fort Naulila to discuss the border question. Schultze-Jena, eager to get news of the food convoy, agreed, not knowing that he would be riding to his death at the fort.

The purpose of the Portuguese actions is unclear; perhaps the local commanders were giving effect to the ancient Portuguese alliance with Britain. But when the news of the attack on the German party reached Windhuk, Governor Seitz interpreted it as a warlike act and decided to assume until the contrary might be established that Portugal had entered the war on the side of the Allies.

The wireless station in Togo that relayed traffic between Windhuk and Berlin had fallen to the British, and weather conditions had not been suitable for some time for direct wireless communication with Berlin, so Seitz had no way of finding out immediately what Portugal's position was.

He decided to send two punitive forces immediately to attack small Portuguese posts near the border. Taking the posts by surprise, they inflicted heavy casualties on the Portuguese without loss to themselves.

Seitz and von Heydebreck considered that an even stronger attack should still be made to dissuade the Portuguese from making retaliatory attacks that might in turn encourage rebellion among the large Ovambo tribe living along the border. To lead the larger punitive expedition they chose Major Franke, who had distinguished himself in the Herero uprising and had several times renewed his three-year tour of duty in South West Africa.

Elaborate arrangements were made to ensure the success of the expedition. Food and water supplies, which in the latter case entailed the drilling of new wells, were established along the route. As a result, the expedition, consisting of 600 men and two artillery batteries, did not reach the border until December 16.

Franke's force hoped to approach Fort Naulila undetected through the thick bush, but the Portuguese had obviously been on the alert, for the Germans were met by a hail of gunfire as they emerged from the bush. Franke immediately ordered his artillery up, and the first shots exploded the enemy's arsenal and set part of the fort on fire.

The Germans now came under heavy small-arms fire on their left flank and machine-gun and artillery fire on their right. The Germans began to suffer casualties from this fire and from askari snipers hidden in large baobab trees that had been left in the cleared ground round the fort. Franke's horse was shot under him and he was wounded in the head and had to hand over command to Captain Trainer.

The Portuguese were ensconced behind barbed wire in trenches reinforced with palisades, and neither the German artillery nor machine-guns could dislodge them. Trainer ordered his men to go in with hand grenades, and these breached the defences. A machine-gun putting the attackers under enfilading fire was knocked out by the artillery with shrapnel, and soon the Germans were storming into the fort.

The Portuguese fled, leaving more than 100 men dead and many wounded. Three officers and 63 men were captured by the Germans, who also seized quantities of weapons, 17 ox-waggons and valuable supplies.

When news of the attack on Fort Naulila reached Berlin there was consternation, for the German government had no desire to get involved in a war with Portugal, at least not while they were still embroiled in gruelling hostilities with Britain and her allies.

There was equal consternation in Lisbon, where there was a matching anxiety to avoid war with Germany and to maintain Portugal's declared stance of neutrality. Seitz insisted that he had not received confirmation of this neutrality until after the attack on Fort Naulila.

Both sides tacitly agreed to take no further action.

What had prompted the Portuguese to adopt the attitude that led to the Naulila incident is unclear. A likely explanation is that the Portuguese authorities had been persuaded by their old allies the British to prevent the Germans from getting supplies for South West Africa from Angola.

The upshot was that the Germans lost the supply column from Lubango and had in addition to abandon hope of obtaining any more supplies through the Portuguese territory. However, the Portuguese now withdrew their forces from southern Angola, leaving the Germans free to concentrate their forces against the growing threat from the South Africans in the south.

References

1. Von Oelhafen, p. 80.
2. *Ibid.*
3. *Ibid.*
4. *Ibid,* p. 72.
5. *Ibid.*

19

Commando Charge

Sixty days after the South Africans had landed at Walvis Bay, Botha was ready to begin his dash across the desert to strike at the heart of the German colony.

The ports were in operation and linked by rail, his supplies were flowing and his men were ready. His first move was a strong thrust eastward to chase the Germans from the positions from which they had been observing Northern Force's preparations. For the first few days the Germans wisely put up little resistance, knowing that they were within range of the six-inch guns of HMS *Astraea* as she stood close inshore.

In quick succession Northern Force captured Nonidas, Goani-kontes, Heigamchab and Rossing.

It was not only the *Astraea*'s guns that worried the Germans; they now had their first encounter with the burgher commandos and the speed and unorthodoxy of their movements.

After Northern Force had taken Goanikontes, O'Shaughnessy, the war correspondent, reported that captured Germans had 'paid a high tribute to the extraordinary mobility of the burghers and expressed astonishment at the utter boldness and dash which characterised their movements'.[1]

So swiftly did the burghers ride that the Germans did not have time to set off a huge remote-detonation mine that they had prepared at Goanikontes. When the South African sappers discovered it and dug it up they found that it contained 37 cases of dynamite, a crate of old horseshoes, another of pipe flanges and one of detonators.

One sapper noted that he exploded 15 mines in quick succession, the last of which 'scattered its contents of lumps of iron all round myself and one man at a distance of two hundred and fifty yards; at the suggestion of my man we had taken refuge behind an ant-heap about eighteen inches high and, luckily, we were not touched'[2]

The burghers' tactics 'were as great a surprise to ourselves as they were to the enemy', wrote a member of the Rhodesian contingent.

'They kicked him as he turned his back – and kicked him hard. Not content with that, they followed him from daybreak to sunset, cutting off a man here and there, galloping, shouting, mad with the ecstasy of the chase. At night they returned tired and dusty, their horses caked with sweat, smiling like schoolboys as their eyes fell on the dejected figures of their captives. They had ridden throughout the day in "columns of lumps" that would have sent a British drill instructor into a state of madness, but they had done their work as it should have been done'.[3]

That the fighting was not all one-sided, or without chivalry, emerges from the diary of Hunter of the Imperial Light Horse. On January 21 he wrote: 'An unfortunate event occurred this morning. Our patrol went out as usual in the morning and a section of four men were told off to occupy a position next to a pigeon-house. This place has been occupied every morning up till now without mishap. The cruiser *Astraea* usually lies out in the bay and in such a position that her guns command the whole of the plain towards the back of the town. Yesterday the *Astraea* left for Walvis Bay and unfortunately left the coast clear for the Germans, who in the night came to within three miles of our defences and took up their positions at the pigeon-house. Our four men cantered up as usual to this place, quite unsuspectingly, when

Separated for a while from their horses, Union cavalrymen ride with their saddles on the railway from Walvis Bay to Swakopmund. The man in the left foreground has on his hat one of the veils that when pulled down were supposed to provide protection from the blowing sand. (Cape Archives)

In a contemporary photograph a white-suited man is dwarfed by the sand dunes that confronted the Northern Force as it struck inland from the coast. (Cory Library, Meara Collection)

suddenly the concealed Germans opened fire, killing poor old Burnett and wounding Dyke so badly that he died that evening, while one of the four, Woodland, was captured.'

On January 26 Hunter wrote: 'Another unfortunate affair this morning; some of our fellows being surprised, one man, Wally Reid, being badly wounded, five bullets having hit him. In the evening a German picket came in with a white flag, to bring in poor Reid, whom our fellows had been unable to find. The Germans we are fighting against here are a very sporting lot. They allowed Woodland to write two letters to his people and to Captain Ross, and gave morphia to Dyke to ease his pain.'

Colonel Skinner himself had a narrow escape when his horse was shot while he was out with a patrol. Only by grabbing the stirrup of one of his men and running for all he was worth alongside the trooper's horse was he able to reach safety and avoid being captured by the pursuing Germans.

Having given himself some elbow room, as it were, Botha now had to make a major tactical decision. His main objective was Windhuk, not only because it was the capital of the colony but because possession of it would cut the railway axis on which the German defence strategy was based. With Windhuk threatened, the enemy would be forced to withdraw all his forces north of the capital or see those in the south cut off.

Between the coast and the capital lay a stretch of territory 'of a character probably unparalleled in any part of the globe. It is an unqualified waste of sand and granite rocks and kopjes, without a drop of water or a vestige of life.

'Across this wilderness all the food and water had to be transported . . . with the advancing columns. The Germans were themselves fully convinced that an advance in force into the interior from Swakopmund was an undertaking beyond human power.'[4]

When the Union forces had landed at Walvis Bay a Swakopmund newspaper had assured its readers: 'We do not think the British will permanently establish themselves at Swakopmund. There is nothing to get here and to make Swakopmund a base for an invasion of the interior seems, to anyone who knows the country, to be a step without any prospect of success. The British commanding officer will therefore probably content himself with hoisting the Union Jack and steaming away.'[5]

Botha had indeed hoisted the Union Jack, but he had not steamed away and now he proposed to take his army across the supposedly impassable desert and hoist the flag in Windhuk.

Two options were open to Botha in his drive on Windhuk: he could either fight his way along the railway line towards Usakos, or he could take a short cut along the usually dry bed of the Swakop river to the wells at Riet.

From Swakopmund, Usakos was 80 miles away across the desert; Riet was only 60. But the Usakos route would give him the use of the railway to move his supplies, provided he was willing to advance at the pace of the track-layers as they rebuilt the line torn up by the retreating Germans. All the two-foot narrow gauge railway from Swakopmund to Rossing had been pulled up by the Germans and stacked at Usakos, but beyond Rossing long stretches had been left intact.[6]

A decision had been taken to replace the narrow gauge track with standard South African three-foot six-inch gauge. It was estimated that it would take three months to complete the line as far as Usakos.

Defence Headquarters in Pretoria impressed on the general that they favoured the Usakos route and had in fact allocated transport on the assumption that he would choose that option.[7] Botha's staff estimated he would need 400 mule-drawn waggons to keep his force supplied in advancing independently of the railway; and DHQ had sent him only 40!

He had hoped that McKenzie in the south would by now have begun his advance from Garub to Aus and so put additional pressure on the German defences. But McKenzie had reported that he was not yet

Soldiers at Walvis Bay at work on one of the many trenches that the Union forces dug in South West Africa but which had seldom to be put to use for defence against German attacks. (War Museum)

ready to move because, although he now had three mounted brigades, the last to arrive was still waiting for its horses to recover from the sea voyage and besides the water resources at Garub were still inadequate.[8]

All of this meant that Botha would be taking a great risk if he chose the Swakop river option. But at the same time he knew that if he advanced along the railway he would have to sacrifice the mobility of the commandos, which was one their greatest assets. And then he would have a hard job keeping those restless souls happy if they were forced to dawdle along at the pace of the railway gangers. If there was no fighting or chasing to be done they were quite likely to begin demanding to return home to see to their farms, just as they had done from time to time during the Boer War.

With characteristic boldness Botha chose to advance along the river, with or without sufficient transport, with or without the approval of Defence Headquarters.

No sooner had he made his choice than the heaviest rains for years fell in the hinterland, and the Swakop river came down in one of its rare floods. The water sank quickly into the sand, but some would remain just below the surface, accessible to digging. If ever there was a good omen, this was one.

By March 15 Botha had, by putting every available vehicle on the job, built up five-and-a-half days of supplies at Husab; and he decided it was now time to make for Windhuk.

The infantry brigades were posted along the railway to guard the construction crews and in forward positions at Nonidas.

The force that would attack Windhuk consisted of two mounted brigades. The 1st Mounted Brigade had as its right wing the Krugersdorp, Potchefstroom A and Potchefstroom B commandos under Colonel Commandant Piet de la Rey. In the left wing, led by Colonel Commandant L A S Lemmer, were the Marico, Lichtenburg, Bloemhof and Wolmaransstad commandos. The brigade's 2 290 rifles were supported by a four-gun battery of the Transvaal Horse Artillery.

The brigade was commanded by Colonel Coen Brits, who had

As they retreated along the railways, the Germans destroyed the line behind them to prevent the South Africans from using it. This photograph of a section of line being dynamited was taken near Karibib. (Cory Library, Burton Collection)

served with distinction in putting down the rebellion. Brits had previously shown his special style of dash in the Boer War while serving as a commandant under Botha.

Collyer described Brits in these words: 'He spoke no English (at any rate never used it), had a genuine contempt for anything like the formal methods of a regular army, which he expressed in telling terms, and was a law unto himself, except that he had for General Botha a great affection and offered him an unvarying and unlimited personal loyalty. He paid little attention to anyone else.

'He was of forceful character and, like so many of his countrymen, of splendid physique and a stout fighter, but lacked some of the essential qualities of generalship.'[9]

Brits nevertheless went on to become a brigadier-general and served as a major-general under Smuts in the campaign in German East Africa.

Reitz says of Brits: 'He stood six foot six inches, did not know a word of English, drank enormous quantities of alcohol without turning a hair, and was celebrated throughout the Transvaal for his racy wit and Rabelaisian stories.'

He was perhaps the antithesis of the commander of the 2nd Mounted Brigade, Colonel J J Alberts. Although he too had served in the Boer War as a commandant, Alberts had been less prominent than Brits, according to Collyer, but was 'a man of influence – a Member of Parliament – and much easier to work with than his fellow brigadier'.[10]

The right wing of Alberts's brigade was led by Colonel Commandant Badenhorst; it comprised the Heidelberg A and B commandos, the Standerton A and B commandos and the Ermelo A commando. On the left wing, under Colonel Commandant R Collins, were the Bethal, Carolina, Ermelo B, Middelburg A and Middelburg B commandos. The total strength of the brigade was 2 564 rifles, and it had a four-gun battery of the Permanent Field Artillery.

For the drive on Windhuk Botha thus had 4 850 mounted riflemen and eight artillery pieces.

All the senior officers in the force were veterans of the Boer War and had served through the rebellion. They had been hand-picked by Botha and were all known to him.

'Employed on the lines to which they were accustomed and led by a commander who was a master of their tactics, they were a formidable force', said Collyer.[11]

Blocking their way along the Swakop river was a German force estimated to be about 2 000 strong with four artillery batteries. They were entrenched in strong positions in the high hills at Riet and Pforte, with their batteries and their machine-guns well placed to sweep the open ground over which the South Africans must advance.

On the left bank of the river bed (and therefore on the right flank of the South African advance) was a 2 000-foot hill, the Rietberg or Langer Heinrich, overlooking the settlement of Riet in the river valley. On the other side of the river were more high hills, the Husabberg, then the Pforteberg and beyond them the Geisibberg.

There were only a few gaps in this natural barrier. Through one of them, between the Pforteberg and the Geisibberg, ran an old railway, known as the Khan line, linking Karibib with Swakopmund. The little settlement of Pforte lay in this gap, and further inland along the railway was Jakkalswater. The Germans had built a branch line from Jakkalswater almost to Riet and thus could move troops and guns by rail almost up to their front line.

Between the South African forward base at Husab and the German front positions just beyond Riet was about 10 miles of entirely waterless territory.

O'Shaughnessy found himself describing this battlefield in somewhat awed terms as '. . . country which for its utter desolation is surely without parallel in any portion of the world; interminable miles – *sans* vegetation of any kind – of dreary, sandy wastes out of which arise, in a variety of heights and a confusion of order, unscalable granite rocks of massive proportions, intermingled with smaller series of serrated, barren ridges. Not a drop of water, not a sign of life – a truly forsaken wilderness.

'Through this remarkable territory meanders the dry course of the Swakop River, between wondrous gorges of such awe-inspiring appearance that the voice is instinctively hushed at this terrible form of grandeur, in fearful expectation of a sudden encounter with the "Old Gentleman" himself, armed with horns and trident complete.'

Into this dramatic arena rode General Botha and his 5 000 horsemen before daybreak on March 20, after a 30-mile march through waterless desert the previous day. Up in the hills the Germans were watching, and waiting behind their machine-guns and their cannons.

The South African plan of action was that Brits's 1st Brigade on the right flank would try to chase the Germans off the Langer Heinrich Berg and drive up the Swakop River to seize Riet. On the left flank Alberts's

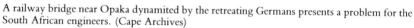

A railway bridge near Opaka dynamited by the retreating Germans presents a problem for the South African engineers. (Cape Archives)

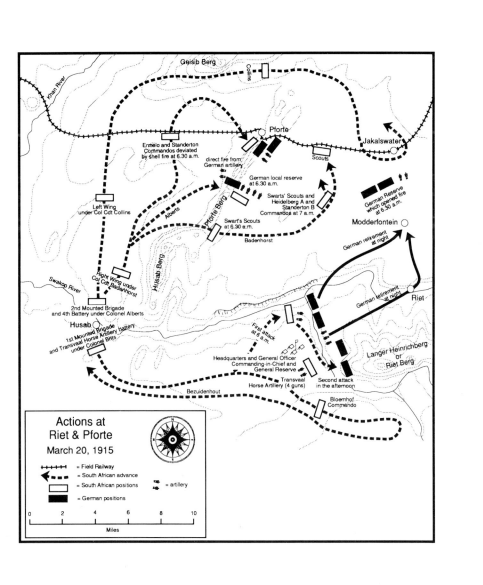

Geisib Berg

Khan River

Collins

Pforte

Jakalswater

Ermelo and Standerton
Commandos deviated
by shell fire at 6.30 a.m.

direct fire from
German artillery

Scouts

German local reserve
at 6.30 a.m.

German Reserve
which opened fire
at 6.30 a.m.

Left Wing
under Col Cdt Collins

Alberts

Pforte Berg

Swarts' Scouts and
Heidelberg A and
Standerton B
Commandos at 7 a.m.

Swart's Scouts
at 6.30 a.m.

Modderfontein

Badenhorst

German retirement
at night

Husab Berg

Swakop River

Right Wing under
Col Cdt Badenhorst

German retirement
at night

Riet

2nd Mounted Brigade
and 4th Battery under Colonel Alberts

Husab

1st Mounted Brigade
and Transvaal Horse Artillery battery
under Colonel Brits

First attack
at 6 a.m.

Langer Heinrichberg
or
Riet Berg

Headquarters and General Officer
Commanding-in-Chief and
General Reserve

Transvaal
Horse Artillery (4 guns)

Second attack
in the afternoon

Bezuidenhout

Bloemhof
Commando

Actions at
Riet & Pforte

March 20, 1915

N

+-+-+-+ = Field Railway
◄━━ = South African advance
▭ = South African positions
▰▰ = artillery
■ = German positions

0   2   4   6   8   10

Miles

2nd brigade would try to capture Pforte and Jakkalswater, with Alberts attacking in the centre and Badenhorst and Collins leading flanking movements on the right and left respectively.

Before dawn broke the cliffs were echoing to the sound of gunfire as Brits launched his attack. But his force soon ran into difficulty. The Germans there were in a particularly strong position against the steep banks of the Swakop River.

'Huge castellated rocks in profusion afforded impregnable cover, while machine-guns – in the use of which the German forces, here as in East Africa, were adept – skilfully posted, enfiladed the open approach across the river bed'.[12]

As Brits's commandos charged across the open ground in the early dawn light they came under heavy machine-gun fire and, with the instinct of the Boer to seek cover in such a situation, they swerved left into a dry spruit. There they remained pinned down for much of the day.

The outcome of the attack now depended largely on an attempt by the Bloemhof commando under Commandant Bezuidenhout to circle round to the right and attack the German positions from the rear. Bezuidenhout was to try to cut through a pass in the mountains that was shown on the map. But the map turned out to be wrong; there was no pass and no way by which his commando could get through.

Bezuidenhout therefore turned back; but instead of linking up with Brits's main force, he headed back to the starting point at Husab. Having taken this extraordinary action, he omitted to tell anyone else about it, and Brits was left to come to his own conclusion later in the day that the attempt had failed.

When he realised that, Brits sent 300 men on foot up the Langer Heinrich to try to turn the enemy's flank. Fighting its way from ridge to barren ridge under the blazing sun, this force slowly pushed the enemy back until, just before nightfall, only the highest peak was still held by the Germans. But by this time the battle had been won elsewhere.

On Brits's other flank his men remained pinned down in front of the hills. When he sent in reinforcements they ended up in the same predicament, trapped out in the merciless heat. It was left to the artillery, therefore, to take the action to the enemy; and that the Transvaal Horse Artillery did with skill.

A gunner with the THA recalled afterwards that the German guns were consistently overshooting while the South African guns were finding their mark.

'We had them guessing after a while as to the number of our guns, as our left section would fire at them and then stop and we would open on the right'.[13]

General Botha had set up his command post just behind Brits's forward positions. Moore Ritchie gave an illuminating, if flowery, description of the scene: 'As the tall chief-of-staff moves aside you see a figure on a little camp stool. The left hand is just under the hip, binoculars are in the right; up go both hands with the glasses; down they come. He speaks to the chief-of-staff; there is a favourite gesture – the arm is jerked out horizontally, the hand pointing loosely, and dropped again.

'The face is powdered with fine sand and dust; during the day he has been allowed a small beaker of water from the artillery. A favour indeed. That is Botha – Louis Botha, commander-in-chief, the man who leads us. And on either flank, well screened little knots of men are grouped round the guns – and 'Hampang-ky-yao' they go in our ears, their reports carrying ten miles back into the desert, where our transport hears them as muffled thunder.

'And look up as you hear that screeching whistle; the enemy's shells burst in the depression round us on both flanks: "Pa-ha-ha!" They look like slabs of cotton wool against the brazen blue sky.

'And all afternoon the heat strikes up at you, overpowering, like the breath of a wild animal. Then the wind rises and the sand shifts in eddies. Veils and goggles are useless. They can't keep out that spinning curtain of grit. The horses rattle the dry bits in their mouths, trying to get some moisture.'[14]

The German guns were withdrawn during the night after the Germans had realised that the position had been made untenable by the outcome of the action over at Pforte. At dawn their positions were occupied by the THA.

'We went over their gun-pits and found pieces of shrapnel all over', the THA gunner wrote. 'As a matter of fact, in one of the gun-pits we found no fewer than five separate pieces of shrapnel from five different shells. The whole of the detachment must have been blotted out or wounded. How they got their guns away is a mystery.

'We found eight dead unburied and several wounded; also a big grave, about thirty-five feet by ten feet, in which they had buried most of their people . . . A shell had struck the arm of a limber and blotted out the drivers and most of the mules.'[15]

While Brits's men were pinned down in front of Riet, the Boers were having much greater success over at Pforte. There, too, the approach to the German positions in the hills was over flat ground with no cover. Alberts, however, had moved his men up at night ready for a charge at daybreak. He sent the Ermelo and Standerton commandos circling to the left to try to get a foothold in the gap through which the railway line ran. Meanwhile Swart's Scouts (each commando had its own scouting unit named after its leader) were sent to seize the gap

General Botha in a pose that became familiar to his officers and bodyguard – seated on his camp chair following the action through binoculars. Here, he is watching his forces attack German positions at Goanikontes on the drive inland up the Swakop River valley. (Cape Archives – AG)

between the Husabberg and the Pforteberg.

The Ermelo and Standerton commandos ran into heavy artillery and machine-gun fire that forced them to go to ground opposite Pforte. Swart's force, however, stormed through their gap in a typical Boer mounted charge. Alberts immediately sent two commandos under Badenhorst galloping in behind them. The Germans poured heavy machine-gun fire at them, but they made elusive targets in the thick clouds of dust raised by their racing horses and casualties were negligible.

In true Boer fashion, once the commandos had breached the gap they did not stop but stormed on, turning in behind the enemy and cutting the railway line between Pforte and Jakkalswater.

That forced the Germans to pull back the artillery that had been holding up the Ermelo and Standerton commandos and, in the lull in the artillery fire, these commandos charged forward and seized positions in the hills overlooking the railway gap.

'Within one hour after launching the attack, the foremost troops were in action on the railway line eight miles away', Collyer notes in his account of the battle. 'The success attained at the start and the enterprise displayed by the subsequent manoeuvres were mainly due to the swiftness of the commandos, which still characterised the spirit of the Boer forces as manifested in the [Anglo-Boer] War.'

From the hills overlooking the railway gap, Commandant Piet Botha of the Standerton commando could see little but the great clouds of dust raised by his charging horsemen and now hanging thick in the windless morning air. Now and again he could catch a glimpse of artillery firing down below him and hear the thundering of the guns.

Botha was puzzled by the fact that the artillery was firing to the east, away from his own advance. He did not know then that these were German guns that had been turned round to fire at Badenhorst's commandos as they seized the railway line east of Pforte and at Alberts's guns and horsemen as they forced their way through the Pforteberg.

Botha decided that the only way to find out whose guns they were was to go down and have a closer look. Leaving his men in position, he climbed down the hillside through the dust and suddenly found, to his consternation, that he was in the midst of a German artillery battery.

Realising that they were more surprised than he was, Botha coolly demanded to see the battery commander and to him announced: 'I have come to discuss the terms of your surrender'. Looking from the solitary South African to his sweating gun crews and back again, the astonished German replied: 'On the contrary, I think it is you who must surrender to us.'

Botha insisted that the Germans were surrounded and had no option but to surrender. The German officer, still seeing nobody with Botha, was equally insistent that the South African was a prisoner of war. Botha was wondering how he was going to get out of this awkward situation when one of his own men came stumbling through the dust, apparently looking for his commander.

'What's going on?' asked the bewildered burgher. Instantly Botha turned to the German and said, 'Here is one of my men come to see why you are taking so long to surrender. This is your last chance.'

With two Boers now boldy confronting him, the German officer was at a loss. Just then a shell from one of the guns that Alberts had brought through the Pforteberg burst over the German battery. As the Germans ducked, Botha and his man made a run for it and escaped into the surrounding dust cloud.[16]

Collins had in the meantime taken his men in a wide sweep beyond the railway, turned eastward along the foothills of the Geisibberg and then swung south to cross the railway again and attack Jakkalswater. This 40-mile trek through the night was intended to cut off the retreat of the Germans and prevent reinforcements from coming up from Karibib.

Collins not only cut the railway and seized Jakkalswater station; he also captured a troop train bringing up German reinforcements. But his triumph did not last long, for his manoeuvre brought his force within range of the guns of the German reserves stationed south of Jakkalswater.

Bursting among the horses of Collins' dismounted men, the German shells wrought havoc: 43 of the horses were killed. Without artillery of his own to reply with, Collins elected to withdraw from Jakkalswater, abandoned the captured troop train and left the riders of the dead horses to become prisoners of the Germans.

Like Bezuidenhout he decided to go back to Husab, and nearly became involved in a fight with Alberts's force, which at first mistook his men for Germans.

At Pforte the action had become an artillery duel, as Alberts's guns had gone into action. A German account of the battle [17] records that two of the German guns were knocked out by the South African artillery early in the engagement and half of the gun crews were killed or wounded. At one point the burghers charged the guns on horseback, firing from the saddle. The Germans beat off the attack, but it left the battery commander dead.

When the German troops, commanded by Major Weiss, withdrew to cliffs near the railway pass, the South Africans sprayed the cliffs with shrapnel from their four guns. Encircled by his foes, with no hope of receiving reinforcements, running low on ammunition and food and with his casualties mounting, Weiss surrendered. The South Africans moved into the enemy positions to find dead and wounded Germans and horses and mules lying thick round the German guns.

The rest of the German defenders of Pforte, under the command of Lieutenant Steffen, stuck it out for a while in the strong positions that they held in the railway pass. When their telephone line was cut they were unable to communicate with the rest of the German force, having previously lost their heliograph. Seeing shells bursting near the train at Jakkalswater and hearing the gunfire of the action there, they concluded that they were cut off. In the afternoon the South Africans brought up two guns and began firing shrapnel. With his men now suffering heavy casualties, Steffen surrendered at 3 p.m.

With Pforte in the hands of the South Africans, the railway cut and commandos threatening to capture the heights overlooking Riet, the Germans withdrew during the night towards Karibib and abandoned the wells to the invaders.

It was a most satisfying victory for Botha. He had lost 13 officers and men killed, 41 wounded and 43 taken prisoner. But he had cost the enemy 16 dead, 21 wounded and 264 prisoners and had captured two guns. He had seized the copious wells at Riet and put his forces in a good position to clear the desert and advance on Windhuk.

The official history of the campaign assessed the victory thus: 'The result of the day's operations was that the pick of the German troops had, with considerable loss, in one day been turned out of strong and carefully prepared positions which topographically were ideal for their purpose. They had every advantage: interior lines, local knowledge of the intricate terrain, water and railway transport nearly to their fire positions.'

With a little boasting that was perhaps pardonable in the circumstances, the official history adds: 'The reasons of [the Germans'] subsequent reluctance to try tactical conclusions with the Union troops are thus not difficult to conjecture.'

A despatch in the Transvaal Leader of April 15 from its correspondent in the field gave most of the credit for the victory to the artillery.

'Though every possible credit is due to the splendid work of our commandos, going straight into action as they did, after the severest marching over the desert here, and behaving with the utmost bravery and dash, the factor that gave the invading army this position of inestimable importance after a day's fighting was the supremely skilful work of the Union artillery.'[18]

At the end of the battle the South Africans' horses were too spent to pursue the retreating Germans. The next day Botha put together a force from the least exhausted horses and men and sent them to reconnoitre in the direction of Modderfontein. They found the German positions abandoned – so hastily, in fact, that they had left behind documents that made it clear that the main body of the German forces in South West Africa had been deployed at Riet-Pforte.

Up till then Botha had not known whether the enemy had sent strong forces in the south against McKenzie. Now he knew he could safely order McKenzie to advance.

In their precipitate retreat from Modderfontein the Germans neglected to alert a hospital train that came steaming along the branch line from Jakkalswater – straight into the hands of the South Africans. When they found that it was a hospital train they signalled for instructions to headquarters, and on Botha's orders it was allowed to return along the line to Karibib.

The burghers did, however, seize useful quantities of stores found at Modderfontein.

Even with these, Botha soon found that he could not keep his force fed with the inadequate transport that Defence Headquarters had provided. He had no alternative but to send most of his force back to Swakopmund, where the men and animals could be fed from the ships. It was galling to him to have to ask the burghers to trek back across the desert to where they had started from after they had fought so well and won so handsomely. It was equally distasteful to the men, who were keen to push on and end the campaign.

A garrison of 600 soldiers from the Durban Light Infantry was moved up to Riet under Colonel Wylie. The burghers returned to Swakopmund to while away the time recalling the excitement of their first battle in South West and the lucky escapes, such as the time during the fighting at Jakkalswater when some of Collins's men noticed a German tugging frenziedly at something in the bush some distance away.

A couple of the Boers galloped off and captured the German, and only then discovered that what he had been pulling at was the detonating wire leading to a huge mine buried precisely where the troop was standing. If the mine had exploded the entire troop and its horses would have been blown to bits.

References

1. O'Shaughnessy, p. 187.
2. Morris, Keith, *Louis Botha, or Through the Great Thirstland,* William Stevens, London, p. 49.
3. Morris, p. 54.
4. Saxon Mills, p. 452.
5. O'Shaughnessy, p. 203.
6. Collyer, p. 59.
7. *Ibid.*
8. *Ibid,* p. 62.
9. *Ibid.*
10. *Ibid,* p. 64.
11. *Ibid,* p. 65.
12. *Ibid,* p. 67.
13. Morris, p. 60.
14. Moore Ritchie, p. 37.
15. Morris, p. 61.
16. Collyer, p. 71; O'Shaughnessy, p. 195.
17. Ungleich, p. 142.
18. Adler, F, *The Transvaal Horse Artillery,* p. 32.

CHAPTER

20

The Burghers

Surveying the field of battle from his elaborate defences at Pforte, the German commander looked to the west and saw armed horsemen galloping in a great loose mass towards him.

Then they seemed to disappear when they came under heavy fire from the German cannons and machine-guns. This was not only puzzling but also infuriating to the Germans, who had carefully calculated the ranges and fields of fire before the battle and had confidently expected that their target would be there to receive the fire.

Soon afterwards the German commander saw more horsemen charging in an amorphous mass from the east. And then the force that had disappeared in the west reappeared, yelling and charging through the dust and shooting from the saddle – and sometimes even hitting their targets!

It was all too much for the sense of order of a soldier schooled in the rigidity of Teutonic military thinking.

'This is not war,' he shouted in angry protest. 'This is a hippo-drome!'

The story was told by a German officer captured at Pforte and repeated, with slight variations, by O'Shaughnessy[1] and Whittall.[2]

This officer may not have been the only German to think of a Roman chariot-racing arena when he saw the Boer commandos in action. Neither was he the only one to fail to find an answer to the Boer tactics, which were the complete antithesis of straight-lined German military tradition.

Even the English-speaking element in the Union Defence Force, moulded in British traditions almost as rigid as the Germans, sometimes found it difficult to come to terms with the free-wheeling unorthodoxy of the burgher commandos. Not that they ever complained about it – they had seen it work too well in the Boer War to reject it in this one.

In many ways the commando tactics were perfectly suited to the campaign in German South West, which gave scope to sweeping cavalry movements and unorthodox approaches.

'Without the commando influence, many mistakes in this campaign might possibly not have occurred,' says the official history of the campaign, 'but then also several tactical achievements would certainly not be on record today.'[3]

The official history, written soon after the end of the war, notes that South African military tradition had been greatly influenced by the commando system, which for more than a century had been 'the organisational basis of many military operations and also influenced the evolution of South African tactics.'

Traditionally the Boer commando had no fixed numerical strength. Since each commando was drawn from the inhabitants of a particular district its size tended to be proportionate to that of the local population. Heavily populated districts fielded more than one commando. It followed that almost everybody in the commando knew each other well. The leaders were men of strong personality and influence and the natural leaders of the community from which the force was drawn.

'As a minor tactical unit the commando is an ideal organisation', says the official history, '[but] in grand tactics it requires very careful handling. The relations between the men and officers in peacetime make routine discipline rather difficult, but the subtle influence of the officers over the men enables them to get much more out of them in a forced march or a "hot corner" than is possible in a regular unit.

'The tactical initiative of the commando is thus a joy to the staff just as their behaviour in combined operations is always a source of considerable concern.'[4]

Given that background, it is not surprising that the Germans found it difficult to work with Maritz and his rebel commando when they attempted to operate together at Upington and elsewhere.

Major Burton, the medical officer, records (without citing the source of his information) that the Germans had a very low opinion of the Boer rebels fighting with them. They complained that the Boers were uncooperative and had no idea of obedience or discipline. Burton quotes a German as saying that 'if it strikes a Boer to do so he will leave his work, go out of the firing line and boil some coffee, even if his superior officer stands next to him and swears – unless his officer has a good sjambok and a strong arm. It is sad for the Germans to have such allies whom we cannot trust.'

The difference between the German regular soldier and the burgher commando was perhaps the difference between the Boers who poured opportunistically through the gap at Pforte and the officer on the *Gneisenau* who shot the seaman when he left his gun to quench his thirst.

As noted previously, the Germans in South West were at one time assured by one of their newspapers that the German troops had nothing to fear from the South African troops as 'they are mostly taken from dissipated farmers and fat-bellied sluggards. It will, therefore, be an easy matter to finish them off.'

It is doubtful that these bombastic sentiments, written by a civilian in an office in Windhuk, were shared by the German military commanders, who knew the Boers' record in the South African war and in some cases had fought beside them. The commanders were nevertheless unprepared for the unorthodox attack that swept at them across the desert.

The official history notes that the Boers' long tradition of using his rifle in combination with his horse for defence and hunting had produced 'a soldier who can deliver quick, sure and economical fire, while availing himself of every scrap of cover as he works forward, who can ride over almost any ground and who uses his horse to rush the fire position from where he will have the best advantage over his opponent.

'But his traditions lean towards independent action; fire control is difficult; and manoeuvre control would have been impossible were it not for the commando influence.'

Tradition had so strong an influence in the commandos that 'the recruit knows what his commando had done when his father was a member of it; he knows further what is generally done on commando and what not, and therefore has a general knowledge of elementary tactics.'

The Germans, who carried their rifles slung down in front of the saddle, found it strange that the South African mounted brigades should carry their rifles with the butt in a bucket behind the saddle and the muzzle held by a strap looped over the right arm. The style is shown in this picture of men of the 2nd Mounted Brigade at Otavifontein. Many commandos seemed to prefer to carry their rifles in one hand, however. (Cape Archives)

These factors meant that 'tactically the commando operates more by instinct than on command. Like a herd of antelope, moving off or wheeling simultaneously, the commando performs many operations without command and with a spontaneity that gives them a whirlwind character.

'On getting fire unexpectedly the head of the column will extend automatically and with inconceivable rapidity, and will further almost invariably do what a skilled tactician would have commanded under the circumstances – either by making use of the ground on which deployed or by charging forward or backwards to a better fire position.

'Every trooper of a commando knows nearly as much about the general situation as the commanding officer. The information of the scouting patrols had been discussed the night before, the commandant had told his friends what the general's opinion was, and the family spirit of the unit, after having digested all the information available, seems to suggest the best course for all concerned when the time for action comes.

'What may be called the herd instinct – not unkindly, but appreciative of all its qualities that have contributed to the success of this campaign – is also to be seen on the march. No orders (and no disorders) in the early morning or midnight march-off. The men wake, saddle and move off at the appointed time, the only discoverable intimation of which may have been a remark by the commandant on the previous night on the bad luck of again having to march at 1 o'clock.

'The operations of a commando are thus spontaneous and natural, while those of a regular unit appear artificial and restrained by comparison. But while the high qualities of initiative, cohesion, individual efficiency and the rapid appreciation of a situation are very valuable, the inclination to independent action is always a danger.'

Some officers were able effectively to combine burgher traditions with Defence Force discipline. 'In general, the troops had the good qualities associated with the commando, while Defence Force training had developed the ability to operate brigaded.'[5]

Collyer confirms the views in the official history. He adds that the burghers 'were, of course, fine horsemen and, though an extraordinary notion to the contrary sometimes finds expression, admirable horse-masters. Their horses, trained to stand when their riders dismounted to fire – an advantage which did away with the horseholders usual in trained armies and swelled the firing line accordingly – hardy and handy and moving at a pace which combined the maximum speed with the minimum physical demand on the riders, or their mounts, together with a frugal mode of life, conferred on the commandos their extraordinary mobility.'

Even an experienced horseman like Burton, when he was attached

The South African burgher commandos were never particular about smart uniforms and by the time they reached Windhuk they would not have graced a full-dress parade. This photograph, taken at the *Rathaus* as Botha received the surrender of the town, shows a typical commando group in the foreground. It also shows how some of the motor vehicles at the left have during the hard drive from the coast been reduced to makeshift wooden bodies somewhat resembling the ubiquitous jeep of the Second World War. (Namibia Archives)

to General Myburgh's commandos, found it 'no easy thing to keep pace with the young burghers from the Eastern Transvaal, who rode like the wind that dies down at sunset.'

As a result he developed a 'half-crown' that compelled him to sit at a strange angle and gave rise to much teasing by the young burghers. Burton exacted a rough revenge: when his worst tormentors came to him for treatment of whatever ailment he smeared their palates with a mixture of castor oil and quinine, which ensured that they would have a bitter taste in their mouths for days.

Collyer found that the Boers' tradition of mobility left them with an inadequate appreciation of the use of artillery. It was their reliance on the rifle that dictated their avoidance of hand-to-hand fighting and the practice of always keeping a way of retreat open.

'A reluctance to push home an attack, of which there were several remarkable instances in the larger battles of the [Anglo-Boer] War, was emphatically not due to want of courage, for in this respect the burgher was the equal of any other soldier. It was chiefly the consequence of the view that, having repulsed the enemy and having inflicted heavy loss upon him , it was merely stupid to give him any chance of retaliating in kind.'[6]

Collyer, who had observed the Boer from both sides, first in the Anglo-Boer War and then in the campaign in South West Africa, believed that 'individually they probably represented the mounted rifleman at his best.'

In the field, the commandos relied heavily on their scouts, of which each mounted brigade in South West Africa had a force of between 25 and 50, each known by its commander's name. The boldness and efficiency of the scouts enabled the commandos to move rapidly over long distances, knowing that the scouts would inform them of any potential trouble ahead.

But as Botha's chief-of-staff, Collyer was often frustrated by difficulty in getting information from burgher commandants who 'were apt to forget that they were part of a whole and not virtually indepen-dent as they had so often been in the Anglo-Boer War.'

This failing was demonstrated at Riet when Bezuidenhout, instead of informing brigade headquarters when he discovered there was no pass through the mountains, simply returned to base; and when Collins nearly exchanged shots with Alberts when he failed to send word that he was retreating from Jakkalswater.

Another weakness of Boer tactics was shown at Riet when Brits sent his men in a headlong dash into a position from which they could neither advance nor retreat.

On the other hand, the strength of the Boer method was brilliantly demonstrated when the commandos, led by Swart's Scouts, swept through the gap at Pforte and, quickly assessing the importance of the breakthrough, charged on without waiting for new orders from head-quarters, to split the German defences and ensure victory for the day.

The niceties of Boer tactics were not appreciated by everyone, least of all by the foot soldiers. An infantryman in the Transvaal Scottish is reported to have said: 'The commandos that are with us, with no particular uniforms, gave a prehistoric touch to what otherwise might be an up-to-date campaign. They are not too good at drill, but their uncouth and simple methods of going for the enemy paralyse him before he knows where he is.

'A commando sighting the enemy will chase after him in a motley crowd, with rifles at all angles, waved or slung, all shouting; when they have come within reasonable distance they will dismount to take the covers off their rifles and then chase off again, firing from any position that strikes them. Such form of attack is not what the modern Hun is used to.'[7]

A member of the Rhodesian contingent who marched unwillingly on foot throughout the entire campaign, and later became famous in another sphere of combat, was perhaps inspired by bitter memories of commandos cantering past his own sore feet to record, later in his life, this sour comment: 'I have ridden with colonial troops and shot with colonial troops and been shot at by colonial troops and I have no hesitation whatever in saying that the Dominion and colonial troops are, on average, with remarkably few exceptions, damned bad horsemen and damned bad shots'.[8]

The Transvaal Scottish footslogger, however, formed a different opinion of the horsemanship of the burghers.

'We passed some burghers the other day when we were on the train', he wrote. 'They were riding along the line when the webbing equipment of one of our fellows [i.e., haversack, ammunition belt containing 150 rounds of ammunition, bayonet and other appurtenances], which was hanging on the coupling outside the end truck, fell off. So we shouted to a burgher to have it sent along by the next train. The son of the soil, however, just spurred his horse, galloped back for the equipment, picked it up with his rifle without dismounting, gradually overtook the train and handed it back to the fellow in the truck!'[9]

Morris commented that although the burghers lacked discipline they were thoroughly amenable to orders and remarkably quick in their movements.

'An instance of their alertness occurred during the advance to Windhuk. The Boers were having breakfast in the early dawn when a patrol brought in a report. General Botha gave an order, a staff officer blew a whistle, commandants got hurried instructions, the burghers mounted and in what appeared to be a few seconds were clear of the camp. "I never saw anything like it in my life," said an officer of the Engineers, an old campaigner.'

The burghers were issued with the same uniform as the cavalry regiments: khaki shirt or jacket, khaki riding breeches, leggings and a wide-brimmed hat or pith helmet. Further into the campaign it tended to become more individualistic.

Dr Walker, the medical officer, recorded early in the campaign that 'there is nothing uniform about them. Many of the men wear a coloured handkerchief about the neck . . . Bandoliers are carried over each shoulder and under the opposite arm. The rifle, for which they have a cover, is carried in a bucket attached to the saddle. They have no bayonets. An overcoat, a large water bottle, a mess tin, a haversack and one blanket constitute their equipment.'

Commandos were identified by a feather or a piece of coloured cloth on the hat, Walker said.

'Each man has brought his own horse and saddle. Consequently, the horses, if useful, are a very miscellaneous lot as regards colour and size.'

Most of the officers, said Walker, 'look very Anglicised in khaki drill tunics and breeches, irreproachable leggings, boots and spurs, with helmet and Sam Browne belt complete. They are thus very easily distinguished from their men, which is not a very wise arrangement for men going on active service'.

Before the commandos sailed from Cape Town the medical officers were instructed to conduct medical examinations, and Walker recalled that 'as we had no instructions to go upon, we just threw out a few who on account of defect or decrepitude were obviously unfitted to undertake the rigours of a desert campaign.

'On the whole, these men from the northern Transvaal are a well set up lot. We passed several tough old boys well into the sixties.'

Later in the campaign Walker wrote about the commandos including 'many fine old backvelders, who nearly all fought against us in the Great War, as they call the Boer War. Most of them have wounds to show; one has eleven, with two British bullets still in him, yet he is now willing to extend the British Empire since General Botha is doing so'.

According to Walker, the Boers 'will stand rifle-fire all day . . . but they are nervous about the big guns and don't like the machine-guns'.

By the time they got well into the campaign many of the Boers had exchanged their army issue British Lee-Enfield rifles for captured German Mausers, which they preferred, as they were of better quality, more accurate and were considered to inflict a deadlier wound.

By that time Walker noticed that the burghers had become even more nondescript in their dress:

'The burghers never look like fighting men and when off their horses they look less like soldiers than ever before. Much of their original clothing has been worn out and the necessary substitutions have not always a military cut. Quite a number of men are entirely clothed in German uniforms, which may lead to complications should fighting occur.'

While Burton was riding with General Myburgh's brigade the commando he was with came to an abandoned farmhouse outside which stood several waggons. On one of them an inquisitive young burgher found a sack stuffed with women's clothes. He dragged the sack round to the back of the house and after a while reappeared, mounted on his horse and presenting a sight that had the commando hooting with laughter.

'On his head there was a large, broad-brimmed lady's hat with a full-sized ostrich feather. A gaily coloured scarf was wound round his neck and his torso was compressed by a tightly-laced set of corsets. Over his riding breeches he wore a pair of loose, white "unmentionables" trimmed with lace below the knees. Long white gloves and a speckled sunshade completed the rig-out.'

The 'only woman in the commando' rode to the head of the column and 'for quite a long time this male commedienne, by her grimaces, antics, winkings and coquetry amused and helped us on our otherwise dull way.'

When the fun palled the burgher removed the outfit and stuffed it back into the sack, which he left on a large flat stone at the roadside 'where no one ever touched it lest it explode.'

Walker found the burghers 'a very peculiar army, wanting in discipline in camp, yet full of dash, energy and endurance in the field. I doubt whether any other troops would have made the sudden dash on Jakkalswater and Riet.'

Lieutenant-Commander Whittall of the Royal Naval armoured cars became an open admirer of the burghers and marvelled at the chances they took in their tactical operations.

'Some of the chances that were taken were enough to raise the hair of any officer not trained in the guerrilla school of war, but the justification of them was that they always came off as they were intended.'

By way of example, Whittall mentioned a dash made by the brigades of Manie Botha and Myburgh to cut the railway at Karibib after the Pforte-Riet battle.

'The two brigades marched the best part of a hundred miles in three days, through the waterless country, cut the railway as intended, and then went off into the blue for another eight days of strenuous marching, and that on a few strips of biltong which the men carried in their pockets.

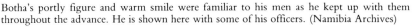

Botha's portly figure and warm smile were familiar to his men as he kept up with them throughout the advance. He is shown here with some of his officers. (Namibia Archives)

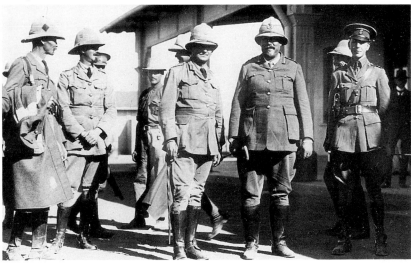

'For eight days these men lived on what fresh meat and game they could pick up by the wayside. The horses had to subsist as best they could, grazing a little on such sparse desert vegetation as might occasionally be encountered. And their experience was that of the rest of the mounted troops – they went out and did, as a matter of course, the apparently impossible, though it must be said that the wastage of horseflesh was terrible.'

True to the traditions of the 'Silent Service', Whittall was more reserved in his prose than were some of the more jingoistic writers who described the campaign. But even he was extravagant in his praise of the soldierly qualities of the commandos.

'They were simply wonderful, those burghers', he wrote. 'Why the Boers were able to keep the field for so long against overwhelming numbers in the Anglo-Boer War is no mystery to anyone who saw their work in German South West Africa.'[10]

Tradition had a lot to do with the performance of the commandos. A strong factor, almost certainly, was that most of them simply liked the life 'on commando', hardships and all, and the adventure of it all. But one of the most compelling reasons for their presence in the desert was their extraordinary regard for General Botha.

If there is one quality that emerges strongly from descriptions of Botha it is his ability to inspire loyalty and affection, a quality that helped him both as a politician and as a soldier. Fighting men under his command not only liked him, they also had confidence in him as a military leader. Many of the burghers trusted Botha's judgment above their own.

'The whole of the burgher article of faith . . . was summed up in the very simple formula: "Louis Botha says so",' Whittall observed.

In Swakopmund he met Botha for the first time when the commander-in-chief invited him to tea.

'Simple and unaffected as he is in manner, no one can meet and talk to Botha for five minutes without coming under the spell of his magnetic personality,' Whittall wrote. 'He compels you at once to the conviction that this is indeed a leader of men. Charming and direct in conversation, he impresses you as one who is absolutely sure of himself and inspires you with equal confidence in him. There is an undefinable and subtle something about him – some elusive quality which cannot be put into words, but which makes you cease to wonder what it is that has made him the trusted and revered leader of his people. And even so, you do not know why.'

There is no doubt about one of the qualities that made the burghers follow Botha: they expected their leaders to lead from the front; and that he did. He did not sit at some safe place in the rear to await the outcome of the action but commanded his men in the dust of battle, as at Riet, where he set up his command post beside Brits and alongside the artillery, hearing the German shells whistling over his head and bursting behind him.

Collyer notes that 'in German South West Africa General Botha, and in German East Africa General Smuts, were either with or immediately behind, and in the closest touch with, the fighting troops throughout their advances. The presence of their commander was looked for by the commandos, whose soldiers would have entirely misconstrued the action of a commander who conducted their operations remote from them'.[11]

Collyer recorded that 'throughout the campaign Botha rode with his commandos and travelled, as they did, without a tent.'

Sometimes Botha travelled in his big green Vauxhall staff car, but often he rode his horse at the head of his troops. Moore Ritchie described how, riding with the bodyguard, his mouth dry with thirst, he could barely make out, in the swirling dust ahead of him, the figure of Botha on his white horse.

'Then out of one cloud in a brazen sky, a few drops of rain fell. I counted five on my bridle hand. Rain on the edge of the Namib desert! It was ludicrous, too bizarre, the last straw. A deep roar of ironical cheering went up. The commander-in-chief looked round and laughed.'[12]

A South African soldier whom he does not identify is quoted by Morris as saying in a letter: 'There is no more popular man at the front today than General Botha. The portly and kindly presence of the South African premier in his smart khaki uniform is as cheery and welcome to the sand-begrimed and sunburnt troops as the news would be that Prussian militarism has been effectively crushed.

'General Botha is daily with his troops . . . A few cheery words, a couple of kindly directed and interested inquiries to a fatigue party shovelling sand, carrying coal or digging trenches has a wonderful effect, and General Botha is continually touching the human side of his soldiers. By the time this campaign is over he will assuredly occupy a much larger share not only of his people's esteem but of their unstinted loyalty and affection.

'Among his commandos his presence sends a flutter from end to end of the camping ground. With the infantry, the great bulk of which is made of British-born and British colonials, General Botha's appearance is the immediate cause of cessation of work and the sign for loud and hearty cheering.'

The esteem in which Botha was held by the troops is illustrated by Moore Ritchie's description of the scene when he landed at Walvis Bay.

'A figure well known to us all crossed the gangway and climbed to the boat deck of our steam tender. We had not seen the commander-

Fussed over by her husband and some of the officers, Annie Botha settles into a chair on a flatbed railway truck for a train trip. No other information is available but it is reasonable to assume that Mrs Botha was travelling to Swakopmund after disembarking from a ship at Walvis Bay. (Cape Archives)

in-chief in personal command since the past bitter days of the rebellion. A great cheer split the morning silence and echoed over the bay to each transport at anchor. With a smile of genuine pleasure, General Botha brought his hand to the salute.'

Some of the South Africans were puzzled when Botha brought his wife and daughter-in-law to Swakopmund on a British warship, together with several cows and hens. Walker suggested that the womenfolk were there to nurse him through an illness, a stomach ailment whose exact nature was not known, but for which Botha's doctor had prescribed a diet of eggs and fresh milk.

'Mrs Botha, née Annie Emmett, a kinswoman of Robert Emmett, the Irish revolutionary, at once set up housekeeping in a building just north of the jetty.'

Walker passed by the house and saw that 'the general's clothing was drying in the yard and his fowls were in the same place, acting up to their responsibilities, with a cow or two as well standing about.'

Mrs Botha looked in at the military hospital in Swakopmund and was shocked at the conditions and the laziness and incompetence of the male nursing orderlies. She quietly went about improving matters without provoking a medical mutiny.

As far as her husband was concerned, she seemed to be an able nurse, for the general was able to take his position effectively enough in the front line at Riet.

After that engagement, Botha went on a sea voyage, but not for his health; he sailed south to Luderitzbucht to see about getting Southern Force moving again.

McKenzie was now ready to make the big advance that Botha was anxious to achieve and his troops were about to fight their biggest battle of the campaign.

References

1. O'Shaughnessy, p. 194.
2. Whittall, W, *With Botha and Smuts in Africa,* Cassel, 1917; p. 122.
3. German South West Africa; part II of the official history of South African participation in the Second World War; Government Printer.
4. *Official History*, p. 35.
5. *Ibid*, p. 13.
6. Collyer, p. 40.
7. Morris, p. 13.
8. Sir Arthur 'Bomber' Harris.
9. Morris, p. 14.
10. Whittall, p. 67.
11. Collyer, p. 74.
12. Moore Ritchie, p. 45.

21

Forward Leap

The South Africans' advance across the desert from Luderitzbucht had been slow because they had had to fight for every yard against the sand and thirst, enemies that had proved more formidable than the Germans.

Before beginning his advance inland, McKenzie had told Smuts in a despatch from Luderitzbucht: 'I feel that the very difficulties of the desert, which make the enemy think they are secure against me, will lead to their destruction.'

The kind of thinking he had in mind was demonstrated by this report, published in a German newspaper before the first landing: 'If the British land any considerable force at Luderitzbucht they presumably intend to push forward along the [railway] line by way of Aus and Kuibis to Seeheim to unite with the force alleged to be coming through Ramans's Drift and working up from the south.

'But such a plan possesses so many almost insurmountable difficulties that it is inconceivable that it can actually have been adopted by the British commander.'

But that was, of course, precisely what Botha intended to do.

In the beginning the pace was necessarily set by the railway construction teams, for the troops and their horses were dependent on the railway for their supplies; it was their lifeline through the desert.

There had been some fighting, but skirmishes rather than serious engagements. There had been enough, however, to make the normally flippant Robinson take a sober look at the realities of warfare:

'One of the few kind things of war is the little time given to one to think. There are, of course, memories that one carries away – memories of men writhing in agony; of men whom one had known and liked making bestial noises while they died; and of horses shattered and maimed and looking pitifully bewildered in their pain.

'But the pictures are mercifully blurred. The brain at such times is too drunken with excitement to do more than record the bare facts.'[1]

Since the first landing at Luderitz in September the South Africans had inched forward along the line of rail to Kolmanskuppe and then Grasplatz, to Rotkoppe, Haalenberg, Tshaukaib and Garub, a total distance of no more than 70 miles.

Now, in March, they were still 15 miles from Aus, where the Germans had set up the wireless masts removed from Luderitzbucht and from where their aircraft operated. Set in hills rising high above the desert floor, the settlement was well placed for defence.

To the natural defences the Germans were believed to have added strong fortifications. The Intelligence Department at Defence Headquarters in Pretoria was convinced that the Germans were going to make a strong stand there and that its capture would be a formidable undertaking.

While appreciating the logistical difficulties of moving an army across the desert, Botha wanted Aus to be captured as soon as possible so that Central Force could then threaten the Germans defending Keetmanshoop and points south against Southern Force and perhaps persuade them to retire to the north.

McKenzie's customary dash appeared to have got bogged down in the desert sands, however, and he showed no immediate sign of moving on Aus from Garub.

One of those who found it difficult to understand McKenzie's reluctance to advance was

Brigadier-General Sir Duncan McKenzie, Commander of the Central Force. (Natal Carbineers)

Lt-Col J R Royston, commander of the Natal Light Horse. Royston, who had his own reputation for dash (he was commonly known as Galloping Jack) was typical of what might be called the irregular officers produced by the British Empire in its colonies, and who had a penchant for raising their own units in times of war and naming them after themselves.

During the Zulu War he had formed and led a cavalry unit known, inevitably, as Royston's Horse. When war broke out in 1914 Royston was living the life of a gentleman farmer on his estate in Natal. He immediately proposed to Smuts, the Minister of Defence, that Royston's Horse should be re-formed for service in German South West. Smuts accepted the proposal but attached insufficient importance to the

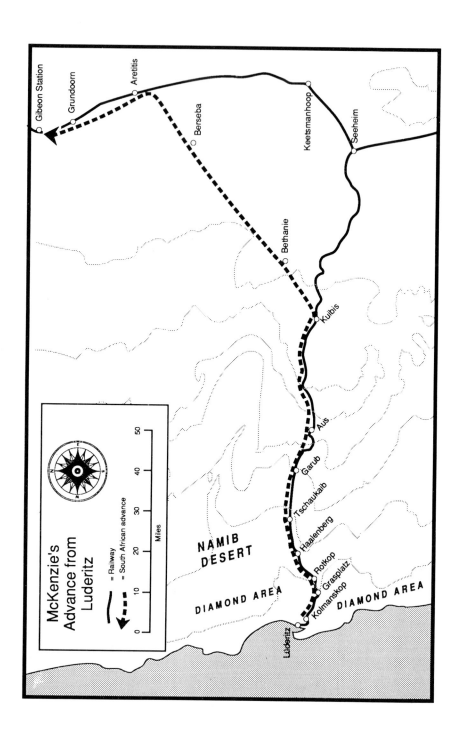

McKenzie's Advance from Luderitz

= Railway
= South African advance

Miles
0 10 20 30 40 50

NAMIB DESERT

DIAMOND AREA

DIAMOND AREA

Gibeon Station
Grundoorn
Aretitis
Berseba
Keetsmanhoop
Seeheim
Bethanie
Kuibis
Aus
Garub
Tschaukaib
Haalenberg
Rotkop
Grasplatz
Kolmanskop
Luderitz

vanities of English gentlemen to accept the name. He decreed that the unit should be named the Natal Light Horse but he allowed it to have four squadrons instead of the customary three, says Napier Devitt in his biography, *Galloping Jack*.[2]

Within ten days of beginning recruiting in Pietermaritzburg and Durban, Royston had a full complement of 600 men, all with previous service and including several Australians. After helping to put down Maritz's rebellion, the NLH arrived in Luderitzbucht in January. McKenzie formed it into the 9th Mounted Brigade with another Natal unit, the Umvoti Mounted Rifles, and the 2nd Imperial Light Horse, under Royston's command.

According to Devitt, Royston bluntly accosted McKenzie, whom he knew well, over his reluctance to attack Aus. He claims that McKenzie replied: 'I can't; I am waiting for three aeroplanes to locate the Germans.'

Royston's explanation of McKenzie's tardiness seems highly fanciful. McKenzie himself had already given his reasons, the most cogent of which was that the water resources at Garub were not yet sufficient to sustain a force big enough to attack the German defences that were believed to exist at Aus.

The official history supports him: 'The strong positions of the enemy and the want of water for the Union troops made a direct attack inadvisable before strategic pressure from the other Union forces had influenced the situation'.[3]

By the time General Botha disembarked at Luderitzbucht to discuss the situation McKenzie appears, however, to have been ready to move on Aus. According to some accounts Botha at their meeting on March 29 bluntly ordered McKenzie to start his advance.

Collyer, however, says that McKenzie reported his force assembled and ready to advance. Beyond giving the order to advance and suggesting the use of mounted troops on both flanks, Botha left it to McKenzie to conduct the operation.[4]

The radio at Aus had been silent for two nights, suggesting the possibility that the Germans had withdrawn. McKenzie sent Royston to find out. (According to Royston's account, it was his idea and McKenzie accepted it but Collyer makes it clear McKenzie was acting on orders from Botha.)

As is found so often with Royston, his account of the entry into Aus differs from others. It seems clear that Royston's force, riding at night, entered the pass giving access to Aus without opposition.

According to Rayner, the first South African troops to enter Aus were the Transvaal Scottish, who went in with fixed bayonets, cheering loudly because they had beaten the cavalry into the town. This gave rise to an untrue story that the regiment had driven the Germans out at bayonet point.[5]

Royston, on the other hand, told Devitt that he rode into Aus on April 1 to find that the only living inhabitant was a solitary baboon walking down the main street. Three dead 'Hottentots' were swinging from a tree from which the Germans had hanged them.

While there may be doubt about whether Royston entered Aus first, there is some corroboration of the story about the Hottentots, which was the name commonly given at the time to Namas. They may have

Aus, shown here in an aerial view, was one of the most strongly fortified of all the German positions. (Cory Library, Meara Collection)

been the members of De Meillon's intelligence unit who were captured when he was killed near Aus and executed. As they were inhabitants of the territory they were probably regarded by the Germans as traitors or spies and liable to the customary penalty.

The Germans had been withdrawing for some time from Aus, but quietly, so as not to alert McKenzie and his comparatively powerful force, which they estimated at 1 800 mounted troops, seven infantry battalions and 12 artillery pieces. The last troops and civilians pulled out on the night of March 30.[6]

That the Germans had at first been prepared to make a strong stand at Aus became clear when the South Africans entered the town. They found elaborate defensive positions running along the hills for five miles. There was an intricate system of trenches, reinforced with timber

208

and containing dugouts, telephones, orderly rooms, lookout posts with armoured protection and 36 gun emplacements linked by an artillery road. To the rear were horse lines, labourers' quarters, an officers' dining room, workshops and even a slaughterhouse and butcher's shop.[7]

Clearly McKenzie would not have been able to drive the Germans out of these positions without a hard fight and heavy losses. He was saved from that by the advance of Van Deventer's force from the south and Berrange's from the east, both of which threatened to isolate the defenders of Aus from the central railway spine.

It was only five days after the evacuation of Aus that Van Deventer entered Kalkfontein, the southern terminus of the line, and only 13 days later that the South Africans occupied Seeheim, cutting the railway between Aus and Keetmanshoop.

In this situation there was no point in defending Aus, and the Germans had no option but to abandon their fine fortifications.

Walking through the virgin trenches after the South African occupation, the eloquent Major Jones of the Transvaal Scottish must have expressed the views of many of his countrymen when he disgustedly summed up the situation as 'a fitting finale to a flaming fiasco'.

Botha's victory at Riet-Pforte ten days earlier may also have persuaded Franke to put his southern force in a position for a quick withdrawal to north of Windhuk if Botha should threaten the capital.

Franke's strategy was now dictated by the realisation that his forces in the south were hopelessly outnumbered. He did not know precisely the South African strength but against his 800 men,[8] General Smuts, now commanding the Southern Army, had 8 000 men and 18 guns, although not all of them could be deployed offensively.[9]

The Aus that the South Africans entered was a dry and deadly place. Before pulling out the Germans had done their usual thorough job of poisoning the wells with dead animals and tins of creosote with holes punched in them and mining and booby-trapping the village and its defences. The wireless masts had been removed.

The South African engineers worked day and night to clear the poison from the wells and repair sabotaged pumps.

'When pumps eventually worked, we drank greedily', the Reuters correspondent reported. 'The wells promptly resented being overworked and ran dry. The climax came when the surface water was exhausted and some of the animals, which had already been 48 hours without water, had not yet drunk.'

Nine days passed before the water situation had improved sufficiently to enable McKenzie to make his next move.

McKenzie has been criticised in several quarters for being laggardly in attacking Aus. If he had attacked earlier, however, the Germans would still have been there and might have put up a resistance that would have cost the South Africans many lives for a position that they later entered without opposition. On the other hand, McKenzie's force would then have been in a position to do earlier what he did next: strike across country to the north-east to cut the main railway at Gibeon and trap the German forces in the south of the territory. If he had been successful in that he would have shortened the campaign considerably.

When he did make the move, however, McKenzie did it fast and well and reached Gibeon only a day after the retreating German force under von Kleist and still in time to block their escape to the north – if his plans had not gone wrong.

His first orders from Botha were to reconnoitre towards Bethanie. He set out with the 7th, 8th and 9th Mounted Brigades (about 1 500 rifles) and the Twelfth Citizen Battery (six field guns). The 9th Brigade set out first, with the others each following a day behind the other to avoid overtaxing water resources along the way.

Approaching Schakalskuppe, the 9th Brigade found the track barred by a newly erected fence. Suspicious sappers probed around the end of the fence and found 15 big mines that would have exploded if the column had fallen for the German trick and ridden round the fence. When the engineers exploded the mines pieces of shrapnel fell 250 yards away.[10]

The brigade bivouacked for the night at Schakalskuppe, where the well gave out before the horses had had a drink. Next day they found a

Kilts in the desert: men of the Transvaal Scottish on parade in South West Africa. The Scottish were the first to enter Aus. (SADF Archives)

small spring at Kuibis, the first open water they had seen so far in the campaign, but it was unable to cope with the demand and ran dry before the whole column had watered.

At Bethanie they found water, but it was heavily alkaline and irritated the men's throats. Next day they set off to cover the 44 miles to Besondermeid across rough going that was so hard on the horses that many of the men got down and walked to spare them. When they reached Besondermeid they found open water.

'We revelled in it, bathed in it, washed our clothes in it,' said the Reuters correspondent.

That evening scouts reported the enemy making for Berseba ahead, and the column saddled up and rode out to cut off the Germans. Watching from a high krantz was a German scout, who waited until the column was riding through a rocky gorge, then boldly joined it, unnoticed in the poor light. He stayed with the column until it halted about six miles from Berseba. Then he slipped away to report to the German garrison in the town that the South Africans had bivouacked for the night and would not reach Berseba until morning.[11]

But the spy was wrong. After giving his men a few hours' sleep McKenzie roused them and rode on in the dark towards Berseba. On the outskirts of the town they ran into a German picket, which opened fire and then retreated in haste, with the South African column galloping at their heels into the town.

The garrison put up a stout resistance, for it had orders to delay the South African advance to protect the retreat of the main German force under Captain von Kleist, which was then only 20 miles to the north. But after being surrounded it surrendered.

Reinforcements sent by von Kleist arrived too late to do anything more than fire a few shots into the sleeping South African camp before fleeing, pursued by the 8th Brigade, riding with stripped saddles. The brigade chased the fugitives for most of the day over atrociously rough ground and captured a few, until they came up against a rearguard posted by von Kleist on the north bank of the Fish River, and gave up the chase as night fell. The brigade spent a bitterly cold night without greatcoats, blankets or food.

Near Berseba McKenzie again indulged his predilection for getting involved in action with his troops rather than ensuring his own safety to enable him to fulfil his duties as commanding officer. In his biography his son says that when lights were seen in the distance 'the GOC took the scouts and went and scuppered two Germans with three wagons and more livestock and brought them back to the bivouac . . .'

At the Fish River the three brigades joined up again and the reunited division halted for a few hours to allow its worn-out horses to take advantage of the fairly good grazing near the river. But after only a short rest McKenzie pushed on. The troops were now on short rations – a quarter pound of biscuits, two ounces of mealie meal, a half-ounce of coffee and an ounce of sugar a day for each man.

Near Aretitis they struck the main north-south railway and followed it. At Grundorn the engineers found that the telegraph line was intact and tapped it. In intelligence terms, they struck gold.

From messages passing over the wire the South Africans learned that the Germans at Gibeon were unaware that McKenzie was so near.

'Where are the tommies?' was one inquiry, to which the response was: 'Don't know.'

Another message said: 'Scouts report seeing enemy's patrols yesterday. Don't believe it; they only saw dust.'

A message from Mariental said: 'Captain reports it quite impossible for the English to be near Gibeon'. A message from Maltahohe: 'Tonight we hear that the English are before Gibeon. Don't believe it. Saw dust. As far as we know the English have not crossed Fish River yet. Intend leaving tonight, with women, for Kalkrand.'

From Gibeon to Mariental the message was: 'Telephone operator here hears that English are coming, but it's nonsense. Quite impossible. Do not know what is happening. Troops moving about.'

Another communication reported: 'Line between Tses and Keetmanshoop occupied. Was able to damage lines only slightly owing to shortness of time. From Tses onwards better results. English horses tired. Mules unshod and in poor condition. Some died in streets of Berseba. English moving along Fish River route. Noticed their lights in laager. Strong party moving in advance.'

But the message that seized McKenzie's attention was this one from Gibeon to Mariental: 'In event of this place being taken by the English it would be possible to establish a new post. Troops leaving tonight'. And then: 'Intend leaving tonight by last train. Will disconnect instrument as instructed.'

Throughout the campaign the South Africans were able to pick up valuable information through the Germans' carelessness in either neglecting to cut telegraph lines as they retreated or failing to use code when transmitting messages by wireless. The information that McKenzie got from the line tap at Grundorn was some of the most valuable of all. It told him that the Germans were preparing to evacuate Gibeon that night and that there was a train standing in the station. If he moved fast he might cut them off and capture them.

Soon afterwards scouts brought back confirmation that there was a train getting up steam at Gibeon station and reported great activity round the station five miles east of the village. Supplies were being carried from the village to the station.

Von Kleist had reached Gibeon with the main southern force on

April 25, only the day before the Union forces tapped the line. He had received telephoned instructions from Franke in Windhuk to load as much material as possible on to the train standing in the siding at Gibeon station and then go north on the train that he had been using to blow up the track as he retreated from Keetmanshoop.[12]

Von Kleist reasoned that McKenzie's rapid advance from Aus to Berseba must have exhausted his men and horses and he would have to give them a few days' rest. That would give von Kleist a day or two to carry out his instructions from Franke.

He therefore decided that there was no need to send out patrols or post guards round the camp.

Far from giving his men a rest, McKenzie was planning an immediate strike. When his scouts confirmed the gist of the intercepted messages he called his brigadiers together and outlined his plan of action.

At eight o'clock that night a party of scouts and engineers set out with orders to circle round east of Gibeon station and blow up the line to the north to prevent the train from getting away.

The scouts were led by Captain Bertram Nicholson, who later became Government Secretary in Swaziland. The engineers were under Captain Grier.

Royston followed them 45 minutes later with the 9th Brigade and a regiment from the 8th, with orders to skirt wide round the station and place his force to the north of it to block the retreat of the Germans when McKenzie made his attack from the south at dawn.

References

1. Robinson, p. 41.
2. Devitt, Napier, *Galloping Jack; Reminiscences of Brig Gen Royston;* H F & G. Witherby Ltd.
3. Official history, p. 51.
4. Collyer, p. 79.
5. Rayner, p. 105.
6. Ungleich, p. 116.
7. Juta, p. 84.
8. Ungleich, p. 118.
9. Collyer, p. 56.
10. Rayner, p. 133.
11. Morris, p. 76.
12. Ungleich, p. 122.

22

Victory at Gibeon

The night was clear but the moon was not yet up as Nicholson with his scouts and Grier with his engineers rode out into the veld on their mission of sabotage.

The going was rough and rocky and they left it to their horses to pick their way through the dark, steering them only on a course across the railway line and then wide to the east of Gibeon station. Not knowing that the complacent von Kleist had dispensed with patrols, the little force rode with caution.

After about two hours Nicholson turned the force westward to the railway and they rode up to the line about two miles north of the station. While the scouts kept watch, the sappers, working as quickly as they dared, placed demolition charges under sixteen lengths of rail. It was 11 p.m. when they finished. Then they withdrew to watch the charges explode, saw the rails leap into the air and knew that their job was done.

But now they had to make their escape, avoiding the patrols that the enemy were certain to send out, for the Germans would know as soon as they heard the explosions what was happening.

The German patrols were indeed quick to arrive, for they knew from the sound that the explosions were caused by dynamite and that could only mean that the South Africans were sabotaging the railway line. But Nicholson led his party well, and long before daylight they passed through the pickets of the main force, which McKenzie had in the meantime moved up to within two miles of Gibeon station in preparation for the attack at dawn.

McKenzie's staff had heard the explosions and needed only Grier's confirmation that the railway line was severed. The train had been trapped. Now it was up to Royston to trap the Germans and prevent them from getting clear to ride north and join Franke's main force near Windhuk.

Royston was already in place on the railway line north of the station. But Galloping Jack, never as brainy as he was brave, had positioned his force badly. He deployed them only half a mile beyond where Grier had blown up the line, and out in the open, with no cover and only about 80 yards from a culvert that the Germans were later that night to use with devastating effect as a machine-gun nest.[1]

At some point the moon rose and brilliantly lit the scene but it is unclear whether this happened before Royston deployed his men or afterwards. Collyer says that the moon was up when Royston made his dispositions, and even in the bright light he failed to notice the culvert or the fact that the drainage ditch beside the railway embankment would give good cover to the enemy.

Some accounts say that the Germans brought their artillery to bear only later in the action when the rising of the moon gave them enough light. At any rate, the Natal men soon found themselves in an untenable position.

Royston had deployed three squadrons of the Natal Light Horse on the railway embankment, facing west, with a fourth squadron in reserve a short distance to the rear. Two squadrons of the Imperial Light Horse were extended on the right of the NLH and the Umvoti Mounted Rifles were to the left rear of the ILH.[2] Because Royston had placed his men so near to the station, it was not long before they were encountered by the patrols that von Kleist had been sending out continually ever since learning that the line had been blown up. In fact, Royston was still getting his men into position at 2 a.m. when a patrol arrived on the scene and the Natal men were forced to open fire, alerting von Kleist to the arrival in his rear of more than a mere sabotage party.

The Germans quickly brought up reinforcements with artillery and machine-guns, and from the cover of the culvert and the drainage ditch they poured a heavy fire into the Natal men.[3] Caught out in the open, they were soon being cut up by shrapnel and machine-gun fire.

At about 3 a.m. Royston went off to the rear. Collyer says he went to order up the Umvoti Mounted Rifles.[4] A letter written by Royston some time afterwards suggests that he went back to 'get away the horses under cover from the big guns'.[5] Why he did either of these things himself instead of delegating the job to a subordinate is not known.

In his absence the commander of the ILH, Lieutenant-Colonel Davies, decided, in view of the heavy casualties being suffered, to order the ILH and the NLH to retreat to where their horses were. When Royston returned he ordered a general retirement.

Royston in his account to Devitt told a different story. He said that he was giving orders for the German machine-guns to be rushed when he heard the order to retire being given on his right front. The next thing he knew was that a whole squadron of the NLH under Captain Bamford had been captured.

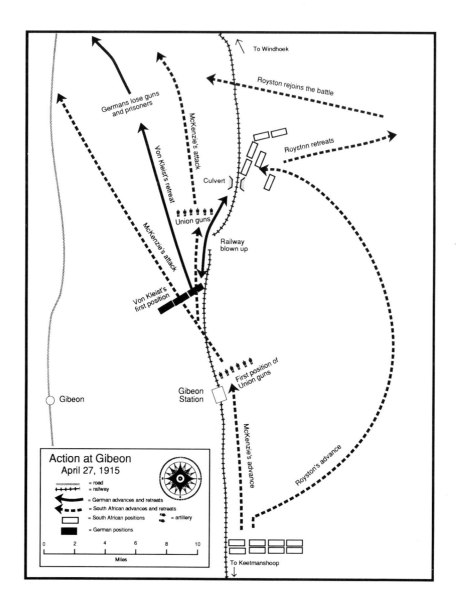

To Windhoek

Royston rejoins the battle

Germans lose guns
and prisoners

McKenzie's attack

Von Kleist's retreat

Royston retreats

Culvert

Union guns

Railway
blown up

McKenzie's attack

Von Kleist's
first position

First position of
Union guns

Gibeon

Gibeon
Station

McKenzie's advance

Royston's advance

Action at Gibeon
April 27, 1915

xxxxxxxxxxxxx = road
⊦⊦⊦⊦⊦⊦⊦ = railway
= German advances and retreats
= South African advances and retreats
= South African positions   = artillery
= German positions

| 0 | 2 | 4 | 6 | 8 | 10 |

Miles

To Keetmanshoop

216

Rayner says that when the order to retire was given the South Africans were so near to the Germans that the order had to be whispered from man to man to prevent the Germans overhearing it. Because of a gap in the line, 72 men of the NLH (Royston's own regiment) did not hear the order and were left behind.

Shortly before dawn they found themselves surrounded and had to surrender.

By that time more than 70 of Royston's force had been put out of action: 24 killed and 49 wounded. Some of those killed had been hit by as many as 30 bullets from the enfilading machine-gun fire.

Royston withdrew his force three miles to the east of the railway to await daylight.

'I went carefully over the ground next morning,' Rayner wrote afterwards, 'and it seemed little short of a miracle that any of the men were left alive to see the morning light.'

One of the South Africans killed was Major John Watt, who had led the charge of the NLH into Berseba. The adjutant of the regiment, Captain Bamford, described the major's death in a letter to his brother, Sir Thomas Watt, the Minister of Posts and Telegraphs in South Africa:

'It is hard to tell you about your brother. He was the finest man we had in this regiment, my best friend and the biggest-hearted man I have ever met. He fell early in the fight at 2 a.m. on the 28th, leading men up a railway embankment under heavy fire.

'He was shot almost under one arm, right through the heart, and died immediately, saying only, 'Oh My God!' He was just a few yards from me and Warby a few yards further on. We were under the heaviest fire from rifles, Maxims and guns, that any man present had ever experienced.

'Your brother's, Park Gray's and my own horses were standing together and [were found] literally riddled with bullets in the morning. Several other shots hit him, one going through the field-glasses I am sending. It was the first shot that killed him instantaneously.

'There is no time to tell you the whole story of the fight – a brilliant stand made by 150 NLH all night against 800 Germans. I will tell you all later.

'Major Watt was a close companion right through for the past eight months. I was with him at Keimoes, Kakamas, Kleis and all the other fights in the Rebellion. On the 23rd of this month when we took Berseba he led a charge of C Squadron, NLH.

'We buried him on the night of the 28th outside Gibeon Siding station in a grave on the right of our other brave fellows who fell.'[6]

When Royston withdrew and the trapped NLH men surrendered, the Germans assumed that they had defeated the main South African force and celebrated joyously. While their doctors attended to the Union wounded, the Germans shook each other by the hand and gleefully broke the captured rifles over the wheels of their supply waggons.

But their joy was short-lived. McKenzie was already moving up with his main force to attack. And Royston, mortified by his reverse, was waiting out in the veld with the survivors of his force to rejoin the battle and attempt to restore his prestige.

Two hours before sunrise, McKenzie opened his attack. He sent a squadron of the 1st Natal Carbineers in extended order towards Gibeon station. Lieutenant-Colonel Montgomery was sent out on the left with three squadrons of the Carbineers and Lieutenant-Colonel Woods with the 2nd Carbineers went out on the right.

Two squadrons of the Natal Mounted Rifles under Lieutenant-Colonel Arnott were in reserve, one squadron of the NMR escorted the artillery and another escorted the transport in the rear.

Von Kleist had grouped his forces west of the railway and two-and-a-half miles north of the station.

'The Germans, who were carefully herding their prisoners, were in no way hurried by the rifle fire that greeted them from our screen as it advanced in extended order against them', the Reuters man wrote. 'But their attitude completely changed when a shell from the 12th Battery boomed overhead.

'At the first sign of dawn the train was sighted, with its white steam belching forth, and the guns were immediately trained on it. Two shells were fired. The white flag was immediately hoisted on the train.'

The Union troops were unaware that the train they were shelling was loaded with tons of dynamite. 'It was well for us that a shell did not actually strike the train. Had one done so, and fired the explosives it contained, there would have been no living being within a radius of half a mile of it.'

The German guns now opened up on the advancing South African forces, but with his flanks being threatened by the Union cavalry, von Kleist was forced to retreat.

'At first advancing under cover of the guns, our mounted men manoeuvred with conspicuous precision', reported the Reuters representative. 'They maintained perfect extended order; they advanced, dismounted, fired, mounted and advanced again with disciplined smartness.'

Leaving a strong rearguard, von Kleist, outnumbered in both guns and men, tried to withdraw his main force. One of the German guns was destroyed by a direct hit and as the rearguard was outflanked, the Germans destroyed the remaining gun and two machine-guns and followed the rest of the force in retreat.

'The artillery raced from position to position,' the Reuters man recorded. 'The mounted men . . . gained more ground. The German guard were hustled beyond hope and in a very few minutes all the prisoners were again in our hands.'

The brisk pace of the action is evident from Addison's account, the brevity of which is in itself testimony to the speed of events.

'As soon as first light came we were in our saddles awaiting the order to ride. We were in Karroo bush country interspersed with rocks and stony ridges, while the Germans used the road to get away, so we had to gallop in the rough to catch them.

'As we sat on our horses awaiting the order to attack, the morning star was blazing in the east and some must have wondered if they would see it next morning again.

'We were on the left of the road in extended columns of troops when suddenly Major Edwards of the Natal Field Artillery came at full gallop down the road, and soon we heard the whips going like pistol shots as the guns came flat out along the road . . .

'As soon as our guns opened up we got the order to gallop. Needless to say we were all keyed up with excitement, and it was astounding how our excitement infected our horses. The poor brutes had been ridden nearly to a standstill during the forced marches, and yet on the day they went like oat-fed hunters after a fox. I have ever since had the greatest regard for the ordinary South African-bred horse.

'The fight itself is a a bit hazy. I remember we galloped from ridge to ridge, leaping over bushes and boulders and opening fire on the Germans on the road. We took it in turn to hold horses so that everyone could have a shot at the enemy . . .

'Riding back over the battlefield, it gave us a shock to see dead and wounded men and horses along the road. I robbed one corpse of a tin mug as I had lost mine, and was a poor second when there was anything to drink.'

In the the heat of the action the captured NLH men came close to being fired on by their own side as they were being hustled along the road by the retreating Germans. In the early morning light the pursuing Natal Carbineers saw them only as shadowy figures and were about to open fire when an officer realised that the men on foot must be the Union captives and gave the order to hold fire. Within a few minutes the prisoners had been abandoned by their captors and rejoined their own force.

'It was a splendid and dashing piece of work,' the Reuters man reported. 'The main body of the Germans fought, all through, a great rearguard action, but we gave them no time. Their Maxims were handled magnificently, but in horsemanship they couldn't touch us. Our field guns were better served than theirs . . . In the early moments of the chase the artillery rendered invaluable protection to our pursuing troops, enabling them repeatedly to change their position and to keep well up with the enemy.'

Royston came back into the picture as soon as there was enough light, but the details of his action are unclear. Royston's recollection, or Devitt's recording of it, differs from Collyer's account. Collyer says that McKenzie, 'finding Royston some distance away, left his bivouac at 5 a.m. and attacked the enemy in front of him'. His force was 'joined by a squadron from each of the NLH and the ILH, the only cooperation Royston was able to afford.'

Royston, however, tells of leading a charge by 1 500 men 'right through the German lines, across the railway line and over the railway station at Gibeon'. Collyer in fact places the Germans on the other side of the railway line and two-and-a-half miles north of the station.

The colonel's words to Devitt seem to be typical Galloping Jack stuff: 'My mind was this: I didn't give a damn whether I was shot or not. I had lost Bamford's squadron and part of my brigade had returned once and I knew that it was now neck or nothing. I was determined to knock the Germans out or die in the attempt.'

Lieutenant Colonel J R Royston, Commander of the Natal Light Horse. (Cory Library, Burton Collection)

He then describes capturing one of six field guns (the Germans had only two) by jumping off his horse, writing out a message for McKenzie informing him that he had 'taken the guns', sticking it onto part of the gun and then riding off after his men.[7]

McKenzie's son, in his account of the battle, was not complimentary about Royston's actions during the night: 'It was a great shock to the GOC to find [Royston's] force was not in position, in the rear or on the flank of the enemy. He was under the impression they were well round towards their right rear or on the flank of the enemy.'

(Royston appears, in fact, to have been on the Germans' left flank.)

Colonel McKenzie says that soon after the Germans retired for the first time before the South African attack his father received this despatch from Royston: 'On reaching the railway line last night, the enemy surrounded us in large numbers and, having no cover, we had a number of casualties. I was obliged to withdraw a couple of miles to save our horses, my position on the railway was completely enfiladed with machine-guns. Am now moving to cooperate with you.'

McKenzie says things looked serious when his father heard that the Germans had captured 200 men of the NLH.

'Shortly afterwards, however, the 1st Natal Carbineers and Lieutenant-Colonel Park-Gray, who had collected a handful of his men – the NLH – released about 70 of these prisoners.

'It appears that the night before, Royston's force took up a position much too close to the enemy, instead of making a wide detour and setting across the enemy's line of retirement ready to meet them in the morning . . . This ill-conceived movement must have been a tremendous disappointment to the GOC as had it worked as it should have the whole German force would have been accounted for.'[8]

When the German rearguard retreated, McKenzie's troops went in pursuit, and overtook and captured groups and individuals in a running fight over about 20 miles. The Germans made an orderly withdrawal along the road to the north, with the South African cavalry on the flanks having to move as best it could over what Colonel McKenzie describes as 'a sea of stones about the size of ostrich eggs'.

Late that night, with the remnants of von Kleist's force now up in the hills and the South African horses exhausted, McKenzie accepted that he would not be able to overtake the Germans and called a halt to the pursuit. It was nearly midnight when McKenzie began collecting his force at Gibeon village, on the Fish River about five miles west of the railway station.

The Union troops were done in. They had been riding hard since leaving Aus sixteen days before, had been on short rations and had had little rest or sleep. According to one estimate, they had had no more than 30 hours of fitful sleep, in freezing cold and on the hard ground, during the past eleven nights.[9]

'I spent my time either trying to keep awake or trying to get to sleep,' one officer recalled.

The Reuters correspondent reported 'an authentic instance' in which, while the Maxims were pouring a murderous fire into Royston's position in the early morning, one of the NLH troopers was heard, in between the rattle of the gunfire, snoring loudly where exhaustion had overtaken him.

'After the battle was over, and the rally was ordered to take place at Gibeon village, many men never reached there that night at all. Officers passed batch after batch of them lying prone on the ground, holding their horses' reins, but fast asleep. They were left as they were, and gathered up in the morning.'

The Germans left eleven dead and 30 wounded on the field and 188 were captured. McKenzie's spoils, in addition to the train, were two field guns, four machine-guns, a large quantity of ammunition, waggons and draught animals.

Three of his men were killed and 13 wounded in the daylight action, bringing the Union casualties in the battle, together with Royston's losses, to 27 killed and 62 wounded.[10]

A captured German officer was reported to have said after the battle: 'We thought it quite impossible for the British troops to have accomplished such a feat. The British Empire may well be proud of her Colonial troops. Volunteers who can face Maxim fire in the way they did will fight anywhere. I cannot praise the men too highly. The perfect internal order kept while advancing under heavy fire, especially by the Natal Carbineers, and the rapidity with which they dismounted, got into action and mounted again simply astonished me and my comrades. Taking into consideration that it was a running fight, their shooting was excellent.

'We were always under the impression that there was no discipline among the South Africans. The splendid manner in which the troops carried out their movements showed us that we were mistaken. Their artillery fire was excellent and the shooting very accurate. We did not think it possible for big guns to keep up with the advance over such rough country.'

The day after the battle von Kleist took his men on a long trek north, swinging wide of Windhuk to avoid Botha's force, and joining up with Franke north of the capital.

He could not realistically have expected to do more than delay the much stronger South African force that had confronted him at Gibeon. But largely because of his neglect of elementary patrolling and scouting, he did not even delay the enemy. It was perhaps due as much to Royston's blundering as his own skill that he foiled McKenzie's attempt to trap the German southern force and prevent it from joining up with Franke in the north.

Some commentators have suggested that if McKenzie had not tarried so long at Garub he might have got to Gibeon in time to intercept von Kleist's force and capture it, which would considerably have shortened the fighting in the north. At any rate, Gibeon was the end of German resistance in the south.

Collyer's summing-up of the battle of Gibeon is that Royston's failure to notice the culvert from which the Germans mowed down the Natal troopers was 'more than bad luck'. The temporary effect of Royston's action was 'nullified by McKenzie's prompt action and efficient handling of his mounted men, and the operations so well planned by him and so well carried out by his troops, suffer in no way by comparison with the finest marches in this campaign of rapid movement.'

Collyer goes on to say, however, that 'fine though McKenzie's work was, it exercised no effect whatsoever on the course of the campaign, for von Kleist would have pursued precisely the same course if there had been no Union troops nearer to him than their own border. It was pressure in the north that brought him back there'.[11]

It is not difficult to imagine what would have been the reaction of the men of McKenzie's force if they had known that this was how Botha's chief of staff assessed their long, painful trek from the sea. They had lived through the miseries of the sand at Luderitzbucht and through the desert crossing; the heat, the thirst, the terrible boredom while waiting to advance to Aus; the hunger, the flies, the forced marches, the sleeplessness, the cold when they reached the inland plateau in winter. While the cavalry and artillery had at least seen some fighting at Gibeon, the infantry had done little more than march, shovel sand and wait.

But McKenzie's men could at least say that they had done everything that had been asked of them and they had done it willingly and well. They had therefore been good soldiers.

The mounted brigades could take pride in their forced march to Gibeon, and their effort was recognised in the Union government's official announcement of the victory at Gibeon: 'The distance from Bethanie to Gibeon is approximately 120 miles. Bethanie itself is some 80 miles from Garub, the place from which General McKenzie's mounted troops began their advance. The performance of this flying column of our mounted troops over a most difficult and arid country, with little or no transport for the last 120 miles, and fighting a severe and successful engagement at the end of it, undoubtedly constitutes a most brilliant feat of arms and endurance.'

True though that might be, the South Africans had failed to destroy the German forces in the south. Von Kleist had beaten McKenzie to Gibeon and slipped out of the trap set for him there. All the marching, all the hardships; all the toiling by the Union Southern Army, and the dying, had been turned to waste by Royston's failure to block von Kleist at Gibeon.

After Gibeon the Southern Army was disbanded. The mounted troops moved in easy stages to Windhuk, from where they were returned to the Union. This was apparently considered preferable to marching them back to Luderitzbucht across the desert.

They still had a far from easy time, for it continued bitterly cold. One report tells of men lying sleeping near Rehoboth with the wet skins of recently-killed sheep wrapped round their feet in an effort to keep them warm, and of the dregs of a cup of coffee freezing within minutes of being put down.

The monotonous mutton diet forced on the men at Central Force after the action at Gibeon inspired this cartoon by Walter Kirby, who was one of the NLH men briefly captured by the Germans after having been left exposed to scything machine-gun fire. (Hunting the Hun in GSWA – Transvaal Scottish Museum)

'If it were not for the thousands of sheep wandering round the countryside we would all die of starvation because there are hardly any rations to be issued,' Addison wrote in his diary on May 1. 'Some days we get half a biscuit and other days nothing, not even salt, but we can have as many sheep as we want. Consequently, we walk out into the veld, catch a sheep, cut its throat, skin it and bring it back into camp. We all have a huge feed of mutton cooked on the coals, feel fine for a bit, and then the hunger pains start again.

'We all have loose bowels, so it is a sort of non-stop motion affair. It is extraordinary how callous one becomes about killing these unfortunate animals.'

'We are weak and thin and crave for carbohydrates, and when put on guard over German prisoners we are allowed to sit down.'

By May 14 Addison was writing: 'All this living among the rocks, sand and thorn bushes and sleeping on the bare ground under the stars behind our saddles has reduced our clothing to shreds. Nobody shaves, we have no soap; our clothes are stiff with dried animal blood and we look and are the most desperate lot of ruffians on any battlefront.

'The soles of my boots completely came off, so I got a piece of wet bull's hide, wrapped it round each boot, laced it up with wire and let the hide dry on my boots, hair outwards. It worked like a charm and I proudly rode into Windhuk with them. My pants had no seat or knees but a goatskin soon put that right. This ensemble caused considerable mirth but at least my posterior was safe from scorpion stings and thorns . . . '

The hunger pains of the Carbineers were eased somewhat when a Boer family, probably one of several that had settled in German South West and carried on living normally during the war, arrived at the camp with a waggon loaded with mealie meal and great twists of Boer tobacco. The Carbineers, however, considered the prices outrageous at a sovereign for a nose-bag full of meal.

Before dawn one morning, while the farmer and his family lay asleep in the tented waggon, on top of the bags of mealie meal, some men of Addison's troop crept under the waggon, carrying nose-bags. Silently a bayonet was thrust up between the planks of the floor of the waggon and a stream of mealie meal came pouring down into the first nose-bag. Soon nose-bags full of meal were being passed along the chain of men under the waggon.

'I wonder what would have happened if by some mistake the bayonet had been jabbed into the old vrou,' Addison mused afterwards in his memoirs.

'It made beautiful porridge, straight from the farm mill,' he added, with no trace of guilt.

With the disbanding of the Southern Army, an occupation force with headquarters in Keetmanshoop was left in the south to maintain order under a military governor. About 100 civilians, including the mayor, had remained in the town and were treated with consideration by the victors, according to a report in a Windhuk newspaper.

'The womenfolk were treated with every possible respect and with great courtesy by the enemy, who have paid in cash for all foodstuffs requisitioned, and whose personal bearing towards the farmers and their families has in every case been considerate and friendly,' the newspaper reported.

The South Africans found that the Germans had established a large and well-stocked military base in Keetmanshoop, which encouraged speculation that they had intended to give massive backing to a Boer rebellion in South Africa.

Some of the Union troops sailed home from Luderitz, the first transport leaving for Cape Town on May 19.

The 1st Transvaal Scottish, the Rand Light Infantry, the Witwatersrand Rifles and the Pretoria Regiment were sent north to reinforce Botha's force.

Whatever it was that drove Royston soon had him back at war. After his return to South Africa he raised another force, which served with a British regiment in France, and later in the war he commanded an Australian brigade in the Middle East.

General Smuts, who had directed the operations in the south in their later stages, remained in South West Africa for a while, travelling to the north to consult with Botha. But his direct role in the campaign was largely over and he was to continue to play second fiddle to Botha until he went off to German East Africa to lead the South African forces there.

Van Deventer went with him as one of his senior commanders. Botha, for his part, still had a lot of fighting ahead of him in the north.

References

1. Hennig, R, *Deutsch-Südwest im Weltkriege,* 1920.
2. Collyer, p. 90.
3. *Ibid.*
4. *Ibid.*
5. Copies of letters from Royston to Sir Thomas Watt in Cory Library, Grahamstown.
6. Copy of letter in documents of Major Burton in Cory Library.
7. Devitt.
8. McKenzie, p. 319-20.
9. Morris, p. 90.
10. *Official History*, p. 51.
11. Collyer, p. 92.

CHAPTER

23

Other Than White

It was a white man's war that was fought in German South West Africa. Those who were not white played minor parts, though not always without pain.

Some were briefly spectators when the fighting passed through their country. Some were victims, shot by the Germans for helping the enemy. Many were servants of the white armies, on both sides; more than 30 000 black and coloured South Africans served with the Union forces as labourers, drivers and horse-minders.

Some, like the Rehoboth Basters, were combatants, rising up against the Germans and fighting bloody and not always one-sided battles against them.

Although it was not the main intention, the Baster uprising helped the South African campaign by diverting German troops away from major battlefronts.

A people of independent spirit, the Basters, of mixed Hottentot and Dutch descent, have always chosen their own path through life. In their 'Gebied' at Rehoboth, south of Windhuk, they lived almost autonomously. Their relations with the Germans were not always hostile, and during the Herero rebellion some of them served with the German forces.

At the outbreak of the First World War 150 Basters were serving in a mainly Baster company in the colony's defence force. Under the Basters' treaty with Dr Goring they were not obliged to help the Germans against a foreign enemy, but the company was assigned to guard the border near Walvis Bay and later to guard duties along the Swakop River.[1]

This displeased the Basters to a point at which the Germans decided to disband the unit. Some, however, were posted as guards over captured South Africans at prison camps. This pleased neither the South Africans, who objected to being guarded by non-whites, nor the Basters, who argued that it freed Germans for active service against the

South Africans and therefore contravened the Goring treaty.

Baster resentment increased when the Germans commandeered ox-waggons from them after a rainstorm washed away part of the railway line north of Mariental in January 1915. As a result of the growing discontent the Baster chief, Cornelius van Wyk, made his way to the Union lines at Walvis Bay and was taken to Swakopmund to see Botha on April 1. He offered the cooperation of the Basters against the Germans.

Botha made it plain that the South Africans did not want the Basters to get involved in the conflict. He told Van Wyk that the Union government would ensure that the Germans did no harm to the Basters but would insist that they should take no unfriendly action against the Germans.

'My quarrel is with the Germans,' Botha said. 'Your people must be outside the fighting line. I want you to act wisely. Do not get involved in this war.'[2]

Both the South Africans and the Germans appear to have adopted a policy of discouraging the indigenous people of the territory from becoming actively engaged in the conflict. The German policy in South West was quite different from that in East Africa, where they raised a large force of black askaris and relied heavily on those able soldiers to fight off the Dominion troops led by General Smuts. The most likely reason for the difference seems to be that after the difficulties they had experienced in subjugating the Hereros and other tribes in South West they were far less willing to arm them than those in East Africa.

The Union government's refusal to recruit blacks into its fighting forces in South West is probably bound up with the old reluctance of the whites in South Africa to arm blacks in case it encouraged them to turn against white domination.

On his return from Swakopmund, Chief van Wyk urged the Baster Council to prohibit any service by Basters with the German forces. As a result there was increased resistance to attempts by Franke to recruit Basters for non-combatant duties to release more Germans to fight against the South Africans.

Active resistance to the Germans was on the increase. A police sergeant was killed, several farms were attacked and Germans on them killed, and a veterinary station was attacked. On April 17, 45 Baster soldiers deserted from their camp at Uitdraai and marched towards Rehoboth, which was garrisoned by only 13 German soldiers.

In response to the garrison commander's telephoned request to Windhuk for help, reinforcements were sent. With them came the chief of police, representing Governor Seitz, who offered to leave the Basters alone if they surrendered all their guns and ammunition. When the Basters in response handed over a few antiquated rifles, the troops occupied Rehoboth and attacked a force of about 300 Basters who had assembled at Neuras, inflicted heavy losses on them and dispersed them.

Later the Basters reassembled at a water-hole at Tsamkuibis and set up fortified positions round the well. Three companies of German troops with two artillery pieces attacked them on May 8. The troops stormed the position but most of the Basters escaped, leaving five Germans dead.

They would have lived if the attack had been delayed, for as soon as it was over word arrived that the Germans were withdrawing to north of Windhuk because of the South African victory at Gibeon and Botha's advance from the coast.

While the Baster rebellion did not divert a large proportion of the German forces from the fight against the South Africans, it did weaken them sufficiently to have influenced the decision not to make a strong stand in the south. But even if a stand had been made the Germans would still have been compelled by Botha's advance on Windhuk to evacuate the south.

It was not only the Basters who gave the Germans trouble. In other parts of the territory there was unrest and German civilians and even soldiers were attacked after the Germans abandoned Windhuk.

'Disobedience and insubordination by the natives on the farms continued to increase alarmingly,' says von Oelhafen. 'They refused to work, many ran away and they did not hesitate to use violence against white men and women.'

Von Oelhafen says 'natives in the armed forces began to go over to the enemy in large numbers; they knew that their wives and children were mostly in Windhuk . . . He is presumably referring to non-combatants, since the Germans are not known to have used black soldiers other than the Basters, who were used on occasion to guard prisoners of war and the 'Kroo-boys' from Liberia who had worked the surf-boats at Swakopmund and were later put in uniform for non-combative duties with the armed forces.

'From now on,' says von Oelhafen, 'the German patrols were betrayed to the enemy wherever they turned . . .

'Soon there was a dense screen of local native scouts in front of the whole enemy lines, and the enemy made very effective use of this instrument against German reconnaissance . . .

'Insubordination against the Germans went hand-in-hand with treachery; here a farmer would be murdered, there another would be seized by the natives and handed over to the enemy.'

(This reference is not clear, since farmers not serving in uniform were left alone by the Union forces.)

According to von Oelhafen, the Hereros 'thought that a golden age had dawned, and already they saw themselves in possession of the

Germans' houses, farms and cattle.'

Typical of the examples of black cooperation with the South Africans that von Oelhafen gives is this: 'A bush patrol led by Lieut Baron Wolff von Gudenberg was on its way from Otjipaue to Waldau when they became aware that they were being followed by native trackers. The patrol went back to Okarumatero and there encountered an enemy patrol of fifteen rifles and drove them off with the loss of three men, seven horses and two mules.

'The German patrol then made for the water-point at Otjimahengu to water their horses, after which they were set upon by a strong enemy force. After a brief exchange of fire that cost the enemy four men and five horses, the patrol itself lost eight riding horses, so that Lieutenant von Gudenberg ordered a hasty retreat. While galloping back this battle-tested officer fell from his horse severely wounded and soon died in the hands of the enemy, who buried him with military honours in Wilhelmstal.'

Although the black and coloured men serving with the Union forces in South West Africa were all unarmed and acting in non-combatant capacities, their very presence with the fighting forces sometimes exposed them to German fire. In some cases they behaved with great bravery and willingly put their lives at risk for what can only be presumed to be a strong sense of duty and loyalty.

At Sandfontein, for example, when the Transvaal Horse Artillery had to move their guns and horses to a position safer from the German fire, some of the Coloured drivers went out into the storm of bullets and shrapnel with the white gunners to help to do the job.

Much more recognition is now given to the part played by blacks in the First World War.

'The importance of the role of Blacks and Coloureds in the conquest of German South West Africa has received scant attention,' says an article published in *Militaria* in 1976.[3] The article says that '33 556 Blacks served as labourers in the Union Defence Forces between August 4 1914 and August 31 1915.' (All save 1 326 from Bechuanaland and 58 from Basutoland were South Africans.)

But these figures are incomplete because they do not include those who 'were engaged independently and taken to South West Africa by units or individuals,' says the article, quoting from the Union of South Africa Year Book of 1918. 'Nor do they include the Native Artillery Drivers in the South African Field Artillery and other gunner units.'

(Those who were 'engaged independently' almost certainly were the black men who were taken to South West as batmen by officers in the Natal and possibly other regiments. Their numbers are difficult to establish.)

'C/Cpl Mokosi, who later served in the South African Police and was awarded the 1914–15 Star, the British War Medal 1914–20 and the Allied Victory Medal, was one of these men. He served with the South African Mounted Riflemen – Field Artillery Battery between March 10 and July 9 1915.'

The article says that 'the role of Coloured personnel in the German South West African campaign has never received the attention it deserves'. It quotes Captain Ivor Difford, author of the history of the 1st Battalion of the Cape Corps, as saying that 'a large number of Coloured men participated in the . . . campaign as artillery and transport drivers, motor drivers and mechanics, as officers' servants and in various other non-combatant capacities, and performed much useful work'.

Difford's book records that it was the good service of the Coloureds in the South West Africa campaign that prompted the Prime Minister to raise the 1st Cape Corps for combatant service in German East Africa.

Not only black and Coloured people but Indians also may have served with the Union forces in South West, according to the *Militaria* article. It suggests that the Indian Stretcher-Bearer Corps raised by Gandhi for service in the Anglo-Boer War and used again in the Natal rebellion of 1906 may have served with Botha's forces in South West. The suggestion is based on the dates of a medal awarded to a member of the Corps, but no firm evidence is produced.

That local black people were used by the Union forces as scouts is clear but the extent to which they were used is not. According to the diary of Captain C Murray of the SA Medical Corps, which was published privately by his family, about 30 Hereros were employed as scouts by the Union Intelligence Section.

Members of the Bondelswarts tribe, which was later to rise in rebellion against the South African administrators of the territory, were used as guides during the campaign. The leader of the rebellion, Abraham Morris, served as a guide with the Steinkopf intelligence unit of the South African Mounted Riflemen from August 27 1914 to May 7 1915.

Apart from brief acknowledgements like that in *Militaria*, the part of the non-white personnel in the campaign has never emerged from whatever pigeonholes or dusty files it might now lie. One day it will, if it is still retrievable. Someone will find the time to dig it out. But the personal stories, the recollections of the humour and the hardships and the bravery, have probably all died with those who could have told about them.

References

1. Ungleich, p. 127.
2. Collyer, p. 83.
3. Bisset, W M, *Militaria*, March 6 1976, p. 55.

CHAPTER
24

Sailors in the Sands

The Royal Navy left the ocean at Swakopmund and went to war in the desert, on wheels. The sailor crews of the armoured cars sent by Britain to help Botha's army steered inland into the sea of sand. Less than two weeks later they were saving the day in one of the fiercest engagements of the campaign, many miles inland.

The presence of seamen on wheels in the Namib desert seems almost as incongruous as would have been Boers riding round the decks of HMS *Astraea* on their horses. But there is a logical explanation for this military oddity.

During the early part of the war the British forces were confronted with a problem in the defence of their airfields in Europe. The Royal Flying Corps had no troops for airfield defence and the army was too hard-pressed to spare soldiers for the job. Most of the Royal Marines had been captured after the siege of Antwerp. The Navy was the least burdened arm of the services at the time and the Royal Naval Air Service found itself responsible for airfield defences.

And so came into being the Royal Naval Armoured Car Division. At first it mounted machine-guns on ordinary cars to give its fire-power greater mobility and later, the cars were protected with sheets of steel.

By the time it was decided to send some of the armoured cars to South West Africa their presence in the navy had been taken so much for granted that Lieutenant-Commander W Whittall, the commander of the unit, No 1 Squadron, did not bother to explain the oddity in his account of the campaign.[1]

He seems to have thought it perfectly reasonable that he should have set out from England in March 1915 with twelve 'light' armoured cars to go and fight the Germans in the desert. Although he does not acknowledge it in his book, Whittall was a pioneer. His were probably the first armoured cars to go to war in Africa, and certainly the first in southern Africa.

232

What German aerial reconnaissance at first dismissed as water tankers were in fact one of the most effective weapons employed in the campaign – the Royal Naval armoured cars. The armour-plated Rolls Royces carried a Vickers machine-gun in a revolving turret. (War Museum)

He explains that a squadron normally also included three heavy armoured cars, but they were left behind because they were considered unsuitable for conditions in German South West.

The light versions were not exactly flimsy; they weighed about four tons each. Unlike the heavy models, each of which carried a three-pounder gun besides a machine-gun, the light cars had only a machine-gun, mounted in a revolving turret.

Like the steam locomotives landed by the South Africans, the armoured cars had to be fetched ashore in lighters from the ships. They had then to be manhandled with exquisite timing over a couple of planks onto the beach from the lighters as they heaved in the surf.

Botha's chief staff officer, Colonel Collyer, to whom Whittall reported, was of the opinion that the armoured cars could not be used in support of the main thrust along the bed of the Swakop River because they would get stuck in the sand. On his advice Whittall took a trolley along the railway to Nonidas to see for himself. Two officers of the Motor Transport section whom he consulted there scoffed at the idea of the heavy armoured cars crossing the sand that bogged down all but the lightest of their trucks.

Whittall was never able to put the matter to the test, for when he got back he found that the decision had been made for him. Higher authority, apparently convinced that the armoured cars would not be of much use with Botha's fast-moving mounted brigades, had decided to send the squadron to join the 3rd Infantry Brigade, now under Skinner's command, which was protecting the teams rebuilding the Otavi railway after it had been pulled up by the Germans. Skinner's force was then at Trekkoppies, a dot on the map that was about to assume an important place in the history of the campaign.

The cavalry-oriented South African military leaders had some difficulty envisaging a useful function for the ponderous metal behemoths and sent them off to join Skinner's infantry for want of any alternative ideas.

The armoured cars were taken by train to Trekkoppies. As the train steamed out of Swakopmund on April 24 Whittall had to endure some ragging from the South African officers about having to miss all the action, which everyone expected would take place on Botha's line of advance along the course of the Swakop River.

The Union commanders were so certain that the Germans would not attack Skinner's force that they withdrew the two twelve-pounder guns that were his only artillery. The guns were taken away to join Botha's force on the same day that Whittall's squadron set out for Trekkoppies. Skinner himself believed there was a real danger of his being attacked by the Germans; but his protests at losing his guns were ignored by headquarters in Swakopmund.

Whittall was not impressed by the security of Skinner's position at Trekkoppies station when he unloaded his vehicles there.

The two-foot-wide narrow-gauge railway that the Germans had built and were now destroying as they retreated along it was being replaced with standard three-foot-six gauge by the advancing South Africans. Although Botha's main thrust was being made along the Swakop, he would be relying on the railway to supply his force once it captured Windhuk or Karibib.

Skinner's force and the railway construction crews whom he was guarding were dependent for all their supplies, including water, on the line from Swakopmund. But even when the mines laid by the Germans had been cleared and the new track laid there was no guarantee that the trains would get through. Breakdowns, often caused by the brackish water fouling the locomotives' boilers, were frequent, and whenever the line was blocked by a broken-down train Skinner's force was in effect isolated, cut off from supplies and reinforcements.

His camp at Trekkoppies was badly sited for defence as he had no option but to camp wherever the railhead happened to be. Situated in a hollow, the camp was overlooked by a ridge on the right and a line of kopjes in front. Rough ground thickly covered with scrub provided excellent cover for an attacking force to get near to the camp.

All this had been noted by the commander of the German force opposing Skinner, the same Major Ritter who had attacked Kakamas. Von Scheele was now based at Usakos with his Aviatik, and Ritter made good use of it to keep himself and his commander, Colonel Franke, informed of what the South Africans were up to and to harass them with an occasional bomb.

Trooper Hunter of the ILH recalls Fritz flying over the camp while his unit was at Rossing and dropping a shell and several handgrenades. 'He came over at breakfast time and the whole camp turned out to fire on him,' Hunter wrote in his diary, 'but he was never within reasonable rifle range. I had eight shots at him.'

When the Germans had moved their aircraft to the Swakopmund front the South Africans had made a matching relocation of 'Skinny Liz', the home-made anti-aircraft gun. Hunter recorded that the gun 'put several shrapnel shots about him, but it was too difficult a mark.'

A few days later Fritz reappeared and Skinny Liz 'put in some beautiful shooting . . . causing him to steer clear of the camp. He dropped several hand grenades but did no damage'. Hunter's unit had moved up to Trekkoppies when Fritz again appeared in the sky. The camp was at church service that day, but 'Skinny Liz put a few shells about him and he cleared off.'

Skinner must have guessed that Fritz had probably reported the withdrawal of his guns, plainly visible in an open railway truck as they went back down the line to Swakopmund. In any case, he was clearly uneasy and he decided to carry out a reconnaissance towards the German positions and to lead it himself.

His fears were well founded. Fritz had indeed reported to his headquarters that there was no artillery with Skinner's force. His observations and aerial photographs had shown Franke that Skinner's force was no bigger than that under Ritter's command.

Franke saw a chance to give the enemy a blow that would at least slow his eager advance, and he ordered Ritter to attack. The aerial reconnaisance had shown relatively strong infantry units at Arandis, 14 miles down the line from Trekkoppies. To prevent them from coming up the line to help Skinner, Franke ordered a demolition team to blow up the line south of Trekkoppies before the attack was launched.

Ritter's force was to be moved near enough to make a night march to get into position to attack Trekkoppies at dawn. The demolition team would leave earlier to be in place to blow up the line a little before then.

It was Gibeon all over again, except that the roles were reversed – and Skinner was not as complacent as von Kleist had been at Gibeon about the possibility of attack.

For his reconnaissance Skinner took a squadron of the ILH, leaving in the camp the 2nd Transvaal Scottish, the 2nd Kimberley Regiment and Whittall's armoured car squadron.

As Skinner and his men rode north on that moonless night of April 25, Ritter's force was riding south. They nearly collided in the dark, but only Skinner knew it, for only he had taken the precaution of sending scouts out ahead. Yet again German carelessness with reconnaissance was going to cost them dear, as it had done at Gibeon.

Some accounts say that the Germans were on the northern side of the railway and the ILH on the southern, others say it was the other way about; and yet others say they were both on the same side. One account even asserts that some of the ILH stumbled on the enemy at such close quarters that a German officer thought they were part of his unit and brusquely ordered them to keep in line![1]

This is an implausible story, considering that it would have been impossible for so large a force to move so quietly that they would not have been heard by the ILH scouts in good time.

It is tempting to believe that some of the scouts deliberately joined Ritter's column, just like the bold German spy who rode with McKenzie's column at Bethanie, but there is no evidence to support this romantic notion.

What clearly did happen is that the scouts heard the Germans approaching and got near enough to discover that the column included artillery. They quietly withdrew and then galloped back to warn Skinner, who immediately turned his force round and headed back to prepare to defend his camp.

Official accounts allow Skinner the credit, if only by default, of having done this with some dignity. But according to one unofficial account, he returned in precipitate haste, abandoning some Transvaal Scottish infantry pickets to the Germans.

That account came to light after Juta published his history of the Transvaal Scottish, which made no mention of the manner of Skinner's retreat. On reading the book, Major DR Hunt, who was with the Transvaal Scottish pickets up the line from Trekkoppies, wrote to Juta and told him this version, which Juta has deposited with the regimental records: 'The ILH came galloping back through our pickets, past Garub (Karub) station and rode off back to Trekkoppies. General Skinner stopped at the station and told Captain Herschell (OC Company) to clear back to Trekkoppies as fast as he could with his company.

'Then General Skinner and his ILH orderly, Trooper N Harley, rode down to where I was 200 yards from the station, with my half of F Company, which was on picket. The General shouted to me: "Get back! Get back! Here's the German main force! Just here! Get back!"

'I said, "Very good, sir. But I have two pickets on those hills over there". He said, "Never mind your pickets. You must leave them. Here are the Germans! Get back if you can!" He then galloped off with his orderly.'

Hunt says he sent off the half company with a sergeant and sent a bugler with a message to the nearest of the two pickets to return to Trekkopies. He then went to fetch the outlying picket and began marching the men back to Trekkoppies. They found the Germans already at Garub station and made a 200-yard detour to avoid them.

At first they marched a little away from the road, which runs beside the railway line, but later took the road and marched along it, just in front of the Germans, who seemed unaware of their presence, according to Hunt.

'The men, who were very tired, had overcoats and asked to be allowed to drop them, but I made them hold on to them as I did not want to give the show away. The march seemed endless and was like a nightmare. As we got nearer to Trekkoppies, the Germans seemed to move off the road a bit to the west and we met an ILH vedette whom I sent in to report our approach to the camp.'

Skinner's first action back at his camp was to telephone to Arandis to call up the reserve force there, the 1st Rhodesia Regiment, which immediately got into the train standing in the station and set off north as fast as the locomotive could go. Skinner meanwhile deployed his infantry in the shallow trenches that they had been able to dig in the hard ground near the railway to await the attack.

At 3.30 a.m. Skinner's headquarters informed general headquarters at Swakopmund of the situation. GHQ, with enormous optimism and perhaps an even greater sense of guilt for having taken Skinner's guns away earlier, immediately sent off a train carrying two four-inch guns, which steamed into Trekkoppies when they were burying the dead after the battle.

On a cold morning in the desert the crews of the armoured cars, some wearing overcoats, prepare to resume the advance. (Cape Archives)

The nine armoured cars available to Whittall at Trekkoppies were deployed in support of the infantry. Five were stationed at various points up to half a mile in front of the trenches. Two were stationed at the point on the railway where the trenches of the Scottish and the Kimberleys joined. The remaining two were held in reserve with the transport, which was standing by in case the Union forces were forced to rereat.[2]

The cars were about to provide an unpleasant surprise for the Germans, who appeared to be unaware of their arrival in the territory. The vehicles had in fact been spotted in the aerial reconnaissance but had been identified as water trucks!

At 5.45 a.m. two explosions were heard as the German demolition squad blew up the railway line. But again the Germans blundered: they blew it up on the wrong side of the South African camp, on the north, leaving the line to the south intact for the Rhodesian reinforcements to come up. Why the German sappers did not first establish their position from the mileposts along the railway is inexplicable.

The Rhodesians arrived at dawn. They had barely flung themselves into the trenches when Ritter opened his attack with a barrage from his two artillery batteries on the South African camp.

Either from their own records of the place or from Fritz's aerial observations, they knew the range to the yard and shell after shell burst among the South African tents. Instead of being occupied by slumbering Union soldiers, as Ritter thought, the tents were by now all empty. Lying in the comparative safety of their trenches, the South Africans morosely watched their kit being blown to smithereens and no doubt silently gave thanks for the reconnaissance that had saved them from being killed in their beds.

Without artillery to reply, the South Africans could only hunker down and wait.

After a three-hour bombardment, Ritter decided that the South Africans had been sufficiently softened up and sent in his troops on foot, with fixed bayonets. His intention appears to have been to cross the railway line and occupy the ridge. That would have enabled the Germans to enfilade the South African trenches – except that the Rhodesians were now established on the ridge. Before they reached there, however, the Germans encountered the 'water trucks', which began spewing a devastating machine-gun fire. Nasty though the shock must have been for the Germans, they kept up their attack, but shifted it to a point further down the railway line to try to avoid the armoured cars. But again the cars were there, spitting flame, and seemingly impervious to the shrapnel fired at them by Ritter's artillery.

Twice more the Germans moved their attack down the line and each time they were forced by the armoured cars to veer away. By this time

German soldiers surrendering to Major Trew, commander of Botha's bodyguard, and some of his men. The bodyguard, drawn from the South African Police, did more than protect the commander-in-chief; its members served as front-line soldiers, too. (Cape Archives)

they were directly opposite the South African trenches and the concentrated fire of the infantrymen in them.

The cover was good among the rocks and the bushes, however, and all that the Scottish and the Kimberleys could see was 'the occasional glint of a bayonet here and there'.[3]

An attempt by the ILH to ride around behind the artillery and attack it from the rear was thwarted when the Germans detected the movement and interposed two strong detachments to protect their guns.[4]

At mid-morning Ritter ordered an intensified artillery barrage with shrapnel on the Union trenches. Then his troops charged, showing great resolution in the face of the heavy fire from the Union positions, and worked their way to within 50 yards of the trenches. But now the two armoured cars posted at the trenches brought their guns to bear and in the face of that and the intense rifle and machine-gun fire from the trenches the German attack withered. Ritter, realising that he was beaten, ordered a withdrawal.

Skinner immediately launched a counter-attack by the South African infantry and the ILH. But the retreating German artillery repeatedly turned round to open a heavy fire on the pursuers and, without artillery of their own, the Union forces had to abandon a pursuit in strength and content themselves with mopping up the German stragglers and wounded.

But the South Africans were not entirely without artillery. Skinny Liz was there to defend them against Fritz (who flew overhead during the action but took no hostile part in it) and her barrel was brought down to an unusually low angle to fire two shells at the retreating Germans. One was seen to burst among them, but whether it caused any casualties is not known.

Although the broken ground over which the Germans had advanced had limited the mobility of the armoured cars, the secret weapon of the Union forces had played a part in the battle that may have been pivotal. It was at least an important one, counter-balancing the Germans' exclusive possession of artillery.

By one estimate, the German guns fired between 400 and 500 shells on the South African positions.[5] Many of these must have fallen on the empty tent camp. Nevertheless, a major factor in the German defeat was the steadiness of the untried South Afican and Rhodesian infantry, who endured their first artillery bombardment like veterans and kept up a fire that was ultimately responsible for stopping the Germans from storming the trenches.

The German losses were 11 men killed, 14 wounded and 27 captured. The Union casualties were nine dead and 32 wounded.

If Ritter had been able to storm the Union positions or force Skinner to retreat down the line, Botha would at the very least have had to postpone his drive on Windhuk and divert substantial forces along the railway to chase the Germans back. He might even have had to abandon the advance along the line of the Swakop River and take the slower alternative of the railway route.

Ritter's failure now left Botha free to concentrate his attention on severing the Germans' railway spine.

Skinner's force meanwhile moved on up the line of rail to Karub. He and Whittall spent some time walking up and down outside the railway station in earnest conversation. They were unaware that they were walking over a mine comprising 35 sticks of dynamite and two slabs of gelignite.

By amazing chance their feet did not touch the detonating pin, of if they did, it failed to set off the mine. It was only when someone else stepped on the detonator the next day that it was activated but, by an even greater stroke of luck, failed to ignite the explosives, which the sappers then dug up.

'When we came to examine the place,' says Whittall, 'it was clear that on the previous day Colonel Skinner and I must have walked straight over the mine at least twenty times.'

References

1. Whittall, p. 34.
2. *Ibid,* p. 37.
3. Juta, p. 40.
4. Ungleich, p. 151.
5. Juta, p. 91.

25

The Dash for Windhuk

In his advance up the heavily-mined Swakop River valley, Botha could have made good use of a practical mine detector. While the mule-drawn harrow might have been effective along the line of the railway, it was not practical for an army on the march. But other concepts were hatching.

Before the advance on Windhuk began someone got the idea of driving herds of goats in front of the troops to set off any mines in the path. Somehow the relevant military authority was persuaded to part with sufficient funds to buy several hundred goats, and these duly arrived in a bleating mass at Nonidas. But nobody could be found who was willing to look after the noisy, smelly herd.

The sappers were the first to be approached, since detecting and neutralising mines was their responsibility. But they took the firm line that their responsibility did not extend to minding goats. The Remount Section of the cavalry was tried next, on the theory that they were accustomed to looking after animals until they were claimed by someone else. But they, too, drew the line at goats.

Even the Transvaal Scottish were approached, although it is difficult to see what linked goats with Scots in the mind of the inquirer. Perhaps it was a feeling that there was a similarity between the sounds made by goats and bagpipes. At any rate, it is reasonable to assume that the kilted soldiers' rejection of the idea was conveyed bluntly.

Salvation came from the burghers. A helpful commando offered to look after the animals until they were needed for their military duties.

But when that time came there were no goats to be seen in the commando camp, or even heard there. That is, they could not be heard bleating; they could, in a sense, be heard in another way.

'Only a steady frizzling from innumerable campfires broke the stillness of the night,' O'Shaughnessy recorded, 'and an odour quite impossible to associate with the bully beef ration in vogue at that period permeated the warm desert air.'

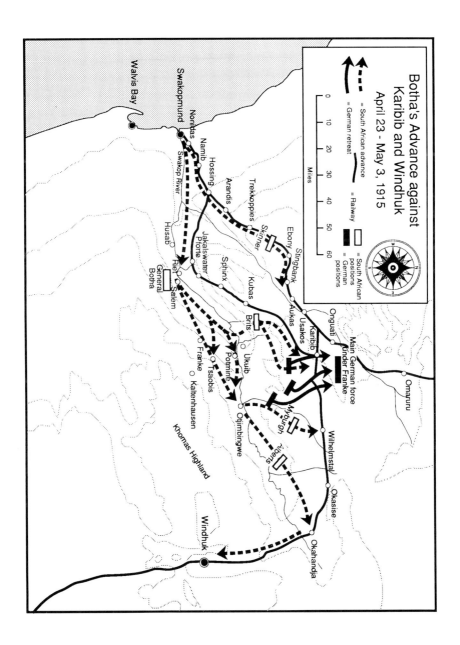

Botha's Advance against
Karibib and Windhuk
April 23 - May 3, 1915

The goats were not the only casualties of the Union troops' battle against hunger. At the end of April the heavy artillery of Botha's Northern Force had become immobilised, not because of enemy action but because the oxen used to pull the big guns had been eaten.

In this case they were consumed with official permission, for the simple reason that there was nothing else for the forward troops to eat.[1] Botha's appeals to Defence Headquarters for more transport waggons to supply his resumed advance along the Swakop River had brought him some waggons but not enough.

In the meantime his force had grown to nearly three times the size it had been when he had been compelled to suspend his advance after the victory at Riet-Pforte a month before and send the mounted brigades back to Swakopmund to be fed from the supply ships. Botha had known that without adequate waggon transport it would be virtually impossible to get a force astride the railway north of Karibib in time to intercept the retreat of the Germans and perhaps bring about their surrender.

By striking straight at Windhuk across the desert he might still not intercept Franke, but he would capture the last of the German wireless stations and complete the 'great and urgent Imperial service' requested by the British. Even that, however, would need more waggon transport than was available. As Prime Minister, Botha knew that the opposition in Parliament to South Africa's participation in the war did not augur well for getting additional funds voted for the South West campaign. He argued to his far-off cabinet that the sooner the campaign was ended the less it would cost; but to finish it quickly he needed transport for his army's supplies.

He sent an urgent appeal to the Union asking that 'every waggon and mule that could be scraped together be sent up'.[2]

And then he put his faith in the burgher commandos and in their ability to travel far and fast with few supplies and still fight effectively. Botha was familiar with the dictum that an army marches on its stomach and he knew that the commandos had given it a new dimension

By the end of April, by feeding his troops straight from the supply ships, he had managed to accumulate enough supplies at Riet to sustain the mounted brigades for five days of operations in the field. He decided that he could risk resuming the advance on Windhuk.

Then came good news. In response to his plea for transport, GHQ said he could have 300 waggons and mules if he could do without some of his heavy artillery. This was a concession he had had little difficulty in accepting since he was already doing without it because its draught oxen had been devoured by his hungry troops.

Botha could now begin his advance with much less anxiety. The supply problem would nevertheless remain acute until the new transport arrived, and it would be up to the commandos to keep going until then. Some of the hardest riding of the campaign was about to begin.

For the advance inland Botha divided his force into two commands. One comprised the 1st and 2nd Mounted Brigades which had fought at Riet-Pforte. They were commanded by Brits, who had been promoted Brigadier-General. In the other were two new brigades, the 3rd, consisting of Afrikaans-speaking commandos from the Transvaal, and the 5th, drawn from the Orange Free State and comprising Afrikaans and English-speakers in roughly equal proportions.

The Free Staters were commanded by Brigadier-General M W Myburgh, who, like all of Botha's senior burgher commanders, had served with him in the Anglo-Boer War.

'Broad-minded and tactful, he numbered many of his English-speaking comrades among his friends,' wrote Collyer of Myburgh. 'He was withal determined and a good disciplinarian and enjoyed the well-deserved confidence of his chief. He was an admirable subordinate who never made difficulties and might be relied upon to carry out his instructions and to use good judgment if called upon to make an independent decision.

'He was tall, even among tall men, powerfully built and the picture of robust manhood . . .'

Myburgh was a Member of Parliament, representing a Transvaal constituency.

Brits's 1st Mounted Brigade, commanded by Colonel Lemmer, had on its right wing the Krugersdorp and Potchefstroom A and B commandos and on its left wing the Lichtenburg, Marico, Wolmarans-stad and Bloemhof commandos, totalling 2 120 rifles. It had four guns of the Transvaal Horse Artillery and a section of machine-guns.

The 2nd Brigade, under Colonel Alberts, had the Heidelberg A and B commandos, the Standerton A and B and the Ermelo A commandos on its right wing. On the left were the Ermelo B, Carolina and Middelburg A and B commandos. Their combined strength was 3 120 rifles, and in addition it had a section of 12-pounders, a section of howitzers and a machine-gun section.

Brits thus had 4 270 mounted riflemen, eight guns and two machine-gun sections under his command.

Myburgh had 4 595 riflemen and eight guns in his force. His 3rd Mounted Brigade, under Colonel H S Mentz, had on its right wing the Wakkerstroom, Utrecht-Vryheid, Paulpietersburg and Piet Retief commandos and Botha's Natal Horse. On the left were the Lydenburg, Pietersburg, Waterberg, Rustenburg and Pretoria commandos. These 2 620 rifles had with them four guns of the 4th Permanent Battery and a machine-gun section.

The 1 970 Free Staters in the 5th Mounted Brigade, commanded by Colonel H W N 'Manie' Botha, the general's nephew, were divided into a right wing composed of the 1st, 2nd and 3rd Regiments and a left wing made up of the 4th, 5th and 6th Regiments. The brigade had four guns of the 2nd Permanent Battery and a machine-gun section.

For his strike inland General Botha thus had a force of 8 860 rifles and 16 guns. In addition he could call on Wylie's 4th Infantry Brigade, now expanded to three times its original landed strength.

To protect his vital lines of communication, Botha had disposed units of the Rand Rifles, the Southern Rifles and the Duke of Edinburgh's Own Rifles along the line from Walvis Bay to kilometre 13 beyond Swakopmund. From that point to the railhead he had deployed the 1st ILH, the 3rd Infantry Brigade, the Royal Naval Armoured Cars, two 12-pounder guns and two four-inch guns.

The Riet-Khan railway was guarded by the 2nd Durban Light Infantry.

Opposing him General Botha now had the entire German strength, von Kleist having moved up to the vicinity of Windhoek. The Germans were along the railway from Karibib to Windhoek and had been patrolling and probing continually towards the Union positions. Apart from a half-hearted assault on Salem they had made no major attacks

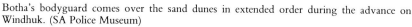

Botha's bodyguard comes over the sand dunes in extended order during the advance on Windhuk. (SA Police Museum)

246

since Riet-Pforte, somewhat to the surprise of the South African commanders.

On April 28 the South African mounted brigades had gathered at Riet for the big push. Wylie's infantry was at Jakkalswater. Botha assembled his commanders and briefed them on the plan of action. Myburgh was to march that evening and head eastwards for Tsaobis, attack it from the south and send part of his force in a pincer movement to attack from the north.

Brits would advance north to Kubas with the 1st Brigade and send Alberts with the 2nd Brigade eastwards to Potmine and Otjimbingwe.

Wylie would stand ready to advance on Kubas along the Khan railway by way of Sphinx.

These movements were to lead to Brits's forces attacking Karibib and Myburgh's swinging north to cut the railway at Wilhemstal between Karibib and Okahandja.

Although he may have suspected it, Botha was unaware that the Germans had already decided to abandon Windhuk without a fight. Franke guessed that the South Africans would send the Southern Army up the railway line to attack Windhuk while the Northern Force would strike for Karibib to cut the northern railway.[3]

Franke's prime concern was to avoid being caught between these two forces. After agonised deliberations between the German military commanders and Governor Seitz it had been decided to leave Windhuk to the South Africans and to move the entire German army and government to the north while the railway through Karibib was still open.

Dr Seitz had moved the seat of government to Grootfontein 23 days before Botha resumed his advance from Riet. The entire civil service and all the documents and records of the administration had already been moved as a precaution.

The military headquarters were moved to Omaruru. Before abandoning the central region, where most of the Germans lived, the administration called up all reserves for the defence of the north. Men who would not normally have been accepted into the military were pressed into service. All serviceable horses were commandeered.

Towns in the central region were left with only a few weeks' supply of food on the assumption that the South Africans would feed the populations of occupied areas.

Before pulling back, however, Franke had thickly mined the routes he thought most likely to be taken by the South Africans in their advance, and had ordered his troops to poison all water supplies as they withdrew.

Thus the advancing South Africans again found that their chief enemy was not German soldiers but mines and thirst.

A captured German flag attracts the keen interest of General Botha. (Cape Archives)

Near Dorstrivier three scouts of the Middelburg commando and their horses were blown to pieces when a hidden German detonated a remote mine as they rode over it.

'The South African soldiers had by this time acquired a useful knack of detecting mines and knowing where to expect them, and the casualties from this source were far fewer than they would have been earlier,' Collyer wrote.

Morris records this description of the march by one of the South Africans: 'We descended into a river bed, where we were met by a single horseman, who kept repeating: "Keep well into the bank." Mines! After crossing a few stony ridges we came to another single horseman, who kept repeating: "Keep in single file – don't stray out." More mines!

'We then began to ascend a range of low mountains or high hills, the most awful place I ever saw. The moon was nearly at the full, which made the effect all the more ghostly . . . A cold, glittering deathliness – not a sign of vegetation or life in any form . . . That was a bad night, winding round and up these mountains, with horses slipping over the loose stones, and I think most of us realised that if our horses failed up there we hadn't much chance.

'On the other side of these mountains we struck an awful streak of soft, floury sand, and, as bad luck would have it, the order was given to quicken pace, which meant a hand gallop. This was the worst we had yet met – like riding through a flour mill in a gale.

'Owing to the lack of water we had to push on and as the sun got higher we began to feel the heat and the lack of sleep. As it got on to midday the water-bottles got empty, and thirst became an added trouble. It was well after midday when we reached Tsamis. Here we found a farmhouse and a well, said to be poisoned with disease germs, and a dry river.'

Suppressing their craving for rest and sleep, the men had to trek on until they found water, for that was a need more vital than sleep.

There were moments of humour amid the hardship, however. It could be hard on the nerves to ride at the head of a column in a night march, not knowing whether mines or an enemy ambush might lie ahead, and so it was with a member of the Middelburg commando. In the bright moonlight a huge baboon suddenly leaped on to a rock in front of the column and gave two loud, harsh barks. It was a startling sight and it is not surprising that to the burgher at the head of the column it seemed very much as though a sentry had suddenly sprung into view and shouted the challenge, 'Wie's daar?'

His automatic response was to yell, 'Vriend! Vriend!'

Understandable, perhaps, but it is equally understandable that the unfortunate burgher's comrades did not allow him to forget the incident for the rest of the campaign.[4]

The rigours of the advance were vividly described by a lieutenant with Mentz's 3rd Mounted Brigade, who recounted how after a hard day's ride his unit was about to get some much-needed sleep when it was ordered to saddle up and join an attack on a German force that had been reported a considerable distance away.

'At twelve we were in the saddle and rode back to a farmhouse, where we found the rest of the brigade riding in all directions to take their places. There was a bit of a scramble round the farmhouse. Incidentally it was discovered next day that it was mined all round and how our people escaped is still a marvel.

'We were on the right flank through the bush. For the first few miles the pace was easy, with an occasional halt but no off-saddle. The pace then quickened, and the fifteen miles seemed to be getting very long. Hour after hour passed, and the fatigue began to tell; you must remember that we had had only scraps of sleep for three nights and three days.

'At about four in the morning, guesswork, the flanking parties closed in on the rough road or track and the pace was increased to a hand gallop. The fatigue became awful. I began to get light-headed. The sky seemed to become a straight wall in front of us and the effect of the moonlight through the dust made me imagine I saw great palaces and churches, with the stars as little windows.

'Then I would pull myself together and look at the men riding in front, and they would turn into funny old giantesses, dancing in the

With Major Bok interpreting, Botha questions captured German soldiers. (Cape Archives)

moonlight. I learned afterwards that everyone suffered from these hallucinations.

'There was no check now; we galloped on and on, mile after mile, over stones, drooping branches, just leaving it to the horse. Those splendid horses! They were far saner than we were and seemed to know there was something ahead.

'Just as early dawn broke we reached the top of a ridge, where a general halt was made. I found we were looking down on to a river bed, with big, willow-like trees in it. That is all I remember, as I was dying for want of sleep. I know the commandos began to move off in different directions; heard a solitary shot fired, and then we moved down through the river bed.

'A couple of hundred yards on the other side we turned sharp to the right and opened out into extended order; all this at the gallop. I glanced to my right and to my surprise saw we were on the outskirts of a little town – Otjimbingwe. A few moments after that we slackened pace and I heard the order, 'Load magazines!'

'All at once there was a regular fusillade of rifle and machine-gun fire. I had no idea they were firing at us as I was too finished to think or care for anything but sleep. I certainly heard some twings of bullets that seemed rather close but was too sleepy to understand. The next thing I remember was being in the river bed with all the others . . .

'In that night's ride we covered from 32 to 35 miles in five-and-a-half hours, most of the way at a gallop, through thick bush, clouds of dust, and rough ground, after having already had three days and nights of perpetual going.'[5]

The commandos' hard riding caught a German company under Captain von Huber-Liebenau in Otjimbingwe 'completely by surprise' but most of the company slipped out before the encirclement was complete.[6] An officer and 23 men were unable to get through the gap and were captured.

Botha, who himself arrived in Otjimbingwe on May 1, now plotted a little subterfuge in his next move. Myburgh was ordered to take his main force along the road from Otjimbingwe towards Windhuk and to stop early on the evening of May 3 at Quaiputz. He was to put up an appearance of camping for the night, but as soon as it got dark he would break camp and turn north for Wilhelmstal, where he would destroy the railway and telegraph lines. From there he would move west towards Karibib and put his force across the Otavi railway and the road to the north.

Before leaving Swakopmund Botha had asked General Smuts to come north and meet him in Potmine for a strategic conference. When he reached Potmine he found Smuts waiting there for him.[7] According to Whittall, Botha reached Potmine soon after the Germans had vacated it. He was accompanied only by a detachment of his South African Police bodyguard. It had been intended that Potmine should be occupied by a much larger burgher force some hours before Botha arrived, but this force did not appear until some hours after Botha had installed himself is the town.

Whittall says that 'if the Germans had not been in such a tremendous hurry to save their skins they might quite easily have bagged the commander-in-chief with the whole of the personal and general staffs.'

In fact, if Whittall is right, the Germans could have captured not only the South African Prime Minister but the Minister of Defence (Smuts) as well.

It seems more likely that it was Smuts alone whom the Germans might have captured, for he was apt to lose patience with slow escorts and go off ahead on his own.

Whittall says, however, that while Smuts was at Potmine he heard how Botha had exposed himself to the danger of being hit by enemy artillery fire during the battle at Riet. Smuts sent for the commander of the bodyguard, Major Trew, and gave him a dressing down for allowing the general to expose himself to danger.

Trew pointed out that he did his best to dissaude Botha from going into dangerous places, but the general always insisted on going his own way.

'You should exercise your authority as commander of the bodyguard and not allow him to expose himself needlessly,' Smuts replied.

'That's all very, sir,' replied Trew, 'but will you tell me what I am to do when the General Officer Commanding in Chief tells me to go to hell?'

Whittall says he never heard whether Smuts was able to give a satisfactory answer.

Botha's insistence on being up with the troops meant that he had to march almost as hard as they did, and Moore Ritchie of the bodyguard tells in his recollections how hard that was. He says he sometimes found that fatigue made him confused about the date when he made entries in his diary.

'You didn't know anything about the date or the day of the week. Existence was just a dateless alternation of light and darkness, of saddle up and off-saddle, of cossack post, of thinking about water – and of yearning with every fibre of one's being for the ineffable boon of a long sleep.'

While he was at Potmine Botha received intelligence that Kubas had been occupied by an advanced detachment of Mentz's force. Over on the Otavi line, Skinner reported that the Germans had evacuated Stingbank. Later Mentz reported signs that the enemy was withdrawing north by road and rail from Karibib.

Smuts left on May 4 to return to the south and on the same day Wylie reported that his infantry had entered Kubas.

Botha now ordered a direct advance on Karibib. A small German force in the town exchanged shots with the approaching Bloemhof commando before retreating. Botha himself rode into the town on May 6 to receive the formal surrender from the mayor and a deputation of leading citizens.

The Union forces had failed to intercept Franke's main force. Governor Seitz had left Windhuk by train and gone north through Karibib on May 1, only three days before Myburgh reached Wilhelmstal and cut the railway.

Once again the Germans had been taken by surprise by the speed of the South African advance, but once again they had slipped through the gap at the last minute. It was a familiar story throughout the campaign, until the final encirclement.

Franke is said to have been astonished at the wide scope of Botha's movements, at the length of the marches that were undertaken and completed, at the ability of the South Africans to move such large numbers of men over these distances and at the speed with which it was accomplished.

Nevertheless he and his commanders consistently exercised great skill in escaping from the pincer movements that Botha invariably employed.

Once Karibib fell the surrender of Windhuk was a formality. But although they had been driven from their capital and herded into the remaining third of the territory, the Germans still had intact most of the force with which they had begun the campaign.

However, while Botha had not yet defeated his enemy, he had radically changed the situation in his favour. In 16 days, with negligible losses to his force, he had moved from his narrow holding on the coast to stretch his command across the breadth of the territory and cut the railway spine on which the Germans had depended for their mobility.

He had driven Governor Seitz and his administration into exile in his own country.

Franke had been deprived of almost all opportunity for initiative. His options were now so limited that it was only a matter of time before he was driven into the last corner.

References

1. Collyer, p. 86.
2. *Ibid,* p. 86.
3. Ungleich, p. 146.
4. Whittall, p. 55.
5. Morris, p. 51.
6. Ungleich, p. 154.
7. Collyer, p. 103.

26

Extended Lines

Now hunger came to haunt the conquerors.

In sweeping across half the territory the commandos had left their supply lines far behind and it would be weeks before the gap was effectively closed.

When the Union troops paraded in Windhuk for Botha formally to receive its surrender they did so with empty stomachs and tattered uniforms. It was the German civilians, silently watching, who were well fed and clothed.

Earlier, when Botha had received the surrender of Karibib, the mayor had told him that the 300 German civilians remaining in the town had supplies for two months.

'They were the only people who for the next few weeks or so would have enough to eat at Karibib,' Collyer said later.

Botha assured the mayor that the civilians would not be deported or interned if they refrained from communicating with the German troops to the north; and they would be allowed to keep their supplies.

The mayoral delegation expressed the opinion that Windhuk would not be defended as there were many women and children there and the same would be true of Okahandja to the north.

'It was clear,' Collyer wrote, 'that the enemy's retirement was complete and that he had transferred the care of his families to his opponent.'

While Botha and his staff were conferring with the mayoral delegation in Karibib a hungry Union soldier, who had had nothing but small quantities of meat to eat for some time, found a bag of meal in what seemed to be an empty house and commandeered it. The owner of the house had not abandoned it, however, but was with the rest of the population watching the surrender. When he learned of his loss he promptly lodged a complaint with the Union troops.

On learning of the incident Botha immediately summoned his

Botha's motor convoy on the road from Karabib to Windhuk to accept the surrender of the capital. Despite their narrow tyres, motor vehicles successfully negotiated deep sand and rough terrain in South West and their success helped to speed the end of the horse in warfare. (Cape Archives – AG)

commandants and made them personally responsible for keeping their own men out of the town.

Collyer writes that 'the next morning the commandants – all physically powerful men – cleared the town by the aid of their strong right arms and put an end for good to any looting, if the very natural reaction of the hungry soldier deserves such a description.'

According to Collyer, that bag of meal was 'the only article of food taken from the civilian population without their own consent and without paying a very handsome price'.

In fact, some accounts say that the Germans took advantage of the situation to charge extortionate prices for the food that they sold to their conquerors.

There was at least one occasion when the conquering troops took more than food from the Germans, but it was not for themselves; there was an element of twisted charity in it. The incident was described by Lieutenant F McE Mitchell of the 1st Transvaal Scottish in a letter to his wife, which is now among the regimental records.

'When our mounted men took possession of one of the small towns on the way to Windhuk,' he wrote, 'they found a notice on the door of one of the empty houses: "We have only been married four months. Please don't damage or take away our things".

'Well, [members of] one of our mounted regiments went inside and found the house was very poorly furnished. So they went round the town and got all the finest furniture they could lay their hands on and furnished the newly-married couple's house in style at the expense of their neighbours and left a note presenting them with the furniture as a wedding present, wishing them luck, etc., and then put a notice outside on the door: "By order of the officer commanding such-and-such a regiment: no one allowed in this house".'

The Union supply lines now stretched 150 miles from Swakopmund by way of the Swakop River and then along the route followed by the commandos in their advance. There was still a desperate shortage of mule waggons, and the mule teams were by now worn out from hauling heavy loads through deep sand and over rocky terrain.

'At this time,' Collyer says, 'supplies with the troops, except for cattle and some grazing, were totally exhausted.'

The rebuilding of the narrow-gauge Khan railway had reached Jakkalswater, but between there and Karibib was 60 miles of rugged, waterless country. Clearly the railway would be unable to cope with the enormous demands made by Botha's forces. It was decided to concentrate on rebuilding the line running through Usakos to Karibib.

Instead of continuing with the rebuilding of this line to the 3 ft 6 in

A few miles out of Windhuk the mayor, wearing white ducks and a matching homburg, meets Botha to arrange the formal surrender of the town. (Cape Archives – AG)

A view of Windhuk, with the railway station in the foreground, and, on the hill behind it, the Tintenpalast (Ink Palace), seat of the government. In the foreground are huts built by indigenous people. (Cory Library, Meara Collection)

width, however, it was decided to end the broader gauge at Ebony and from there relay the old German narrow-gauge track to Karibib, where it would link up with the German broad-gauge line from Windhuk to the north.

This course was chosen even though it meant that supplies would have to be offloaded and reloaded at Ebony and again at Karibib, adding to the time taken to get them to the troops at the front.

'The ten days, from May 5 to May 14, during which small, stray quantities of supplies were sent up by both routes under extraordinary difficulties were a prolonged nightmare for General Botha and his staff and a most trying time for the troops,' Collyer said.

The stiff-lipped Collyer's reference to 'a trying time' was probably a characteristic understatement, and it seems that the hunger continued for much longer than two weeks.

Whittall describes a visit to Karibib several weeks after its surrender, having driven up from Usakos in an armoured car.

'To say that a state of virtual famine existed does not exceed the truth,' he wrote. 'Everyone was on the shortest of short rations. Even the hospitals were living from hand to mouth. The nursing sisters had been living for days on ration biscuit and a little sugarless tea and with hardly any prospect of better conditions in the immediate future.'

Before leaving Karibib to accept the surrender of Windhuk, Botha had another meeting with Smuts, who had come up from Aus, to

257

discuss the next moves in the campaign.

According to Collyer, the energetic Smuts travelled so fast that he outstripped his entire staff, 'of which representatives, if report were to be believed, were to be found shed at intervals along the sand and sea routes as far back as Aus'.

He left Swakopmund with Colonel Hoy but left him behind when he found that the colonel could not keep up. After he left Usakos his transport was held up and he abandoned it and set out on foot. He was found by a patrol calmly walking along the road some miles from Karibib.

One of the troopers in the patrol gave up his horse to the general, and he completed the journey on horseback.

Botha set off from Karibib on May 8 on the 120-mile journey to Windhuk to accept the surrender of the capital. A fleet of 17 cars was assembled to transport the commander-in-chief, some of his bodyguard and a machine-gun section.

The party camped at night by the roadside. Botha, who seldom bothered with a tent when on the march, slept as usual on the ground, under the stars. Crossing sandy river beds the vehicles frequently became stuck. When that happened to his car the general climbed down and helped to push, leaving his staff no choice but to follow suit. The escorting troops were thus treated to the sight of staff colonels and majors sweating and slipping in the sand as they put their shoulders to the vehicle.

At Okahandja the party was joined by General Myburgh and the advance guard of his force. After a second night spent by the roadside, Botha's party early next morning saw rising out of the bush the wireless masts of Windhuk, whose capture had been the primary purpose of the campaign – at least as far as the British Government was concerned.

Outside the town they were met by the mayor, dressed 'in an immaculate white suit and driving a smart phaeton', O'Shaughnessy reported. The little mayor was overshadowed by Botha's 'vast khaki bulk'.

The mayor was sent back to the town so that he could formally hand it over. After giving him a start, the South African column entered the capital in 'a long and imposing cavalcade made up of Botha's 17 vehicles and Myburgh's commandos and artillery'.

With a crowd of German civilians watching, Botha formally accepted the surrender of the town. But it was to his assembled troops that he spoke about this 'great and memorable moment' and thanked them for their 'splendid achievement in overcoming the hardships of the desert.

'When the record of the campaign comes to be written, your march will stand out as one of the most remarkable events in history,' he told them with a hyperbole perhaps excusable in the circumstances.

The Union Jack was hoisted above the *Rathaus* and a proclamation was read declaring martial law over the territory south of the 22nd parallel.

Then business went back to normal in the town, with women chatting in the streets and meeting in the cafés for coffee. The civilians had been primed as to what to expect by a local newspaper. In contrast to the earlier scathing reference to 'Botha's rabble', the *Sudwest* assured its readers that wherever the South Africans, these 'troops of a Teutonic nation', had occupied towns in South West they had conducted themselves 'in such a way as becomes civilised soldiers'. They had behaved 'properly and courteously'. Not only had they paid cash for everything that they needed but 'they did not object in the least to the prices asked by the farmers'.

A few days before the entry of the South Africans the newspaper had gloomily reported: 'The last German troops have just left Windhuk. We who remain behind watched them disappear down the dusty road with heavy hearts and a distinct feeling of envy. For it is very hard for us to remain behind and live under the hostile flag, even though we know that [the enemy's] triumph will be short-lived and that our Kaiser will exact a double penalty.'

The formal surrender of Windhuk at the *Rathaus*, with vehicles of Botha's motor convoy in the foreground, beyond them burghers of Myburgh's force and at the steps of the town hall a crowd of German civilians who came to see their mayor hand over the town to Botha. The Union Jack has been hoisted on the flagpole on top of the building. (Namibia Archives)

South African mounted troops ride down Kaiserstrasse, the main street of Windhuk, after the occupation of the capital. (War Museum)

Some of the South Africans went immediately to inspect the great wireless station, said to be the second most powerful in the world after that at Norddeich in Germany. With its 360-foot masts, each resting on a huge glass insulator, and mile-long aerials, the station covered many acres. O'Shaughnessy reported that the instruments in the operating room had been removed, but otherwise the Germans had left the station intact, apparently in the conviction that they would regain possession after the Allies had been defeated in Europe.

Before returning to Karibib, Botha installed Colonel Mentz as military governor in Windhuk. Mentz had been sent with his force in a probe to the east in the hope of intercepting von Kleist as he retreated northward from Gibeon. The South Africans believed that von Kleist was still marching in a wide detour round Windhuk, but German accounts say that his force went by train through the capital to Okahandja before striking overland again.

The South African version is supported by Denys Reitz, who was sent from Aus by Smuts to find out what was happening in the north. From Gibeon he and two companions drove by car to Mariental, where they were told by scouts from McKenzie's force that von Kleist was slowly falling back, blowing up the railway as he went.

At Rehoboth Reitz's party concluded 'from the trampled spoor round the station and from the general appearance of things' that the Germans had now abandoned the railway line and were continuing their withdrawal by road.

Seated in the open beside the railway line at Giftkuppe, Botha, wearing a peaked cap, listens impassively while Governor Seitz proposes terms for an end to the fighting. (Namibia Archives)

'And on looking north-east, along the way they had gone, we could see a tall pillar of dust where their column was trekking 15 or 20 miles away.'

Von Kleist made such good time that Mentz's probe eastwards from Windhuk was too late to intercept him.

Botha's journey back to Karibib from Windhuk was nearly his last; and the man who nearly made it so was one of his own soldiers.

The mounted trooper suddenly appeared out of the bush in front of Botha's open car, swaying drunkenly in his saddle, and levelled his rifle at the general. The driver of Botha's car, Lieutenant Snow, swerved to one side. The general's ADC, Captain Esselen, leaped from the car and, springing up at the trooper, dragged him from his saddle and brought him to the ground.

The soldier, now in a state of alarm and confusion, staggered to his feet, saluted and explained, in a voice that O'Shaughnessy says had a suspicion of Irish brogue, that he had mistaken Botha for Governor Seitz.

He scrambled back on his horse and zig-zagged off into the bush.[1] Botha let him go; he had more important things on his mind.

Soon afterwards Botha was met by a despatch-rider carrying a message from Governor Seitz, proposing that an armistice be arranged to allow a meeting to 'discuss terms'.

The proposal had been decided at a meeting between Dr Seitz and Colonel Franke and senior members of their staffs. The Governor had argued that the German cause was lost in South West Africa and that it would only be a matter of time before the South Africans secured a total victory. Botha might, however, be amenable to an armistice, as he had accomplished the objectives desired by the British government and his army was exhausted and an increasing drain on South Africa's resources.[2]

Botha agreed to an armistice, and it was set to begin at noon on May 20. It was agreed to hold talks the next day at Giftkuppe, a kopje on the eastern side of the railway about midway between Karibib and Omaruru.

The Germans arrived by train, the South Africans by car. The setting was simple: a tent pitched in the veld beside the railway track with a table and chairs at the flap. It was the first opportunity that the German and the South African leaders had had to size each other up at first hand. Almost all the talking was done by Dr Seitz, whom Collyer describes as a small man but vehement and even aggressive in his bearing. 'He made up for his lack of inches by occasionally impressive utterances, and once or twice threatened his auditors with the displeasure of "sixty million Germans".'

Colonel Franke, 'a soldierly looking man', hardly spoke. Neither did Botha, who gravely listened without interruption to the Governor's proposals.

Before they got down to the main business, Seitz protested that the South Africans were arming the natives, which Botha denied; and he in turn complained that the Germans were still violating the Hague Convention by poisoning water supplies.

Seitz then proposed that the South Africans should retain control of the territory south of the 22nd parallel and the small piece between the parallel and the Windhuk-Karibib railway. A neutral zone would be demarcated between the two forces to prevent any further clashes.

O'Shaughnessy says that at one point Botha indicated that he did not understand what the government meant by a neutral zone and later said: 'I think I understand what you mean by a neutral zone; that was Belgium's position before Germany invaded her.'

The correspondent says officers present at the conference reported that Seitz reacted 'with cool anger'.

Botha then withdrew from the meeting for a private discussion with Collyer, and on his return he told the Governor that he would consider only a total surrender by the German forces. This Seitz rejected.

The talks broke up with an agreement that the ceasefire should end at noon the following day.

Seitz could see no point in a total surrender at that stage. After eight months of fighting the German forces were still largely intact and could possibly sustain themselves indefinitely in the relatively well-watered northern territory. They could obtain food from the Ovambo and operate blockade-running ships with the help of the wireless station at Fort Sessfontein.

The Germans still controlled nearly 200 miles of railway. If their forces were broken up they could switch to guerrilla warfare. They still held more than 600 South African prisoners. On the European front the German forces held the initiative and had launched the offensive at Ypres.

And Franke's forces, by continuing to tie down 50 000 South Africans in South West, were preventing them from being sent into action against the Germans in East Africa or Europe.

All these points were seen by Seitz, and probably Franke too, as sound reasons for rejecting Botha's terms of total surrender.

Botha's reasons for rejecting the compromise proposed by Seitz can be gleaned from Collyer's account. He says that the South Africans formed the impression at Giftkuppe that the Germans were uneasy and that Seitz's attitude 'gave a clear impression of bluff.'

It might also be assumed, although Collyer has not said so, that the South Africans felt that with a little more effort they could force the Germans into total surrender. Having come so far, and having set up an elaborate supply system, it made no sense to turn back, even though they had done what the British expected of them.

They had also to bear in mind that acceptance of Seitz's terms would probably have bitterly disappointed the men in Botha's army, who would have resented seeing victory gratuitously thrown away after they had gone through so much to win it and when it was clearly within their grasp. That attitude might even have been reflected in popular sentiment at home, with political consequences that Botha and Smuts would have wanted to avoid.

Neither Collyer nor anyone else has suggested that another consideration that might have influenced the South Africans was the possibility of gaining conrol over South West Africa and even incorporating it if Germany were defeated in Europe. The idea might not have figured large in Botha's thinking but it is not unreasonable to suspect that it was an ambition cherished by Smuts, since it is exactly what he tried to accomplish after the war.

An intriguing aspect of the Giftkuppe meeting is that Botha appears not to have consulted his government before replying to the German proposals, as he did later on at the final surrender talks. He clearly did not take the German proposal at Giftkuppe seriously enough for that.

Once they had decided to force an unconditional surrender, the South Africans felt they must move fast, for they were convinced that the Germans were planning a 'long withdrawal to the north'. It was thought possible that the regular soldiers in the German forces might even be contemplating an attempt to make their way across the continent to German East Africa to join Colonel von Lettow Vorbeck's forces.[3]

That theory was later said by its supporters to have been given credence by the finding of six large boats propped up beside the railway track at Omaruru. These were the surf-boats that had been used at Swakopmund to carry cargo ashore from ships anchored in the roadstead. They had been brought to Omaruru by rail, and the plan apparently was to take them from there by waggon to the Okavango River and use them to carry the remnants of the German forces across the river, or even for some distance down the river, in an attempt to reach German East Africa.

It was a desperate and even romantic plan but it would have been enormously difficult to accomplish. It would have meant crossing hundreds of miles of British territory, through Northern Rhodesia and perhaps Nyasaland, or through equally hostile territory in the Belgian Congo. Even though there were no strong forces in those territories the South Africans could easily have sent troops, with British approval, by rail through the Rhodesias to intercept the fleeing Germans.

Whatever the purpose was in carrying the boats to Omaruru, 150 miles from the sea, it was abandoned there and so were the boats, and their presence beside the railway remains an intriguing mystery.

The purpose of the exercise must at some time have been recorded in official documents but these have not been found; perhaps they were lost with the many other records of the German colonisation of South West Africa that were destroyed by Allied bombing of Germany in the Second World War.

At any rate, the South Africans were convinced of the need to make their next move speedily. They were still hampered, however, by the transport bottleneck, and Botha, after his last experience, now refused to budge without adequate transport.

He had already planned his next move, though. He would advance along the railway with the 6th Mounted Brigade under Lukin and the 1st Infantry Brigade under Beves.

He would send Brits with the 1st Mounted Brigade in a wide circle to the west to cut south of the Etosha Pan and seize Namutoni and release the South Africa prisoners who were known (from an intercepted wireless message) to be held there.

On the other flank Myburgh would swing out to the east to capture Grootfontein, with the 2nd Mounted Brigade under Alberts and the right wing of the 3rd Mounted Brigade under Jordaan.

Between Myburgh and the centre would be Manie Botha, now a Brigadier-General, with the 5th Mounted Brigade. He would move parallel with and east of the railway and maintain contact with the forces on either side of him.

Once Brits and Myburgh had captured Namutoni and Grootfontein respectively, they would swing in towards each other to close the pincers on the Germans.

It was a classic Botha plan, making full use of the mobility of the burghers on either side of a firm core of infantry.

Some have compared Botha's favourite tactic with the bull's head tactic used by Shaka, the Zulu king. Shaka sent his impis forward in a mass (the bull's head) and then when close to the enemy he quickly sent out from the central mass flanking forces (the horns) which would move round behind the enemy and join up to surround and trap him. It is not certain, however, that Botha was copying Shaka.

While Botha was waiting for his supply system to become ready his force received a new arm. The first aircraft to join the Union forces arrived at Karibib.

Botha and his troops were seeing the birth of the South African Air Force, which many years later was to serve with distinction in the Second World War and in Korea.

References

1. O'Shaughnessy, p. 220.
2. Ungleich, p. 159.
3. Collyer, p. 121.

CHAPTER
27

The Wings of War

The flying machines came to Karibib in May, diving out of a cloudless sky and swooping in over the thorn trees with their engines racketing loudly and emitting castor oil smoke.

The first came in on the 26th, bumping violently over the uneven landing strip. The young pilot pushed up his goggles and climbed down from the cockpit, pulling off his gloves and loosening the strap of his flying helmet, a modern-day knight alighting from his steed, and no doubt relishing the glamour of his situation and the drama of his arrival.

He had not heard the earthbound soldiers cheering as he swooped, birdlike, over their camp, but he could see them waving and he knew they would be cheering – all except, perhaps, those who were trying to calm the horses that had been set snorting and plunging by the sudden appearance of an unfamiliar and noisy monster.

For months the Union soldiers had watched the German aeroplanes flying overhead and occasionally run for cover when bombs came down. And even though the German visits had relieved the monotony of camp life the troops had grown tired of the one-sidedness of it. Now their own side had machines in the air and the pride of it was something to cheer about. Now they would show those Huns!

The aeroplane was still so new a thing then that few of the South African soldiers had ever seen a flying machine except those sent over their lines by the Germans and some had not even seen those.

For many of the troops it was the defiance of gravity that was impressive rather than the look of the machine with which it was accomplished. To some it looked much like a flying bathtub, an article of toilet furniture suspended between two flimsy wings amid a cat's-cradle of struts and wires, with a propeller whirring behind it. An awkward tail hung out behind that and four large wheels fixed below as a reminder of the inevitable brevity of the machine's victory over gravity.

The first South African planes to land at Karibib, French-made Henri Farmans, stand on the airfield that has been abandoned by the retreating Germans. (Cape Archives – AG)

This fragile-looking contraption, with the tail assembly linked to the stubby fuselage by bare metal tubes, was in the image of the Wright Brothers rather than of the Red Baron or Biggles.

Yet it was one of the most modern machines of its kind, this French-built Henri Farman, the first all-steel aircraft ever made, and it was to prove of great value in the campaign in German South West. These 'ricketty engines of war', as one cavalry officer described them, were to change the nature of the campaign, certainly the tactical thinking of the enemy.

For the first time in this war waged over vast distances the Union forces now had the means to observe the enemy from the air, to spy on his movements and his dispositions far ahead of the van and carry the news swiftly back to headquarters.

One of the pioneer aviators, Lieutenant (later Major-General) Ken van der Spuy, recalls in his memoirs that after he had reported to General Botha on a long reconnaissance, the general said: 'You are a good flyer, Ken, but an even better *verkyker*. For weeks I haven't known for sure where so-and-so is or where he is making for. I have therefore not been able to move my troops and plan accordingly. Now I know, and I feel much better.

'This morning, until you came back, I was able to see only so far,' he said, pointing. 'Now I can see for hundreds of miles. Wonderful!'[1]

As with the German aviators, it was reconnaissance and observation rather than bombing or strafing or other direct hostility that made the

267

aircraft useful in South West. In May 1915, when the first South African aircraft went into active service, the technology for mounting a machine-gun on a plane did not exist. There were no aerial dogfights. Even on the Western Front in Europe, if an airman wanted to shoot at an enemy aeroplane he used a revolver, a rifle or a sawn-off shotgun firing slugs.

It was only later, when he was back in action over France, that Van der Spuy conceived the idea of having a Lewis machine-gun hung by straps from the upper wing of his biplane to allow his observer to fire at enemy planes, thereby becoming one of the pioneers, if not the originator, of aerial combat.[2]

Even if they had had the means, however, the South Africans would not have been able to have dogfights with the Germans because by the time the Henri Farmans landed at Karibib the German airmen had virtually been grounded by crashes. They had simply run out of aircraft and, as the South Africans pushed them northward, out of landing strips.

The aerial observation carried out by the Germans at Trekkoppies had been their last fling. There is no record of German aerial activity after von Scheele crashed on May 27, which was three weeks after Van der Spuy made the first test flight of a Henri Farman over Walvis Bay.

So there were no Germans in the skies on the arrival of the South African Aviation Corps, (also known at the time by the Dutch equivalent, Zuid-Afrikaanse Vliegenierskorps).

Ironically, it was a report by the 'traitorous' General Beyers that led to the formation of the Corps. As Commandant-General of the Defence Force of South Africa Beyers had been sent by Defence Minister Smuts to Europe and England in 1912 to attend army manoeuvres and report on the use of aircraft in military operations. His observations on the ground and from the air (he became the first South African general to fly when he made a flight in Germany) convinced Beyers that 'aircraft are going to play a very important part in warfare in the future', especially in reconnaissance.[3]

As a result of his recommendation that a military flying school should be established, the first ten South African military pilots began their training at the private Compton Paterson flying school at Kimberley in 1913. Six of them were commissioned in the newly formed SAAC in the Active Citizen Force in April 1914 and sent to England for further training. All six were allowed to join the Royal Flying Corps at the outbreak of war, and two of them, Van der Spuy and Gordon Creed, served in France, going into war with only about 20 hours flying time in each of their logbooks.

In German South West Africa, however, the need for an air arm was becoming increasingly urgent with Fritz (whichever one he happened to be) making a nuisance of himself by bombing raids and by disclosing Botha's movements to his enemy.

Smuts was keenly aware of how valuable aerial reconnaissance would be in the wide reaches of South West. As Minister of Defence he applied his famous energy and drive to getting South African planes in the air over South West, against formidable obstacles.

The leader of the Kimberley six, Captain Gerard Wallace, was joined in England by four others: Creed and Van der Spuy, who were recalled from France, and Edwin Emmett and Basil Turner.

Turner and Emmett then returned to South Africa to set about recruiting ground crew, who would go straight to Walvis Bay to await the arrival of the planes and pilots. Wallace, Creed and Van der Spuy set about acquiring the aircraft and spare parts.

The need for aircraft in the South West campaign had been seen even outside military circles as early as October 1914. Sir Abe Bailey, who closely associated himself with the South African war effort, tried, together with Hayes Hammond and Sir Leander Starr Jameson, to acquire American aircraft and pilots for the South African force in South West Africa. The Wright double-deckers which they thought of acquiring were found on testing in Britain to be unsuitable.

British aircraft were also considered unsuitable for the conditions in South West, and the French Henri Farmans, powered by 150 hp Canton-Unne engines, were chosen. Getting them was another matter, however. All the Allied services wanted aircraft, and the needs of the force in South West had to compete with other priorities. The South Africans had to beg, borrow or steal whatever they could wherever they could.

It was March before six of the 12 Henri Farmans ordered arrived in Walvis Bay. They had travelled as deck cargo and become badly corroded by sea water, and they had to be restored before they could take to the air, by which time it was early May.

In addition to the French planes, the SAAC had obtained two BE 2C planes and three pilots from the Royal Naval Air Service, but the wooden frames of the British aircraft twisted in the fierce climate of South West and were never used operationally. Both crashed in early flights and were damaged.

The severity of the conditions is illustrated by a report submitted by one of the British pilots, Lieutenant John Cripps, after he had made a forced landing in his BE 2C near Swakopmund after the engine had cut out. As he landed in soft sand the aircraft came to a sudden stop and the undercarriage went up through the wings. The damaged machine was dismantled and the engine and fuselage were carried to Nonidas station and tied to the railway. The two right wings were also taken to the railway line and anchored down with rails in case the wind that is

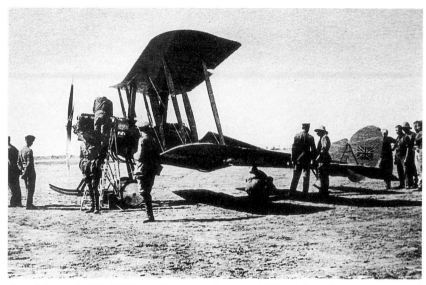

One of the two British BE2C aeroplanes brought to South West Africa. They were never used operationally as the fierce climate warped the wood from which they were made. (SADF Archives)

notorious in the area began blowing. The other two wings were left where the plane had landed.

During the night the wind did indeed get up, and Cripps reported that 'when I got out of my tent I found the two planes (the term used for wings at that time) which had been left at the station had been blown bodily along for about 20 yards. I got some rails and endeavoured to anchor the [wings]. I left them with the rails on them. As soon as my back was turned, a sudden gust took the wings bodily into the air, overturning the rails.

'The wings landed about a mile away near the railway, we found next morning. In the morning these wings were wired to the railway line. About two hours afterwards, another gust took them bodily away again.

'I could not find the wings that I had left where I had landed during the night of the storm but found them quite close to the railway line near the others. All the parts were collected and brought to Walvis.'

Although the British planes were never flown in South West, their pilots appear to have been quickly converted to the Henri Farmans, for, according to O'Shaughnessy, the first two aircraft to fly from Walvis Bay to Karibib were piloted by Lieutenant Creed and by Sub-Flight-Lieutenant Hinshlewood of the RNAS. They covered the 140 miles in an hour and a half.[4]

Karibib was not the first place at which the SAAC planes landed

The sturdy, all-steel Henri Farmans were unaffected by the South West climate and performed well until the end of the campaign. As the engine and propellor were mounted behind the pilot, he had excellent visibility to the front. (Cape Archives – AG)

after taking off from Swakopmund. Hunter of the ILH records in his diary that while his unit was at Karub, about halfway between Swakopmund and Karibib, an aircraft landed there.

'This was a great day as our first aeroplane arrived from Swakopmund,' he wrote on May 9. 'Lovely machine carrying a pilot and an observer.' And on May 25 he noted: 'We heard an aeroplane which had just arrived at camp Karub. Saw on return a fine large Henri Farman biplane. A young South African is the aviator, Van der Spuy.'

Karibib was the first real operational base of the SAAC. There the South African aircraft were able to make use of the airstrip formerly used by the Germans but elsewhere they had to improvise landing strips, often at short notice, as the Union forces advanced. On a few occasions Major Wallace, the officer commanding the SAAC, had to abandon an airfield he had just established and rush the equipment by car to a new site to keep up with the advance.

The responsibility for providing and maintaining airstrips and hangars was given to the man who may have been the pioneer of aviation in South Africa: John Weston. While living in Brandfort, Weston, a civil engineer, designed and built his own aircraft in 1907 but, realising that it was under-powered, he did not try to fly it. He dismantled it and took it to France to have a 50 hp Gnome engine fitted and flew it there in 1910. He brought it back to South Africa with its new engine and made a number of flights in it in 1911.[5]

If Beyers was the first South African general to fly in an aeroplane, Botha may have been the second. While Botha was still at Karibib he paid a visit to the airfield with Colonel Collyer and was invited by Van der Spuy to go for a flight. Collyer, thinking of the commander-in-chief's safety, gave the airman 'a dirty look' but Botha only asked if it was safe. On being assured that it was, he accepted the offer and, with the aid of a ladder, his great bulk was installed in the observer's seat.

'We had scarcely lifted beyond the boundary of the aerodrome when the engine faltered and dropped its revs considerably', Van der Spuy recalled. 'We were then only a few feet above the tall scrub and I had the greatest difficulty in keeping the machine aloft, just skimming the bush and edging warily round trees.

'I was unable to turn towards the aerodrome and had to make a wide and cautious circle before I had the machine facing towards home and safety. I reached the edge of the aerodrome and landed downwind, only just managing to pull up on the extreme opposite edge, bounded by a deep ditch.

'General Botha was helped out, thanked me for the flight and remarked that he would have liked to have gone higher but added that he had guessed that I was meeting with some trouble and did not wish to disturb me in the air by talking.'

Botha remarked with a twinkle in his eye that perhaps flying was not as safe as Van der Spuy had said it was. Later Collyer reprimanded the airman for persuading the general to make the flight.

On at least one occasion Van der Spuy did crash on landing. In his book he blames the crash at Kalkfeld, between Omaruru and Otjiwarongo, on the runway having been made too short. He says he had no alternative but to land as he did not have enough petrol to return to where he had taken off. He ran off the end of the runway into the bush, damaging the Henri Farman and injuring his leg. But Hunter noted in his diary on June 26 that the crash was caused by Van der Spuy landing with, instead of against, the wind because the wrong wind direction had been signalled from the ground.

'Unable to stop, the aircraft crashed into a tree, the carriage part being completely wrecked, also the tail and a few stays smashed. The observer fell right over the head of the pilot and was not hurt. The pilot, however (Van der Spuy, I believe), suffered badly from shock and had to be removed on a stretcher.'

Two other aircraft that flew with Van der Spuy from Omaruru 'landed beautifully,' Hunter says.

Accidents with the aircraft did nothing to shake Botha's faith in the value of aerial reconnaissance, and he made full use of it to the end of the campaign. Van der Spuy says that both Botha and Collyer told him they

Before the campaign ended the aerial bomb had come to South West. This photograph shows an Henri Farman about to take off on a mission with six bombs slung in a rack under the fuselage. (*Star* Archives)

believed the introduction of aircraft had shortened the campaign considerably.

When the SAAC was formed the value of aerial bombing was disputed in military circles and neither bombs nor devices for dropping them existed. In October 1914, while the South African High Commissioner in London was still negotiating for the acquisition of aircraft for the infant SAAC, he was told by the War Office that the dropping of bombs from aircraft had not yet been established as a practical proposition.[6]

But before the campaign ended the South African aircraft had begun dropping bombs on enemy targets. There is a record of Wallace on June 10 asking the Defence Department for a hundred hand grenades, a hundred 16-pound bombs and twelve 200-pound bombs. That bombs were dropped is confirmed by the accounts of South African prisoners of war who were at Tsumeb when the Germans there were bombed by a South African aircraft.

★ ★ ★ ★ ★

It was at Arandis, on the railway line from Swakopmund to Karibib, that a footsore young bugler in the Rhodesia Regiment got his first sight of a German aircraft. Not long afterwards, when his feet had become much sorer, he got his first sight of a South African aircraft.

The two experiences were to change the life of Arthur Harris.

The Rhodesians marched on foot all the way from Swakopmund to Tsumeb, with frequent forays out to one side or the other. They suffered from hunger, heat, dust and thirst. They fought at Trekkoppies and in other engagements.

Along this painful road young Harris took a firm decision never to serve in the infantry again.

'Never again was I going to walk anywhere,' he said later. 'I was going to sit on something.'

It was the sight of the aircraft that convinced the bugler of the folly of walking and his conviction became rocklike when someone remarked (incorrectly, of course) as the South African airman flew overhead: 'He'll be going back to Cape Town for breakfast.'

By then Harris was no longer a bugler, at least not a practising one. He had solemnised his psychological severance from the infantry by burying his bugle at the bottom of a trench outside Swakopmund.

At the end of the campaign in South West Harris returned to his native England and tried to join the artillery, knowing that gunners never walked but rode on horseback or on the limbers. But the artillery was full and could not take him in.

Then he remembered the aircraft that he had enviously watched in South West, and remembered an advertisement that he had seen in an English paper about service in the Royal Flying Corps. So he applied to join the RFC and, with some help from family connections, was accepted.

The former bugler went on to become Marshall of the Air Force, Sir Arthur Harris, well known in the Second World War as 'Bomber Harris'.

Through business interests, Harris later made occasional visits to South Africa. A newspaper columnist in Cape Town, Maxwell Leigh, brought Harris together with two other local residents, Ken van der Spuy and Willie Truck.

Harris, who developed the practice of saturation bombing in the Second World War, must have been intrigued by Truck's recollections of how the German pilots in South West Africa first attacked their targets by tossing hand grenades or shells over the side of the cockpit.

References

1. Van der Spuy, K R, *Chasing the Wind*, p. 82.
2. Silberbauer, D, *Cross and Cockade*, p. 174.
3. *Ibid*, p. 174.
4. O'Shaughnessy, p. 249.
5. Silberbauer, p. 175.
6. *Militaria*, January 2 1970.

CHAPTER
28

Medicine at a Gallop

There was not a tooth in the mouth of the elderly burgher who had come to Major Burton for medical attention and that intrigued the doctor. He knew that the army insisted on its recruits having at least a full set of false teeth.

After all, if an army marched on its stomach, how could it march if its men did not have teeth for filling the stomachs?

When he had finished attending to the burgher's complaint, Burton asked him how he had managed to get accepted into the commando when he had no teeth, and certainly was not wearing false teeth as he sat before the doctor.

'Well, yes, I was turned down by all the army doctors who examined me,' the burgher admitted, for he knew that the commando was too deep into South West for him to be sent back. 'They all said I had to have teeth. But I wanted very much to go with the commando so I went to see my family doctor, old Dr van Niekerk. He knew I was fit and strong without teeth and perhaps he would pass me fit for military service.

'I explained my problem to him and he said, "But of course I'll pass you fit for service, even without false teeth. After all, you're going to South West Africa to shoot Germans, not to eat them".'

This burgher was probably one of very few men who got into the Union forces with such a disability. So great was the demand to sign on that the examining doctors could afford to be selective. Those who were not fit enough were in any case soon weeded out by the harsh conditions under which the campaign was conducted.

Among those who stayed on, the losses through action and illness were relatively light. As is common in wars, more men died of sickness in the South West campaign than were killed or fatally wounded in action.

Official figures show that only 88 were killed in action in a campaign in which it made military sense for the Germans to avoid

The Germans used camels to carry stretcher cases in this way from the battlefield. The stretcher is suspended between the front and back camels and the patient is lying on it with his torso and head shielded from the sun by a canvas screen. The front camel is led by a medical orderly riding another camel alongside it. (Namibia Archives)

battle or fight delaying actions rather than risk heavy casualties against greatly superior forces. A further 25 died of wounds. However, deaths from disease and accidents totalled 153.[1]

The official history says that 'as the country was very healthy and the casualties small, no great demands were made on the medical service. The provision to meet heavy casualties at any time was there, however, and the mounted brigade field ambulances kept up and sustained the same marching records as the brigade to which they were attached.'

Burton with his 'half-crowns on his backside' attests to that. But he also records that the field hospitals and even ambulances were often left behind by the commandos when they made their lightning advances.

Burton – and, no doubt, other doctors with the mounted brigades – kept up with the burghers by travelling light. He packed essential medicines into panniers on pack-horses which soon became accustomed to keeping pace with the commando. The medical demands of the burghers were in any case not heavy.

Walker, who tended to take a lofty view of the commandos, noted that 'the burghers certainly like to have doctors when they go into action, but they expect nothing elaborate. Just a bandage when hit, a

Beside a mule-drawn ambulance waggon a South African soldier has his arm attended to by a doctor. (War Museum)

The hospital ship *Ebani* off Cape Town. With its operating theatres, wards and nursing staff the vessel was able to handle some of the most serious wound cases. (SADF Archives)

A South African soldier holds his hat to shade his head as he is carried on a stretcher to a ship, probably the *Ebani*, moored at the dockside. The vehicle at right appears to be an ambulance. Oddly, the stretcher bearers seem not to be wearing shoes, only socks. (SADF Archives)

little something out of a flask and the assurance that they cannot possibly recover, satisfies.'

'But that assurance must come from a real doctor and they shout loudly until he comes; a Red Cross orderly suffices not.'

Burton, who had a much closer rapport with and respect for the burghers, knew that for their minor ailments they tended to rely on their own resources. Most burghers had in their saddlebags their own 'huismiddels', small bottles of 'druppels' ranging from 'versterk' and 'kraam' to 'benaudheid' and 'witte dulcis' and even a little asafoetida ('duiwelsdrek' or devil's dung).

To treat sore backs Burton sometimes got a medical orderly to rub the patient's back with the axle grease for the waggon wheels, and he does not record having received any complaints about the efficacy of the treatment.

Walker complains strongly in his book about the inadequacy of the ambulances and other transport available to the medical units. Twelve mules were used to pull an ambulance carrying only two men, and the ambulances were badly sprung; even for fit and healthy men riding in one was an ordeal.

He describes thus the arrival in Swakopmund of wounded men from Nonidas in the charge of a sergeant : 'It was a most exhausted-looking procession that came in. The sergeant and his men and the drivers of the four ambulance waggons were besmirched with a paste of dust and sweat. With every jolt of the wheels somebody groaned. For two days and nights the wounded had been exposed to the heat, cold, wind and dust, with little water and less food. Previous to that they had had 48 hours of trekking under the most trying conditions.'

Base hospitals were established in Swakopmund, Luderitzbucht, Windhuk and Karibib. Patients fit enough to travel were sent to hospitals in South Africa by train or ship. The hospital ship *Ebani* was one of the first vessels to arrive off the coast at the start of the campaign and she served until it ended.

As the Union forces moved north they also made use of captured hospitals for the treatment of both South Africans and Germans. Often the German medical staff remained behind with their patients when the German troops pulled out. Walker was impressed by the competence of the German nurses in the Windhuk hospital and was surprised to find that they were accustomed to performing minor operations.

One nurse kept a close and suspicious watch on the South African anaesthetist during an operation on a German patient, constantly feeling the patient's pulse and examining his eyes. She relapsed into a strictly nursing role when the doctor remarked acidly: 'I suppose you think that, not having succeeded in killing a German in battle, I am trying to do so on the operating table?'

References

1. *Militaria*, January 4 1973, p. 58.

CHAPTER

29

Forced March

As the Union army gathered itself for the final push its forces were stronger than they had ever been in the campaign. But so were the Germans.

Despite having lost two-thirds of the colony, the German losses had been relatively small. Their previously widespread forces were now concentrated on a single front and in rugged country easy to defend. They knew that they were making their last stand and that it would have to be a long and strong one if they were to be saved by a German victory in Europe.

Botha thought that the coming battles might be severe, for he was facing a desperate, well-ensconced enemy who had fewer men but more artillery and machine-guns than he had.

The stage seemed set for fierce fighting in the bush-covered hills of the north.

The Union army had at last overcome its transport difficulties. It now had 527 wagons, enough to enable each force in the army to carry with it supplies for two to three weeks.

'For the first time in the campaign, transport which would allow anything more than two days' supply accompanying the fighting formations was to hand,' Collyer noted.

With at least 27 ships plying between Cape Town and the South West African ports to bring supplies there had been a continued bottleneck between the ports and the battlefront. But the astonishing speed with which the railway line from Swakopmund was rebuilt brought it to Karibib by May 15, only ten days after the Union troops had occupied the town.

The line between Windhuk and Karibib was restored a few days later, and the line between Windhuk and Keetmanshoop, linking to Luderitzbucht, was reopened in the middle of June. On June 25 the new railway being built northwards from the railhead of the South African system at Upington was joined to the South West African system at

280

Commando members ride beside the supply waggons as Botha's forces leave Usakos for the final advance. (Cape Archives)

Kalkfontein. Botha's army could now, in theory, get supplies railed all the way from Cape Town if it so desired.

Despite all this transport, however, water would still be a problem at the front, for the advancing army could not carry with it enough water for its thousands of men, horses and mules. Now that the retreating German troops were leaving their own civilians in the hands of the South Africans they were no longer poisoning the wells and waterholes. But these were nevertheless far apart in the region into which the invading force was about to advance and would probably be bitterly contested.

There was another factor that offset the improved supplies. Botha knew from intercepted wireless messages that Franke planned to retreat towards Namutoni if he were pushed out of his strong position north of Karibib. He might even contemplate a retirement into Angola or a desperate trek to German East Africa.

Botha was determined to stop Franke from escaping and to prevent the German forces from posing any future threat. It is likely that, being acutely aware that Franke held more than five hundred South African prisoners of war, Botha wanted to prevent him from taking them with him in an attempt to flee from South West. There was nothing in whatever moral rules might apply to war to prevent Franke from taking his prisoners with him, and even if he did not intend to use them as hostages their presence with his force would inhibit attacks by the Union forces.

Franke must know from bitter experience how fast the Union forces could move, and he would be prepared for it this time. So Botha knew that to surround and trap the Germans he would have to move even faster than Franke would expect. That would mean moving faster than his supply waggons could travel.

Once again the burgher commandos would be called on to ride hard and far out on the flanks, living mainly on what they could carry. And the infantry would have to make some even more arduous forced marches to prevent the centre from becoming too far detached from the flanks.

Rations to be carried by the troops in the advance were to be restricted to mealie-meal, coffee, sugar, salt, biscuits, soap, tobacco and matches.

A week before the advance began Botha went to Usakos to inspect the two brigades there. The inspection concluded with a march past, headed by the armoured cars.

'I think that everyone had expected this part of the affair to be rather humorous, and that the cars would rattle and bump their way past the saluting base, with much clanging of armour and machinery and in any sort of order,' Whittall recalled. 'But, on the contrary, the cars, with their powerful engines turning slowly, simply stole silently past, four abreast and in perfect alignment, their grim outlines relieved by the flaunting White Ensigns which we flew on gala occasions. They made an impressive sight and, as one of the staff remarked afterwards, "No wonder the Huns don't like the look of them".'

Botha then addressed the troops, speaking as usual, in Dutch, with his military secretary translating into English. With typical British intolerance of other languages, Whittall remarked testily in his account of the campaign: 'Why the general prefers to make all his public utterances in Dutch I don't know, since he has perfect command of English.' What the lieutenant-commander overlooked was that many of Botha's troops had not even an imperfect command of English, even though they were fighting under the Union Jack.

During the advance from the coast along the general line of the railway the armoured car crews had by trial and error found the best way to get their heavy vehicles through the sand. Matting, wooden poles, even iron piping were used under the wheels without success, all either being flung out or smashed up by the wheels, driven by the powerful Rolls Royce engines. The answer was at last found to be lengths of angle iron placed under the wheels, and each car was equipped with a supply.

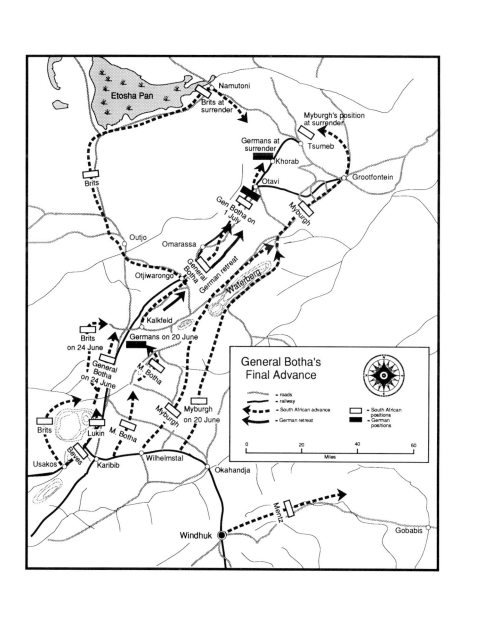

General Botha's
Final Advance

It meant, however, that members of the crew had to retrieve the angle irons as the rear wheels passed over them and run round to drop them in front. This was not an exercise that was welcomed by the British sailors in temperatures of more than 100 in the shade.

A successful technique for crossing river beds was discovered accidentally when one of the drivers, mistaking a signal, charged the dry watercourse at speed. Whittall says that 'with a plunge that threw everything into the air that was not lashed or strapped fast, the leader took the dip, ploughed through the sand, throwing it up in front like the bow wave of a destroyer, and rocked and plunged herself up the opposite bank.'

According to Whittall the cars proved that they could move in the difficult country at least as fast as mounted men, but only by consuming a gallon of petrol and a gallon of water every four miles.

When the advance began on June 18 the armoured cars moved out with Beves's 1st Infantry Brigade, and the Royal Naval officer was inspired to remark: 'I have never seen better infantry anywhere than these five battalions of South Africans who moved out of Usakos on that June morning – and I have campaigned with the infantry of every one of the great military powers and with that of some of the smaller.'

Whittall was especially impressed by the Pretoria Regiment and the Transvaal Scottish.

'As they swung out across the open square that marks the northern-most boundary of the town, it was difficult to think that these spare, hardbitten soldiers were volunteers whose ordinary avocations were those of the peaceful civilian. They looked and carried themselves like veteran regulars who had made campaigning the business of their lives.

'And they were as good as they looked, not only these two crack battalions, but the whole of that wonderful infantry who were now setting out on a march that in a lesser war than this would stand out as one of the highest military achievements of its kind in all history.'

By way of illustration Whittall tells of a soldier in the Kimberley Regiment who approached him during the march and asked whether his unit had a doctor who might give him some Vaseline for his feet. The doctor was summoned, and when the soldier removed his boots and what was left of his socks the medical man said he could not possibly keep walking and had better get into the ambulance. But the soldier refused, so the doctor dressed and bandaged his feet and he walked off with a cheery wave to rejoin his regiment and continue the march.

'And that was the spirit of them all. When the road was hard and long; when they were called on to do a thirty-mile march, with little water and little food, under a scorching sun; when they bivouacked without blankets with the temperature seven or eight degrees below freezing point, it was always the same . . .

284

The pipes and drums lead the Transvaal Scottish at a church parade at Usakos before the final advance. (War Museum)

'Most of these magnificent fellows now lie in soldiers' graves in France. It was they who, after the conclusion of the South West Africa campaign, hastened to form the first splendid South African force that General Lukin brought over . . . It was in stricken Delville Wood that they wrote the page which will remain a storied and a hallowed memory so long as the South African Union and its history shall endure.

'And the story they wrote there was an epic one, as befitted the men of Botha's army who in this African "side-show" had shown the dour stuff of which they were made.

'There have been troops as good as this infantry of Beves. But no general has ever had the supreme good fortune to command better material than these South Africans.'

Fulsome stuff, perhaps; but worth preserving as an honest appraisal of the South Africans by an outsider who was there and whose opinions, in the end, are no more eloquent than the statistics of the miles marched through trying conditions by this unflinching army.

Although Botha's army had crossed the desert strip between the coast and the inland plateau, its water problems were far from over. At few places in South West Africa is there enough water to support an army the size of Botha's force.

From the day when the force began its march to the north it suffered from thirst. The Reuters correspondent describes having trekked the 40 miles from Omaruru to Kalkfeld with only one stop for water at Otjua, only to find on outspanning at Kalkfeld at 3 a.m. that there was not enough water left. Told there was another well farther on at Kalkfeld station, the unit he was with inspanned and trekked on.

At the station a field ambulance unit was trying to water its many teams of mules from a well fast running dry.

'So desperate had become the state of the animals at this stage that as each team was drawn towards the well the mules took charge and, in their mad rush, one or two would tumble headlong across the trough into which the water was being tipped. The officer in charge said he hoped to complete the task in five hours more (they had already been busy for three hours).'

The Reuters man's unit decided to trek on, and the next evening arrived at a farm where a small flow was being pumped from a well. But a squadron of the ILH was there first, and it took three hours to water its hundred horses. Waiting all round the well was a large herd of cattle apparently owned by the local farmer 'clamouring for water at their accustomed place. While our mules and horses were enjoying their turn we were kept busily occupied in the dark warding off with sticks the more desperate rushes of these beasts.'

Morris records an officer in the South African Engineer Corps telling about his unit being stuck for a fortnight in a village, 'very nearly

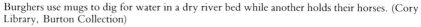

Burghers use mugs to dig for water in a dry river bed while another holds their horses. (Cory Library, Burton Collection)

286

starving and fondly and vainly waiting for supplies to come up . . . We trekked through some eighty miles of pure desert without one single blade of grass, then another eighty miles of stunted bushes and rocks. For the first part of the march, where water was scarcest, whenever we did come to a watering place we found the water poisoned . . . On the march I saw horses try to suck at men's water bottles; in fact, my own did all he could to intercept a cup while I was drinking, and I have seen men pour all the remaining contents of their water bottles into a helmet and give their horses a drink, not knowing a bit when we might strike the next water.'[1]

Botha himself said: 'When I tell you that sometimes we trekked a distance of fifty miles without water and that at the end of the trek the men had to scrape a dry river bed to find water, you will realise all the hardships they suffered. When we brought the horses to the water their tongues were so dry that it was impossible for them to drink and it was necessary to force water down their throats before they would drink.'[2]

★ ★ ★ ★ ★

Botha's advance was being made with a force of 10 000 riflemen, of whom 4 750 were infantry and 5 250 were mounted, and with 32 artillery pieces. Against this force Franke could muster 4 750 men after scraping the barrel to bring in all available reservists.[3] The Germans were still superior in artillery, and had the advantage of being concentrated in prepared positions in familiar terrain, whereas Botha's strategy compelled him to separate his forces widely and over long distances.

A little before the advance began Botha learned that the Germans had taken up well-fortified positions on a line from Kalkfeld on the railway line to the Waterberg plateau to the east. Botha sent Brits out on a flanking movement to the left and Franke, deciding that his forces were too small to avoid being outflanked, once again abandoned his prepared positions. On June 21 he pulled back to kilometre 514 on the railway line to Tsumeb, about nine miles north of where the line to Grootfontein branches off to the east.

There he prepared to make a stand. He issued an order to his forces declaring: 'The time to retire and avoid the enemy is now past. We have arrived at a stage where we must and will fight.'

Franke explained to his troops that previously it had been necessary to preserve the German forces rather than try vainly to defend the whole territory against an overwhelmingly stronger enemy.

'Now everything depends upon our preserving ourselves till the conclusion of peace in Europe, and that requires the greatest exertion and self-sacrifice of everyone.'[4]

Franke knew that Botha's immediate objective was the wells at Otavifontein. To reach them the Union forces had to cross a forty-mile waterless stretch from Omarassa. If he failed to drive the Germans out of their positions at Otavifontein his troops would have to turn about and trek back to Omarassa for water.

The Germans would then have an opportunity to emerge from their well-watered defences and attack the retreating South Africans in the rear.

Franke decided to meet the South African advance at Otavifontein rather than at kilometre 514. Keeping the bulk of his forces at kilometre 514, he posted Major Ritter at Otavifontein with seven mounted companies, three artillery batteries and ten machine-guns.

To protect his eastern flank, Franke posted Captain von Kleist at Asis and Guchab, to defend the mountain passes between Otavi and Grootfontein. Von Kleist's orders were to keep scouting parties watching to the south and east of his position. He was to watch for any attempt by the South Africans to outflank Grootfontein to the east and to defend the passes until further resistance became pointless, and then to withdraw towards Tsumeb by way of Guchab.

After von Kleist's disastrous failure to maintain scouting operations at Gibeon, Franke perhaps thought he was entitled to expect that there would not be a similar failure at Asis and Guchab. It was to be a wrong and costly assumption.

As General Botha advanced northward in the centre with Lukin and his 6th Mounted Brigade he lost contact with Myburgh, who had set out from Wilhelmstal on his swing out to the east, heading for Grootfontein. This development caused Botha no great concern, for it had been expected and he had faith in Myburgh's ability and judgment.

The commander-in-chief was still maintaining communication with Manie Botha's force on his immediate right flank.

At the Omaruru River the troops came across the first running water that some had seen since arriving in South West and hundreds of men walked down to the banks to watch the trickle of water flowing over the sandy bed.

Burton, riding with Myburgh's column, describes how as the Wakkerstroom Commando turned a bend in a rough road on a Sunday morning, a large landmine, exploding just ahead, 'made a terrific noise and hurled upwards through the overhanging dust old horse-shoes, bolts and nuts, scrap-iron and fragments of exploded shell, which fell upon us as we came down the slope of the hill.'

By the time the sappers found the detonating wires and traced them to their source the Germans who had set off the mine had escaped.

But it was the lack of water rather than mines that bothered Myburgh's men. Burton recalls that at times the burghers had to dig as deep as twelve feet into a dry river bed. Where there were wells there were water tanks, but these had always been emptied by the Germans by the time the commandos arrived.

'The only water left in a tank would be the small amount lying in small puddles on the uneven floor of the tank, and the burghers, with dixies and canvas nosebags, knelt down to scoop up the water in a mug or cup. The clear water went into a dixie for himself and dirty water was poured into a nosebag for his horse or mule. Scenting the water, the horses stretched their necks forwards over the walls of the tank.'

Chaplain Meara was marching – and suffering – with the infantry as it followed behind Lukin's cavalry. Near Otjiwarongo he watched water being poured from a tank-cart into a trough for the men to fill their water-bottles.

'A flock of birds flew down to the water, alighting on the helmets and shoulders of the troops and thence into the trough in their eagerness to seek the water. It was quite interesting to see that the troops at once waited until the birds had quenched their thirst and flown off before drinking themselves.'

Meara was with the 1st Infantry Brigade (Transvaal Scottish, Pretoria Regiment, 2nd Kimberley Regiment and Durban Light Infantry) whose men were suffering from hunger as well as from thirst and fatigue by the time they had passed beyond Otjiwarongo.

The retreating Germans have emptied the water tanks and poisoned the wells and the pursuing South Africans are forced to dig for water. Often they found none and had to move on and try again elsewhere. (Cory Library, Burton Collection)

'We have to march long distances between water holes and on half-rations,' the chaplain says in his diary. 'This last march prior to our striking camp this morning was a distance of 26 miles without water. The march that we have now in contemplation from here [Okaputa] to Otavi is about 42 miles and the intelligence inform us that it must be done without finding any water on the way.'

On July 5, the chaplain wrote that 'the men are utterly worn out and we have yet many miles to go. Water is very scarce and we get little of that as well as little food . . . This long and trying march is testing the endurance of the men to the uttermost. In all the regiments there have been men dropping out on the line of march from exhaustion and weariness, from badly blistered feet, etc. The march has been a horribly trying one partly because of the fearful dust and broken roadways and the thorn bushes growing all over the country and edging the roadways so that men's clothes and legs were often torn therewith.'

The South African aircraft were now flying daily on reconnaissance and bombing missions, and Burton recalls having some misgivings as one flew over Myburgh's column. He remembered that the Union troops had been instructed to put out a sheet with a letter marked on it to identify themselves to the airmen.

'But we had no sheets, and any we had would have been torn up for bandages. Our distinctive features were our shabby, tattered, worn-out garments, emaciated horses, mules and donkeys and schanzes [shelters] made of discarded tent canvas.'

At Otjiwarongo Brits set off on his wide detour to attack Namutoni and cut off the enemy's line of retreat. All available motor transport (one report mentions more than thirty vehicles) and petrol were given to him to enable his force to keep itself supplied. He was expected to be out of communication for most of what was estimated to be a 200-mile trek.

On the day when Brits set out, the aerial reconnaissance reported Myburgh, whose column the airmen had sometimes been unable to find, at the Waterberg and in line with the general level of the advance.

At this point in the march the central force entered broken terrain that made it impossible for motor vehicles to operate off the roads. As the armoured cars were now roadbound and unable to be of much use it was decided to return them to Britain so that, in Collyer's words, 'they might be used to advantage in some theatre which would give them a fair opportunity for tactical action which local conditions now denied them.'

When they returned to Britain they took with them the thanks of the South African Government and a statement from the cabinet that 'the conduct of the officers and other ratings of the squadron under all conditions and in all circumstances maintained the high traditions of the Royal Navy.'[5]

South African prisoners of war who escaped from their captors rejoined the Union forces at Omarassa, looking tattered and speaking of hardships in the German prison camps. (Cape Archives)

On reaching Omarassa, Botha ordered a pause in the advance to consolidate his forces before beginning the trek across the waterless 40 miles to Otavi. While the 6th Mounted Brigade was at Omarassa and Manie Botha's 5th at nearby Okaputa, Beves's infantry, the artillery and the Aviation Corps were still a few miles south of Otjiwarongo. Myburgh was at the Waterberg and Brits was somewhere in the west, presumably beginning to turn north for the Etosha Pan and Namutoni.

When the infantry reached Otjiwarongo the Rhodesia Regiment stopped there to garrison the town and the other regiments continued on to Omarassa.

There, several groups of South African prisoners of war who had managed to escape emerged from the bush, tattered and starving, and told of the hardships endured in the prison camps.

Botha now began to worry that the Germans might carry out their apparent intention of retreating to the north-west, in which case they might encounter Brits's column and, being numerically stronger, overwhelm it. The general decided to anticipate any such move by attacking Otavifontein immediately with Lukin's and Manie Botha's forces, without waiting for the infantry to come up, and so keep Franke too busy defending himself to conduct an ordered retreat.

'Forced marches were sustained, without any off-saddles, through-out the night of June 30 – July 1, General Botha riding with the columns, which forged ahead in clouds of dust,' says Collyer.

The South Africans believed that Franke had disposed almost his entire force at Otavi and Otavifontein and that their own forces were outnumbered. They were unaware that Franke had held back part of his force at kilometre 514 and that there were no more than 1 000 Germans opposing the 3 500 men under Lukin and Manie Botha.[6]

Otavifontein was considered by the South Africans to be a difficult position to capture. It lay east of Otavi, below the Otaviberg hills and on the railway line to Grootfontein, which passed through a gap in the hills. The direct approach to Otavifontein lay across a bush-covered valley between the Otaviberg and the Elefantenberg to the south. To the east were more hills, the Eisenberg. Only the Germans concealed in the bush covering the hills could get a clear picture of what was going on in the valley.

Ritter had been told by Franke that he must hold Otavifontein for at least a week until the defences at kilometre 514 (Khorab) had been completed. He had assured Franke he would be able to do so.[7]

Two days later, at daybreak on July 1, the burgher commandos were upon him in their usual dashing style. General Botha left Osib, twelve miles south of Otavi, early that morning, and already Manie Botha and his Free Staters were well into a headlong commando-style advance into the heart of the enemy positions while the Germans, according to Collyer's account, were still scrambling to man their defences.

References

1. Morris, p. 45.
2. *Ibid,* p. 47.
3. Hennig, p. 269.
4. Collyer, p. 143.
5. Collyer, p. 135.
6. Hennig, p. 275.
7. Ungleich, p. 182.

30

Charging into the Unknown

From their positions on the bush-covered hilltops the Germans had watched the approach of the two Union brigades, one on either side of the railway line, their horses and guns raising clouds of dust as they rode across the dry plain.

Manie Botha was on the left side of the railway with his 5th Brigade and Lukin on the right with the 6th Brigade. As soon as they came within range the German guns opened fire. They had measured the ranges and their first shells were on target. But the South Africans, instead of advancing in column, quickly melted into the bush on either side of the line.

According to Collyer, the Germans had not yet occupied their elaborate defensive positions when the South Africans appeared. It is possible that they had not expected Botha to make a night march and appear so quickly in front of their defences. Yet German accounts maintain that German scouts had detected Botha's advance and reported it to Ritter and that by 5 am on the day of the battle the Germans were in their positions.

The official South African history of the campaign says that Manie Botha's 5th Brigade had been ordered to advance to Otjikurume, south of the Elefantenberg, where the Germans were believed to be strongly positioned. The brigade encountered the German outposts while it was still dark 'and rushed them at such a rate that they had no time to let off the rockets and light signals prearranged to warn the main body'.[1]

Manie Botha, 'who appreciated the possibility of the situation, pursued the outposts with his whole brigade instead of continuing his march to Otjikurume as ordered'.

For the South Africans to rush into the valley was like charging into a trap. The usually cautious Manie Botha had not intended to do any such thing; but when, pursuing his retreating enemy, he found himself in the valley, he realised that it would be difficult to gather his men

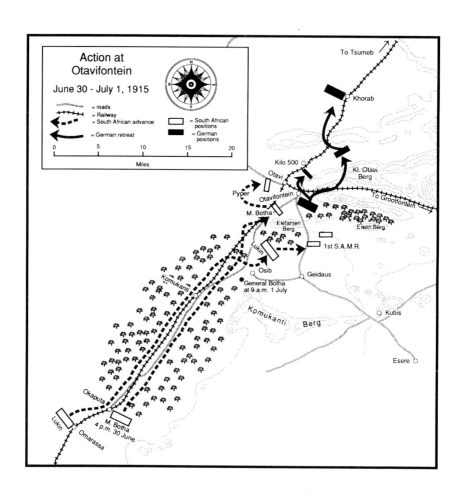

Action at
Otavifontein

June 30 - July 1, 1915

∽∽∽∽∽∽ = roads
＋＋＋＋＋ = Railway
◄━ ■ ■ ■ = South African advance
◄━━━ = German retreat

☐ = South African positions
■ = German positions

0   5   10   15   20
Miles

To Tsumeb

Khorab

Kilo 500

Otavi

Kl. Otavi Berg

To Grootfontein

Pyper

Otavifontein

M. Botha

Elefanten Berg

Eisen Berg

Lukin

1st S.A.M.R.

Osib

Geidaus

General Botha at 9 a.m. 1 July

Komukanti

Komukanti Berg

Kubis

Esere

Okaputa

Lukin

M. Botha 4 p.m. 30 June

Omarassa

General Botha (left) inspects the beginning of the 150-yard trench blown in an approach road to Otavifontein when South African sappers detonated a German mine, the biggest laid by the Germans in the campaign. Having been given advance warning of it the South Africans were able to capture the German soldiers waiting to blow it up when the Union troops passed over it. (Cape Archives)

together and effect a retreat. He decided the best thing to do in the circumstances was to continue advancing.

Collyer says that the 5th Brigade 'had become committed to their tactical enterprise in the manner in which commando units often entered a fight induced by the instinct of the individual to take a sudden line of action . . . and there was no choice between trying to get out or seeing the business through.'

He asserts that 'the rapidity of the advance over the last 10 miles . . . had upset the German commander's calculations, for his outposts came back into their positions with their pursuers on their heels, and he was thus prevented from disposing of his main force as he had proposed to do.'

General Botha, now back in his car, was following close behind his namesake. When he learned where the commander of the 5th Brigade was he became worried that the Germans would send a force in from the east and cut up the brigade. To block any such move Lukin, whose brigade was being held in reserve, was ordered to send a strong force to the eastern end of the Elefantenberg. Later the rest of Lukin's brigade advanced on Otavi by the same route.

A regiment of the 5th Brigade under Lieutenant Colonel Pijper was sent swinging out to the west and came in to attack Otavi from that direction, the open side, expediting its evacuation by the Germans. By noon the Union artillery was up and shelling Otavifontein, and Ritter, who commanded the German forces in the battle, ordered a general retreat. Ritter himself was almost lost to the Germans, with his horse shot under him and his staff clerk captured.

Fighting a rearguard action, the German force withdrew along the railway line to Grootfontein. The South Africans did not pursue them, for their horses were exhausted, Ritter's force was still strong and they had got what they had come for: the water at Otavifontein.

Collyer says that at the end of the campaign Franke's chief-of-staff told him that if the Germans had had just one hour in which to occupy their carefully selected positions 'General Botha and his two brigades would never have got back to Okaputa.[2]

'If the strength of the two forces and the preponderance of four to one in field guns in favour of the enemy is borne in mind, it will be realised that there is much to be said for this opinion,' was Collyer's dry comment.

Extraordinary luck was with the South Africans in one respect. On the road into the valley from the eastern end of the Elefantenberg the Germans had laid the biggest mine of the entire campaign, a huge bed of explosives stretching under the surface of the road for 150 yards and covering the full width of the road. It was over this road that Lukin's brigade made its advance. But because it had advance warning of the

This photograph is identified in various records only as South African infantry on the march in South West Africa but it is thought to show the 1st Infantry Brigade on their extraordinary march to Otavifontein. (SADF Archives)

mine, Lukin's men were able to trace and cut the wires by which the mine was to have been exploded when the South Africans were well placed on top of it. By following the wires they were also able to capture the German soldiers who were waiting in their hiding-place to detonate the mine.[3]

Avoiding being blown up by the mine might not be considered a mere matter of luck if the South Africans knew of its existence. But how did they learn about it? That must surely have been luck. Collyer, who seldom volunteers more information than he considered pertinent to the subject, does not tell us. He says cryptically that 'GHQ had become aware of the position of all mines laid by the enemy as far as Otavi' and says the big mine there was shown on a plan. He does not reveal how GHQ got hold of the plan and this remains one of the mysteries of the campaign. According to some accounts, it was captured and this is the most likely explanation.

Considering the fierceness of the fighting, the casualties were astonishingly low: three Germans dead, eight wounded and 24 captured; four South Africans dead and seven wounded.

Botha's force settled into the pleasant surroundings at Otavifontein, revelling in the sight of greenery and running water after the flinty glare and the thirst of the march north. Botha set up his headquarters in the

After the capture of Otavifontein, South African cavalry form up for the next advance. They know now that it will soon be over – but they also know that the Germans are still strong enough to put up a stiff fight. (Cape Archives – AG)

German barracks to await the arrival of the infantry and news of Myburgh and Brits.

The 1st Brigade swung into Otavifontein on July 6, only four days after the mounted brigades had reached there. They were tattered and dusty, blistered, burned and limping, but marching erect. They had fired no shots, seen no enemy, but they were proud of what they had done and their ranks were in immaculate line as they came in to the skirl of the Transvaal Scottish pipes. Behind the band came the Durban Light Infantry, then the Transvaal Scottish, then the Pretoria Regiment and then the Kimberleys, and finally the heavy artillery.

The mounted troopers already in Otavifontein cheered them as they came in, for they knew what the foot soldiers must have endured.

Not all of them knew that the infantry had even increased the marching pace at the end in response to a request from General Botha that they reach Otavifontein as soon as possible so that they would be there if a ceasefire were agreed on that would halt all further troop movements. If no ceasefire were arranged the general still wanted the infantry in Otavifontein to provide the fulcrum for cavalry attacks on Khorab or Tsumeb.

General Beves addressed his men and congratulated them on their march of more than 300 miles, the last 270 practically without a break, the last 80 in four days, the last 45 miles in 36 hours. This marching, he said, would have been exceptional under normal conditions; in the heat, dust and thirst and on low rations it was a performance of 'the greatest credit.'

Perhaps a better tribute than Beves's unimaginative understatement came from the German commander himself. When he was told that the Union infantry had arrived in Otavifontein, Franke, who may have known when they had begun their march, commented: 'They travelled by train, of course'. He could not believe that they had come so far and so fast on their own feet.

Botha now began preparations to attack the Germans at Khorab, where the main force was now concentrated. He was still concerned about avoiding an enemy advance in strength on Brits. The South Africans were hoping that the Germans were unaware of the movements of Brits and perhaps even of Myburgh.

But Franke had already guessed what Botha was up to. On July 2 the commander of the German garrison at Outjo had come into Khorab with his men and reported that he had been attacked by a strong South African force on June 28. Franke reasoned that a force as large as that which had attacked Outjo must be on a wider mission and he guessed that its purpose was to capture Namutoni.[4]

Franke knew about Myburgh's movements from a report sent in on July 2 by von Kleist from Asis, where he was guarding the gap between

Otavi and Grootfontein. Von Kleist had reported a large Union force approaching from the south, obviously Myburgh's force. Franke had immediately warned Governor Seitz and his administration to evacuate Grootfontein and move to Tsumeb.

The German commander suspected that Myburgh intended to move on from Grootfontein to Tsumeb and that in fact Botha's plan was to encircle the German forces and administration and secure their defeat or surrender.

Franke immediately requested a meeting with Seitz. The meeting was held on July 3 at Khorab and was attended also by the police chief, Lieutenant-Colonel Bethe, and Franke's commanders. Franke said he expected Botha to launch a major attack within the next few days and it would not be possible for the German forces to avoid defeat by the stronger Union army. He argued that it was too late to begin the planned withdrawal to the north-west because the South Africans were too near, the German horses and mules were too weak from lack of fodder to make a long journey and there was only enough maize meal to last the German troops for another three weeks.

Seitz said he did not want to have to negotiate with the South Africans from a position of weakness and asked whether Franke could first win some kind of tactical victory. The military commander's response was blunt: his forces would be destroyed if hostilities were not suspended.

Reluctantly, the governor agreed to seek terms from the South Africans. He drafted a letter to Botha proposing a ceasefire under which the German troops would accept voluntary internment in South West Africa with their weapons. He pointed out that the German troops were now concentrated in strength and warned Botha that further hostilities would result in much bloodshed. He reminded him that the German forces were in a strong position in Europe.

The letter was sent off immediately with an officer carrying the white flag of truce and reached Botha at sunset.

Botha responded the next morning, July 4, with a letter rejecting Seitz's proposals. The knowledge that the Germans were ready to seek terms was welcome to Botha, who knew he could destroy the enemy forces but wanted to avoid the casualties that would result. He did not want to begin negotiating until his plans were complete, until Brits and Myburgh were in position to encircle the enemy.

Grootfontein had already fallen – captured single-handed by an intrepid signals officer, Captain Poole, who had been moving in advance of Myburgh's column to try to set up communications.

Von Kleist, who had concentrated his force at Ghaub, was taken by surprise there by Myburgh on July 4. As at Gibeon, and despite Franke's instructions, von Kleist had neglected to put out adequate sentry posts, on the ground that his men needed a rest. But if he was careless about patrolling, von Kleist was very good at escaping from awkward situations. As at Gibeon, he slipped out of Myburgh's encirclement, but at the cost of several men wounded and 66 captured and the loss of 12 supply waggons. The South African casualties in the engagement were one killed and three wounded.

Von Kleist retreated with the rest of his force to Khorab and the way was open for Myburgh to advance on Tsumeb. His instructions from Botha were to circle round the town to approach it from the north.

Brits's whereabouts were still unknown.

Botha's attention was now focused increasingly on the South African prisoners of war, who were known to be held at both Tsumeb and Namutoni. He wanted to know they were within a South African encirclement before he sat down to talk to Governor Seitz.

References

1. *Official History*, p. 46.
2. See also *Official History*, p. 47.
3. Collyer, p. 140.
4. Ungleich, p. 189.

Behind Wire

In the darkness the four prisoners had no difficulty in finding the hole in the fence that was to be their gateway to freedom.

They had worked on it surreptitiously for days, waiting until the German guards moved away before tugging at the barbed wire and thorn branches, slowly enlarging the hole until they judged it big enough to wriggle through. Then they had covered it again to wait for the right moment.

They had chosen the Kaiser's birthday, January 27, as a good time because the Germans were known to celebrate the occasion in fine style and the guards would probably be less alert than usual. Even on an ordinary day vigilance was slack, for the Germans did not seriously expect any of the South African prisoners to try to escape into the wilderness beyond the wire. When they had arrived at the camp at Franzfontein near Outjo the commandant had told them that the best guard was the desert outside, and that belief had clearly influenced the sentries.

But in planning their escape the prisoners had forgotten about the moon. On the Kaiser's birthday it was large in the clear sky and bathing the whole camp and the desert outside in bright light. The attempt was postponed for three days.

They were an oddly assorted group, united mainly by their common desire to escape. Sergeant A McKenzie of the Upington Commando was the senior man. Corporal H J McElnea of the 1st Imperial Light Horse had been captured near Garub while serving with General McKenzie's force. His horse had been shot from under him in a skirmish. Rifleman O C Maritz was a sturdy Dutchman from the 1st South African Mounted Rifles. Rifleman FM Frantzsen was a powerfully-built Dane who had somehow landed up in the Veterinary Reserve Corps.

They had planned their escape with care. Water was their main worry. Each man had in one way or another acquired three water bottles. They had also made crude but effective water bags, sewn together from stolen canvas scraps. There were two bags for each man. Their only food was sixty 'vetkoeke' – two-ounce pieces of dough fried in oil – that they had secreted. And they had half a bottle of rum stolen from the Germans.

The night of the escape was blessedly dark, and they squeezed through the hole in the fence without being seen. But in their frantic wriggle through the thorns and barbed wire their supplies were seriously depleted. Some of the water spilled out of the bags and several of the water bottles and ten of the vetkoeke and the bottle of rum were left behind in the fence as they ran into the night.

It was a sorry start to a journey they knew must take them across more than a hundred miles of desert and semi-desert before they reached the safety of the Union positions. How they would make it with their derisory supply of food and water must have weighed agonisingly on their minds as they stumbled on through the night.

Then the first miracle happened. It rained – the first rain recorded in the area for several years. The steady downpour continued for hours, obliterated their footprints and made it impossible for the Germans to track them. Sucking up water from the little pools that collected in the rocks, the men squirted it into their water bags until they were full again.

They walked all night, heading due west towards the coast and stopping only to eat. For thirty-six hours they walked in the rain, sleeping fitfully in the downpour and racked by rheumaticky pains.

The clouds cleared and they walked on, through mountains, sand flats and brush country; then more mountains. Their feet suffered increasingly. Then their boots began to come apart, torn on the jagged rocks. They saw lion spoor, and a new anxiety was added to their burden.

When the skies cleared, heat and thirst became serious. McElnea began to lag behind, his feet bleeding through his shredded boots. Maritz took off his own boots and gave them to McElnea and walked on barefoot. They were now passing through the coastal desert and their water was finished.

McElnea began to act strangely, constantly throwing away his hat. Each time Maritz retrieved it and put it back on his head.

And then, when they paused for a rest, they realized that McElnea was no longer with them. He had become separated from them in the maze of rocky hillocks through which they were passing. A search found no sign of him, and the others decided to press on to the coast, which they knew must now be near, in the hope of finding food and water and then returning to look for him.

When they stumbled down to the sea they saw buildings in front of them. They had reached the coast at the old whaling station at Cape Cross. The buildings were badly damaged (presumably from the shelling by *Albion*) but there were tanks containing water. After relieving their thirst, they collected limpets from the rocks and boiled them in an old pot found in the wrecked buildings.

They had also found half a bottle of seal oil and with this they improvised a lamp, which they put in a window that night in the hope that McElnea would see it.

In the morning Maritz and Frantzsen went back to look for McElnea, and near the beach they found the lid of a tin of foot-powder that he had been carrying. But of McElnea himself there was no sight, and they returned to Cape Cross.[1]

Next morning the three filled their water-bags and headed south along the beach towards Swakopmund. Next day they came across footprints and followed them, hoping that they had been made by their missing companion. The following afternoon they saw what looked like a rag on a pole, about half a mile inland. When there was no response to their waving they walked on. Then McKenzie said he could see someone lying beside the pole and they went to have a closer look.

It was McElnea, lying in a scooped-out hollow. He was alive but in bad condition after having gone without water for two days. When he recovered somewhat after a drink of water, he explained that, thinking he was going to die, he had stuck up the driftwood pole and attached an improvised flag to it and then, scraping a shallow grave, had lain down in it.

Maritz now saw a seagull that seemed unable to fly. He chased it and killed it with a stick, and it was boiled in salt water in the old pot. It did not go far between four starving men, but the food gave McElnea enough strength to stagger on.

But soon they could not find even limpets to eat and when their situation was beginning to look really serious they saw Swakopmund in the distance. Hardly had they begun rejoicing, however, when they saw a German patrol cantering towards them. After enduring so much they were going to be recaptured, with salvation in sight just down the coast!

But fortune had not finished with the gallant group. A South African patrol galloped up from Swakopmund and the Germans retreated.

McElnea was too weak to continue walking and had to be lifted onto a horse, but the others made it to Swakopmund on foot – ten days after escaping from Franzfontein. They had walked more than two hundred and seventy miles from the hole in the prison fence.[2]

★ ★ ★ ★ ★

Colonel Grant at Gibeon railway station with German soldiers and civilians. The pipe-smoking man in the white hat could well be Herr Wasserfall, the magistrate who befriended him. (Namibia Archives)

The highest-ranking prisoner in the hands of the Germans was Colonel Grant, the South African commander at the Battle of Sandfontein. Either because of his rank or because of the respect that he had earned among the Germans for his fight at Sandfontein, or both, he was treated with great consideration.

From the battlefield Grant was taken to hospital in Warmbad, where he was visited by his victor at Sandfontein, Colonel von Heydebreck. Another South African prisoner, Rifleman Scholl of the Transvaal Horse Artillery, was assigned to Grant as his batman.

From Warmbad Grant was moved to Keetmanshoop and placed on parole. In his diary, in which he wrote almost daily, Grant records that he was sent books and a cake by a local lady, a Mrs Plichter (Pflichter?), on whom he called to express his thanks.

In November Grant was moved to Gibeon, where he received letters from Captain Welby and the other officers captured with him, who were being held at Outjo. In Gibeon Grant exchanged visits with the magistrate, Herr Wasserfall, and became friendly with the local veterinary officer, Dr Leursen, who lent him a horse to go riding. Together with a young lady schoolteacher they rode out one Sunday to spend the day with a local farmer, Herr Kreiss.

Despite these diversions and his fairly comfortable quarters, Grant was often depressed by his situation, especially when he heard bad news about the war. His entry on December 19 reads: 'The Germans have received news today of further successes to their arms and are displaying bunting in consequence. Feel much depressed. God's will be done.'

On December 24 it was his daughter Marjorie's birthday and Grant 'drank her health in a bottle of German wine, specially saved for the occasion.' But on the same day he records his depression at the news of the 'capture of 130 of our men by the rebels at Stolzenfels'. Next day, however, he was a guest at a Christmas dinner party at Dr Leursen's house, with the magistrate and two schoolmistresses.

A few days later the Germans gave Grant a telegram, from his wife, sent through the Defence Department in Pretoria, conveying greetings to him and the other South African prisoners from 'all the women and children of the 1st Regiment'. Grant asked his captors to pass the greetings on to the other prisoners.

In Gibeon, Grant was given more books by a Mrs Albert Voigts, and on April 13 he celebrated his wedding anniversary with a bottle of wine shared at dinner with a local man whose name is illegible in the diary.

But now the war was coming nearer and Grant was taken in a train with German women and children and hospital patients to Waterberg.

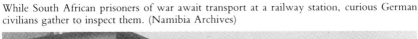

While South African prisoners of war await transport at a railway station, curious German civilians gather to inspect them. (Namibia Archives)

Captured South African mounted riflemen are marched under escort, probably while being taken to a prison camp. (Namibia Archives)

On the way they stopped in Windhuk, and the German officer escorting him took him to a hotel for a hot bath and then to his own house for dinner.

In May he was moved to Tsumeb and given a room in a hotel. There he was visited by Herr Wasserfall, the magistrate from Gibeon, who was being moved to Namutoni and had left his wife in Omaruru. The fortunes of war were turning.

Grant records having gone to an open-air church service in Tsumeb attended by Governor Seitz and his staff on May 23, but he does not mention meeting the Governor.

About this time his diary contains increasingly frequent references to the plight of the lower-ranking prisoners in Tsumeb, who were living in the open in a large barbed-wire enclosure with little shelter. If the Germans were treating Grant with consideration they were showing little for the lower ranks.

The contrast emerges strongly from the account given by another of the Sandfontein captives, P J Young, of his experiences in the prison camps for the men. Young and his fellow prisoners were taken by train in stages north to Otjiwarongo, and from there they marched for two weeks through blistering heat to Franzfontein.

As at Tsumeb, the prisoners at Franzfontein were simply herded into a large enclosure.

'We were crowded into a patch of the wilderness fenced off with barbed wire,' Young wrote. 'There were no living quarters. We got together in small groups, selected a spot of ground and parked ourselves there.'[2]

The prisoners were fed small quantities of meat, mealie meal, rice and coffee beans.

'At the slaughter pole, men with lusty appetites fought for the prize of a billy-can of blood and the animal's entrails.'

The prisoners, now 'streamlined' by their spare diet, sang songs and some made musical instruments and formed a band.

After nine months the prisoners, most of whom were without boots, were given a quantity of rawhide with which to make sandals for a march to new quarters. The long march back to Otjiwarongo was a painful trudge, and even when the men got into railway trucks at the station 'the pain stayed in our feet.'

The prisoners were kept for a while at Otavifontein, where, after being inspected by Colonel Franke, were allowed to have a bath and were given German military uniforms to wear. Their rations were increased.

Franke's visit almost certainly resulted from representations made by Grant to the German military authorities. The Germans had first refused to allow him to see any other captured South African officers or men; but in May he was allowed to visit the men in the camp at Tsumeb. He listened to their grievances, which were mostly about poor food – some of the men were suffering from scurvy. They also complained about being forced to make wooden boxes for German mines and to go out on working parties to dig holes for the mines.

Grant spoke to the camp commandant and got an undertaking that the prisoners would not be employed in making or laying mines or on any other military work.

He was also allowed to visit the sick prisoners, most of whom were suffering from malaria.

On June 14, after being allowed to talk to captive South African officers passing through from Namutoni, Grant had a meeting with Franke and complained to him that both the officers and lower rank prisoners were receiving half rations. He had learned that at Namutoni they had no tables or chairs and were 'having to lie and eat on the ground'. Grant said the prisoners were badly off for clothing; some had no boots and others even had no trousers. Grant said that these conditions were a contravention of the Geneva Convention and asked that they should be put right.

Grant also complained that Sergeant Till of the Transvaal Horse Artillery, who had lost a leg as a result of being wounded in action, was lying on the ground in a stable at Namutoni. The colonel demanded that

South African prisoners of war are taken to the Windhuk station to board a train for a new camp as the Union advance moves north. (Namibia Archives)

prisoners of war who were incapable of further military service should be repatriated.

Franke told Grant that it had been difficult to feed and clothe the men owing to supply and transport difficulties, but now that they were at more accessible places it would become easier. Washing and other utensils had already been sent to Namutoni, he said. Franke promised that Sergeant Till would be sent immediately to a hospital. He evaded the other matters raised, says Grant.

Twelve days later Sergeant Till arrived at Tsumeb from Namutoni, but he was put in a compound with the other prisoners 'under conditions most unsuited for a man in his state'. Grant arranged for the sergeant to share the room occupied by his batman, Scholl.

Young and his fellow prisoners ended up in the compound at Tsumeb, as did Percy Close, a member of the 8th Mounted Rifles who had been captured by Maritz's rebels near Van Rooyen's Vlei in January and handed over to the Germans. Close, who later described his experiences in a book,[3] was in the prison camp at Uitdraai before being moved to Tsumeb.

Close's captors had a sample method of preventing the prisoners from escaping; they simply took away their boots at night. Instead of counting the prisoners at the evening roll-call, they counted the boots.

At Tsumeb Close was reunited with three prisoners who had escaped from Uitdraai, and recaptured in heartbreaking circumstances. The three, Rens, Bennie and Du Toit, took with them on their escape a water-bag that they had made from canvas stitched together with cotton thread pulled from a tunic. They bought food from local blacks and stole some from a farmhouse. They lived off the land as much as possible, once eating a nest of guinea fowl eggs and on another occasion roasting what they thought was a tortoise, only to find when they broke open the shell that it was empty.

Close recounts that the three, making for the Union lines in the south, passed so near to Windhuk they could see the masts of the wireless station. Three weeks after breaking out of Uitdraai they ran into a picket, the last one between them and the Union lines, and were recaptured.

Close tells how some of the prisoners put on plays in the compound at Tsumeb, those playing the female roles wearing dresses made out of provision bags. This would suggest that at Tsumeb, at least, conditions were not so bad as at Namutoni, where men went trouserless for want even of provision bags, and at Franzfontein, where they went about barefoot when their boots fell apart.

One of those who spent the entire campaign behind wire was Wally Clark, who was well known in South Africa as a soccer player. He was captured by Maritz in October, 1914 when he accompanied Colonel Bouwer to take a message to the rebel leader, who handed him over to the Germans. Clark's recollections, as recounted in the South African press after the campaign, were that the treatment of the prisoners varied according to who was in charge of them.

At first the prisoners were hit with rifle butts and abused by the German guards. At Ukamas, however, they were well treated, and given blankets and plenty of food. While passing through Windhuk on the way to Franzfontein they were jeered by crowds in the streets and locked in the local gaol without food. Clark's recollections of Franzfontein matched those of Young: hunger, cold and hardship.

Grant's diary records that when he visited the men in the Tsumeb compound on June 28 he found that their food rations had improved and they were getting a rum ration. (Close remembers it as arak, which he says came with a tobacco ration.)

New arrivals entered the compound from Otavifontein at the end of June, and Grant asked for permission to visit them, but it was refused. The Germans told him that 53 prisoners had escaped from Otavifontein (presumably those who rejoined the Union forces on the advance from Karibib) and the rest were being punished. Grant learned that 12 of the escapers had been recaptured, and four had been shot when they ignored an order by their pursuers to halt.

On June 22 Grant was told to vacate the room in which he had been living in the hotel at Tsumeb as it was wanted for Colonel Franke, who was moving his headquarters to Tsumeb. Grant was accommodated in a little wood-and-iron cottage beside the prison compound.

The approach of the Union forces was now producing increasingly visible effects on Tsumeb. The prisoners saw huge quantities of stores and weapons being destroyed or hauled away.

'Wagonloads have been going all day and for the greater part of the night,' Grant wrote on July 3. One of the things destroyed was the yellow Taube aircraft that the prisoners had seen at the airstrip when they had been taken to work there. The prisoners had always made a point of doing as little work as possible on such occasions, and now the guards made even less effort than before to get them to work.

Artillery pieces and other weapons were being dumped in the deep lake near Tsumeb, the Osikotosee. Grant says some materials were being put in the copper mine, but he may have been confused with the dumping in the lake.

Excitement began to grow in the compound as the German activity made it clear that the Union forces were drawing near. On July 3, according to Grant's diary, the Government officials arrived from Grootfontein to establish the administration, in so far as it existed, at Tsumeb.

The camp at Tsumeb, where the South African prisoners lived in the open, most of them without shelter of any kind. Grant succeeded in getting their conditions improved by complaining to the German commander-in-chief. (Cory Library, Burton Collection)

Excitement grew feverish, both inside and outside the prison compound, on July 3 when a South African aircraft flew over the town.

'The alarm sounded and everybody was rushing about,' Grant says. 'The cause was soon apparent. It was one of our aeroplanes. It sailed over at about 10.15.'

Close says the prisoners were told to 'lie low and keep quiet'. The guards outside the barbed wire were reinforced.

'We saw the aeroplane coming towards Tsumeb. We waved tunics, shirts and hats and shouted ourselves hoarse for joy.'

Close says he heard afterwards that the pilot realised that those waving were South African prisoners and not Germans and refrained from dropping bombs on them.

The German troops opened up a heavy rifle fire on the aircraft as it circled overhead at a height Grant estimated at about five thousand feet.

'It was a most beautiful sight, watching the complete disdain with which the aeronaut and aeroplane treated the sniping,' Close records. 'The machine curved ever so gracefully in the air and passed over the station, where it dropped two bombs.'

Grant says the plane dropped three bombs, its target being 'a convoy near the railway station going to Osikotosee'.

On the same day the colonel records making one of his now frequent visits to the sick prisoners in the hospital and asking the camp commandant to issue canvas groundsheets to the men as shelter from the sun and dust. The men were 'extremely uncomfortable' in their compound in the middle of the village.

Colonel Grant was summoned by the military commander at Tsumeb, Major Wehle, and told that there would probably be a fight at Tsumeb during the next few days, and he was concerned that the prisoners of war might try to escape during the fighting. He told Grant that the guards had orders in that event to fire not only at those trying to escape but into the camp itself, and therefore it was 'highly desirable that they should remain quiet.'

Grant replied that it was only right that the prisoners should know that and requested permission to inform them. It was granted, and he went to the compound, accompanied by Captain Medding of the German military staff.

'I explained the position to the men and asked whether they wished my advice,' Grant says. 'They all said yes. I therefore told them they should remain quiet as any overt act such as a large number attempting to rush the guards would probably cost many lives for no adequate purpose; that any who attempted such action should previously reflect that they would be endangering the lives of their comrades who were remaining quiet.

'The bare possibility of my men being shot down like sheep was a terrible one for me to contemplate.

'The men all seemed to accept my advice, the seniors especially. They pointed out there was nothing to indicate their camp was a prison camp and that it was likely to be fired on in an action.

'I therefore got a promise from Hauptmann Medding to place two large Red Cross flags over it. I also subsequently suggested to Major Wehle that the men be provided with entrenching tools in order to entrench themselves and have some cover in case of attack. This he assented to. He promised that it would be done in the morning.

'The men were apparently very glad to see me and cheered lustily. They were all in good spirits, due, I think, to the aeroplane visit this morning and the knowledge that our forces are near. I shook hands with most of the seniors and chatted for the few minutes I had with them. Poor fellows, my heart went out to them; they were all very brown, bearded and dirty and their camp a miserable one. Most of them have no shelter but I hope this is being remedied.'

On July 4 Medding told Grant that on account of the presence of women and children in the town it had been decided not to have a fight in Tsumeb.

'The fight would occur some distance out. If our troops enter he has been instructed to surrender.'

With Medding's permission Grant told the men of the decision and 'impressed on them the necessity to remain quiet for the sake of avoiding fighting in the town'.

July 5 is noted in Grant's diary as 'a day of suspense'. In the morning it was reported that five squadrons of South African troops were about six miles away and could be expected at any time. The day wore on with no sign of them.

'This evening Captain Medding informed me that an armistice would commence tomorrow at 7 a.m. I also had to promise that I would not attempt to communicate with our troops.'

Grant's last entry on that day, his last day of captivity, is: 'We all feel rather jumpy and cautious tonight.'

References

1. *Nongquai.*
2. Young, p. 163.
3. Close, Percy L, *A Prisoner of the Germans in South West Africa*, Maskew Miller.

CHAPTER

32

The Jaws Close

As the German leaders debated whether to fight, flee or surrender, Botha's pincers were closing in the north.

Myburgh and his force, weary and tattered but still full of dash, had gone past Grootfontein and were beginning their swing to come onto Tsumeb from the north.

At one point in their headlong advance they had gone without water for two days in the burning heat and the dust. At night they had endured cold so severe that after they had obtained some milk at an isolated farm it was handed out to the men in frozen lumps.[1]

When Burton approached another farmhouse near Grootfontein for milk for his patients he got a startling response from the man who came to the door.

'No, voetsek, you damned khaki; I have no milk for you,' the man shouted and slammed the door in Burton's face. Only later did he learn that it was the farm of Andries de Wet, leader of the Vrij Korps that had fought with the rebels, and his brother Piet.

While Myburgh was making his circle to the north, Brits's force was approaching Namutoni along the southern edge of the Etosha Pan. This was prime game country, and the commandos often had to stop to allow large herds of zebra to cross their path. Meat was obviously not in short supply at this time. At Rietfontein one of the burghers shot a lion, according to O'Shaughnessy, who does not say whether it was for sport or in self-defence.

Although Botha did not know it, Brits was only a day's ride from Namutoni when Governor Seitz sent another letter to Botha on the afternoon of July 4 asking for his detailed terms for ending hostilities. In his reply, received by the Germans the following day, Botha demanded the surrender of the regular troops in the German force but said the reserves would be allowed to resume their normal occupations.

Seitz now proposed a meeting with Botha to discuss terms. Botha agreed and set the meeting for 10 a.m. on July 6 at kilometre 500 on the

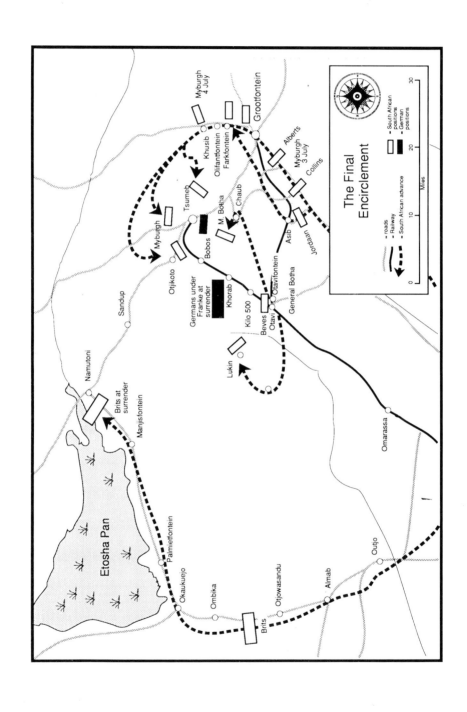

The Final Encirclement

Etosha Pan

Grootfontein

Myburgh 4 July

Khusib
Olifantfontein
Farkfontein

Alberts
Myburgh 3 July
Collins

Tsumeb

Chaub

M. Botha

Myburgh

Otjikoto

Bobos

Germans under Franke at surrender

Khorab

Kilo 500

Beves
Otavi
Otavifontein
General Botha

Asib

Jordaan

Lukin

Omarassa

Sandup

Namutoni

Brits at surrender

Manjisfontein

Palmietfontein

Okaukuejo

Ombika

Otjowasandu

Almab

Brits

Outjo

Legend

- = roads
- = Railway
- = South African advance

☐ = South African positions
■ = German positions

Miles
0   10   20   30

railway, about a mile north of Otavi station.

Botha proposed a local armistice betwen the German force at Khorab and the Union forces at Otavi. Collyer says that special care was taken to exclude Brits and Myburgh from the cease-fire.

'The scope of the armistice was definitely and purposely restricted so as not to interfere with Myburgh's movements and to avoid embarrassing Brits, the circumstances of whose position was quite unknown at GHQ, he says.[2]

Botha also made it clear that he could not accept any terms without their being approved by his government.

To ensure that the local nature of the armistice was understood and accepted by the Germans, Collyer himself went to the German lines under a white flag of truce. He discussed the arrangement with the German general staff officer, Captain Trainer, to make sure that the armistice terms as set out in Botha's letter were not misinterpreted.

At Namutoni events were assuming a farcical character. On the afternoon of July 5 a German officer who had been out on patrol spurred his sweating horse into the Foreign Legion-style fort and reported that the Union troops were approaching. The German commander, apparently reasoning that it was pointless for his garrison of 110 to resist a superior force, immediately hoisted a white flag and ordered the wireless equipment destroyed. On his instructions his men began destroying the huge stores of military equipment in the base to prevent its falling into enemy hands.

While this was going on the senior South African officer in the prison camp, brushing aside the guards, went up to the German commander and demanded that as the white flag was flying and the fort therefore surrendered, the destruction of war material must immediately stop and the prisoners be given charge of the weapons and of the surrendered camp.

Astonishingly, the German commander agreed, and the South African prisoners suddenly found themselves in charge of the fort. But there was still no sign of the Union forces and when at sunset they had not arrived the Germans began to realise that it had all been a bit premature. They demanded their weapons back. The former prisoners refused.

After much argument a compromise was reached: the weapons would all be stored in the guardroom, which would be jointly guarded by both the Germans and the South Africans.

As the night lengthened with no sign of the Union troops the embarrassment of the German commander deepened but there was nothing he could do about it now.

It was not until eleven the next morning, July 6, that Brits led his force into Namutoni formally to accept its surrender. It turned out that

315

the German officer who had reported the approach of Brits's force had actually seen only a motorised scouting party and had assumed that it was the main force.

There are other versions of Namutoni's surrender, but this one, although bizarre, seems to have a ring of truth to it in that it was told in detail to Saxon Mills by Lieutenant B Wahl, who had been one of the South African prisoners in the camp.[3]

While Brits was approaching Namutoni on the morning of the 6th, Myburgh was riding up to Tsumeb. He was unaware of the armistice arrangement but even if he had been he would not, by Botha's definition, have considered himself bound by it. Franke, however, assumed that the armistice covered Tsumeb as it was only 20 miles north of Khorab, where he had his main force.[4]

When the Germans at Tsumeb saw Myburgh's force approaching from the north-west, Whele sent out Captain von Alvensleben under a white flag to inform him of the armistice. This was at 6 a.m., according to the German accounts. Myburgh, not knowing of the armistice, suspected a trick and kept advancing. By 6.15 his force was within range of the German artillery at the Tsumeb fort. The artillery officer, Captain Haussding, decided that as the armistice did not take effect until 7 a.m. it was his duty to open fire, even though he could see von Alvensleben

During his final confinement at Tsumeb, Grant lived in the little cottage in the centre of the picture, overlooking the open camp where the other prisoners were kept. The photograph was probably taken by a member of the South African force on the day Tsumeb was captured, for on the left is the red cross flag that Grant persuaded the Germans to put up as Myburgh's force approached the town. (Cory Library, Burton Collection)

riding with the Union forces and still trying to persuade them to observe the armistice.

Haussding opened up with all of his four guns and the first shells burst directly above the South Africans (and von Alvensleben), who promptly scattered, but not before several had been wounded. Haussding, with rigid devotion to duty, kept firing sporadically until 7 a.m., then stopped to comply with the armistice.

Burton says that as Myburgh's force approached Tsumeb two German officers rode out under a white flag and 'almost breathlessly asked why we were advancing during the armistice. Our leaders said they knew nothing about an armistice, although they had heard news of the Germans suing for peace.

'And while this discussion continued, suddenly two shells in rapid succession exploded directly above our commandos halted on the road. A part of the first shell wounded a horse severely in the neck. The second, which exploded over our heads, wounded three men and a fourth burgher near me had his eyebrows singed by flames and his face covered with black powder.

'While attending to him I found a large hole in his balaclava cap and a larger hole in the back of his overcoat.'

The Germans had the range exactly and fired a total of 11 shells, leaving Burton convinced that it was a marvel that nobody was killed. Many of the commandos were young burghers who had never been in a stiff fight, and at the first shell they sought cover behind rocks and in dongas and even up in trees.

'No one was more amazed at all this than the German officers with the white flags and all they could say was that the German gunners had made a mistake, which they would correct if allowed to go back to the town.'

The Union commanders gave them an ultimatum that if the town were not surrendered within the next two or three hours it would be attacked. There was no response to the ultimatum and the commandos rode into the town without resistance.

Grant was just getting out of bed when he heard the German guns open fire. He counted about 11 shells and assumed that the South Africans were advancing on the town and that Wehle, who had taken up a position the previous evening 'just outside the eastern side of the village' with about 150 men, was opposing them.

Grant hurried down to the German military headquarters, where he found 'Major Wehle and a lot of German officers looking very perturbed. In the midst was a South African who came up to me at once . . . The South African officer was much excited and stated that after the German officer [with the white flag] had met our troops and delivered the message [about the armistice] the Germans had opened fire after 7 a.m. and actually while our people were speaking to the bearer of the flag of truce and consequently our people suspected a fraud and pushed on into the village.

'Just then, about 9 a.m., we heard cheering from the prisoners of war, so I hurried down with Hauptmann Medding. We found that a party of South African troops under Colonel Jordaan had come in. They were accompanied by the officer who had taken out the flag of truce.'

Grant introduced Jordaan to Medding, and then more South African troops came in under Colonel Collins.

'The situation was extraordinary. The Germans remained under arms and our men were facing them at a few yards' distance. In the meantime an argument was going on between Major Wehle and Hauptmann Medding and the two colonels of our side, the Germans stating that we had infringed the armistice and our people maintaining that the Germans had fired after 7 a.m.

'Then followed a comparison of watches and it was found that all the watches of our people were nearly an hour ahead of the local time. This explained matters to some extent. It also turned out that the German artillery had fired in error.

'It was then decided to wait for General Myburgh, who was expected any minute. In the meantime, on my advice, Jordaan withdrew his men about 100 yards from the Germans as there was an element of danger in having the men so close opposite one another.

'Myburgh eventually arrived and we all withdrew up to the [headquarters] where we had a conference with Wehle and Medding, the result being that the town was surrendered.

'General Myburgh then walked down to the prisoners with me and made them a speech telling them that this was the proudest day of his life . . . Of course, the men were rapturous.

'In the late afternoon the disarmament of the German troops took place. I could not help feeling sorry for them. "A fellow feeling, etc.".

'Jordaan and Collins dined with me.'

From inside the prison compound the men had a somewhat different view of the events. Close says that the first the prisoners saw of their rescuers was when two Union soldiers came riding into the town 'without even a white flag, fearless of the consequences, yet hoping to be the first to tell the prisoners that their release was at hand.

'The cheering of the prisoners was tremendous and continuous. We stood at the barbed wire fence and heard what they had to say.'

Later more Union troops rode in and the prisoners, still confined behind their fence, gave them vetkoek, bread and coffee. The troops were allowed to water their horses 'and all morning they came in to do so'.

One man rode over to speak to the prisoners and was told by the German guard to go away. The burgher told the guard to 'go to hell' and the guard walked shamefacedly away 'to wild cheering from the prisoners'.

According to Close, General Myburgh was flying a white flag of truce when he rode into the town. When he went down to speak to the prisoners 'he stood on a chair at the gate of our enclosure and told us what his men had come through in order to release the prisoners'.

He kept saying : 'The gate is now open to you'.

The prisoners appear to have taken him at his word, for, according to Close, they swarmed out of the enclosure and roamed the town, talking to the worn-out burghers and helping themselves to souvenirs such as German bayonets.

'Spirits of both kinds flowed in the camp that night,' Close says. 'Good fellowship existed everywhere. General Botha was the hero of the hour and a most grateful admiration for General Myburgh was universally felt.'

Close recalls that there was great disappointment among the prisoners on learning that the war was still being fought in Flanders and that Constantinople had not yet fallen.

When Burton rode into the town with Myburgh he went to the prison camp and saw the prisoners being guarded by German sentries with fixed bayonets. The guards made no attempt to stop Burton as he opened the gate of the compound and went into what he saw was 'a

German soldiers captured at Otavifontein contemplate a future in which the only certainty is confinement in a prisoner of war camp. (Fort Wynard Museum)

piece of flat ground with no buildings or tents'. He soon found the men whom he was looking for: Dr Godfrey Dalton and Dr William McCowat, with whom he had been at medical school in Edinburgh and who had both been captured while serving with the Union forces as medical officers. They were now acting in the same capacity in the prison camp.

Burton walked up to them and asked them the time. They glared at him and said: 'It's just 12.30, but you will have to stick it out like the rest of us'. With his beard, sunburned face and ragged garments, Burton had looked to the doctors like one of the prisoners. Only when he identified himself did they see who he was and warmly invited him to have a cup of coffee.

Burton asked where he could find Colonel Grant, and Dalton pointed to a small house opposite the enclosure and said: 'Our gallant colonel lives there alone. He walks with a limp and has become weak and very deaf, so be careful, because he does not like to be shouted at.'

Burton decided that before approaching the colonel he would walk about the town. He went into a general dealer's shop and asked for bread, something he had not tasted for six months. The storekeeper, who must already have adapted himself to the new reality of a South African occupation, sold him a large loaf for a shilling. Burton took his prize to a bench under a big tree on the trunk of which was a notice warning that the road leading out of town was heavily mined and dangerous

Burton ate half the loaf but, to his great disappointment, the bread was 'coarse and gritty and seemed to have sawdust in it. I threw the rest away.'

At 4 p.m. Burton knocked on Grant's door. The colonel unlocked and opened the door 'and loudly asked what I wanted him for.' Burton saluted and handed over a letter from his father, who was one of Grant's closest friends.

'He opened the letter and then seized me by the hand and invited me in,' Burton wrote in his diary. He spent the next hour asking Burton about King William's Town, their common home town.

'He was still lame and very deaf and spoke about his gallant officers and men and was glad that the campaign was over and peace declared.

'I bowed myself out of his sitting-room and thanked him for his courage and wonderful stand at Sandfontein when left in the lurch by the defection and treachery of Lieutenant Colonel Maritz early in the campaign,' Burton says. 'We never met again.'

References

1. O'Shaughnessy, p. 229.
2. Collyer, p. 147.
3. Saxon Mills, p. 457.
4. Ungleich, p. 196.

33

Surrender at Kilo 500

While Myburgh was being shelled at Tsumeb, members of Botha's staff were setting up a large tent alongside the railway line at kilometre 500 and furnishing it with a table and chairs. The German delegation arrived for the surrender talks promptly at 10 a.m. by train from Khorab.

This time, in contrast to the meeting at Giftkuppe, Botha did most of the talking. Governor Seitz again rejected unconditional surrender, but Collyer says that 'His Excellency, however, bore traces of anxiety and worry on his face, and no longer exhibited the pungency of comment and self-confident air which had been observable on the first occasion of meeting.'

Collyer, who believed that 'the helplessness of an adversary was a sure passport to General Botha's sympathy', says the general tried to mitigate the soreness of defeat for the Germans.[1]

He undertook to recommend to the Union Government that the German officers be released on parole with their small arms and be allowed to live anywhere in the territory, provided they notified the South African authorities of their place of abode.

The non-commissioned officers and men of the active force would be interned and would be allowed to keep their rifles but would not be allowed ammunition.

The reservists would all be allowed to return home and resume their jobs and would be allowed to keep their rifles and a quantity of ammunition for self-defence against the possibility of marauding blacks.

All the guns as well as the stores and transport of the German forces were to be surrendered. Botha was insistent on the artillery being handed over.

His readiness to allow the reservists to go free arose from his realisation that they would be needed to help to repair the war damage to the economy of the territory. He probably reasoned that South Africa would have charge of South West Africa after the campaign and the

In the sparse shade of a thorn tree, Botha awaits the arrival of the German delegation at kilometre 500 to sign the surrender terms. On Botha's right are Colonel Collyer, his chief-of-staff, wearing a peaked cap, and Major Weisk. On Botha's left are Major Bok and Captain Esselen. (Cape Archives)

healthier the economy the lesser burden it would be on the Union's resources.

Botha's consent to some of the Germans keeping their arms had already been contravened, unwittingly, by Myburgh, who, with what seems to have been a strong sense of irony, was disarming the Germans at Tsumeb, arming the freed South African prisoners and putting them in charge of their former captors.

As he took his seat across the table from Seitz and Franke, Botha still had no confirmation that Brits had reached Namutoni or that Myburgh had yet occupied Tsumeb. In the course of the conversation with the Germans, Botha and Collyer subtly drew from them the confirmation they needed that both places were in South African hands.

The confirmation of the capture of Tsumeb came partly from Franke himself when he complained that Myburgh's attack on the town was a violation of the armistice. In response, the South Africans produced the written agreement excepting Myburgh and Brits from the ceasefire. The meeting at kilometre 500 was adjourned to allow the draft terms to be telegraphed to South Africa for submission to the Union cabinet. The armistice was extended to all forces in the field, with effect from noon that day.

In a cable to his cabinet recommending approval of the terms, Botha told them that 'we are in a position where we can afford to be generous'.

Franke agreed to allow a South African officer to go by rail through the German lines to acquaint Myburgh and Brits of the situation. Franke also allowed the South Africans to use the telephones under his control to speak to the Union commanders in the north.

That would have enabled the Germans to eavesdrop on the conversations if they had been able to follow Dutch, and Franke no doubt had people on his staff who could. But the South Africans found a solution to that: when they did not want the Germans to know what they were saying they spoke in Zulu.

In the German camp there was by no means unanimity about surrender as they awaited the response of the Union cabinet to the proposed terms. Before the meeting of July 6 some of the younger officers had been in favour of an attempt by the German force to break out to the north before the South African pincers closed. But Franke appears to have taken a stand against any such action, regarding it as too late and bound to fail.

One of Franke's main concerns, according to Hennig, was to ensure that the German artillery pieces would not be taken into the South African forces and used against German troops elsewhere. He repeatedly

It is all over except for the final formalities. At kilometre 500 Governor Seitz and his party have alighted from the railway carriage drawn by the locomotive behind them and are being escorted by Botha to the tent where the surrender document will be signed. (Cape Archives)

came back to this point during the negotiation of the surrender terms. He was not over concerned about the older guns that comprised the majority of the German artillery, but he felt strongly about the modern guns being turned against their makers.[2]

Collyer, on the other hand, seemed to the Germans to appreciate how useful their guns would be to the Union forces and argued strongly that they should be surrendered to the conquerors.

Franke went to great lengths to establish the views of his officers on the question of surrender itself and on the terms. The older officers tended to take the view that they were being asked to lay down their weapons too soon; the greater part of the German forces in the colony were still intact and well-armed, even though food supplies were low. Some wanted to fight on a while longer to preserve their honour, others wanted to fight to the last man.

The artillery officers were strongly opposed to surrendering their guns. Orders had been given that all the guns should be destroyed to prevent their falling into the hands of the Union forces, but the order appears to have been countermanded by Franke in the belief that the South Africans had agreed that the guns need not be surrendered.[3]

Some guns were thrown into the Osikotosee, but at least 37 guns fell into the hands of the South Africans and some, at least, appear to have been used against the Germans in East Africa.

The guns aside, Franke believed that there was no point in fighting on when the only result would be the loss of more lives. He told Seitz that he would fight on if the Governor asked him to but as the responsible commander of the German forces he would do his best to avoid the reckless spilling of blood.

In the end a majority of the German officers agreed to surrender on the South African terms; but there is some doubt whether the terms that Botha sent to his government for ratification were clearly understood, even by Franke.

Manie Maritz, the rebel leader, who appears to have played little part in the German defence, now bowed to fate and, with a handful of followers, set off north to escape into Angola.

The Union cabinet's acceptance of the surrender terms was tele-graphed to Botha at 3 a.m. on July 8, but with amendments. The main one was that the officers would be allowed to keep only one pistol each and the other ranks one rifle each, all without ammunition. Only officers who signed a parole would be allowed to keep their horses.

Botha immediately sent the revised terms to the Germans with the request that they be accepted by 5 p.m. the same day.

The new terms, although different only in minor respects, were received with unhappiness by some of the German officers and there was prolonged argument among them. Some advocated rejection of the new terms in favour of the original terms. Others again argued in favour of renewing hostilities and going down fighting, with honour.

Franke pointed out that renewed fighting would inevitably lead to a South African victory that would enable Botha to impose whatever conditions he chose.

The Germans now had essentially four alternatives: surrender on Botha's terms; a resumption of fighting in the hope of winning better terms; a fight to the end or breaking up the German forces into small groups to wage guerrilla warfare until the Allies were defeated in Europe.

Some officers argued that Botha would accept the original terms if he were pressed as he would want to avoid further hostilities to save lives on his own side and to prevent further damage to the economy of the territory.

All day the arguments raged. As the clock ticked close to 5 p.m., Seitz sent a message requesting a two-hour postponement. To this Botha agreed. Still the Germans remained locked in dispute. Some simply could not bring themselves to accept what they regarded as the dishonour of defeat, especially as the German armies were advancing in Europe. In what appears to have been an attempt to gain time, Seitz sent Botha a letter requesting a further meeting to clarify ambiguities in the terms.

Outside the tent at kilometre 500, Botha talks to Franke at the right. In the foreground Collyer is talking to an officer, probably his counterpart, the German chief-of-staff. (Namibia Archives)

German artillery surrendered to the South Africans at Khorab. Franke tried hard to insert in the surrender terms a provision that would prevent the more modern guns from falling into the hands of the South Africans and then being turned against German forces in another theatre of the war. (Cape Archives)

Botha received the letter at 7 p.m. and immediately replied that if the terms were not accepted without amendment by 2 a.m. on July 9 he would resume hostilities.

The South African troops were ordered to stand by for an attack on Franke's position at Khorab. Lukin would attack from the west, Manie Botha from the east and Beves from the south. Unless the order were countermanded, they would begin to advance at 2.30 a.m.

As the hours dragged by, Botha and his staff sat in their headquarters in the old German barracks at Otavifontein and drank cup after cup of coffee and waited.

A few miles outside Otavi on the railway to the north, a solitary South African officer waited in the dark night, muffled against the cold, with the engine of his car slowly turning over as it stood beside the track. He kept looking at his watch as the hands neared 2 o'clock.

The deadline passed and there was still no sign of a train coming down the line with the German response. Botha had told the officer to wait until 2.30, then leave.

At 2.30 he looked once more at his watch and walked towards his car. Then, through the bush, he saw a light. He waited. The light drew nearer, and now he could hear the puffing of a locomotive.

In a few minutes the engine slowed to a stop beside the lights of his car and from a single carriage behind it stepped a German staff officer, Captain Virmond. He solemnly handed a sealed envelope to the South African, who leaped into the car and sped off towards Otavifontein.

At Botha's headquarters preparations were being made for the resumption of hostilities when the car roared up to the door. The envelope was opened and smiles broke out all round the room. The Germans had accepted the surrender terms. The campaign was over. Orders for the advance to be called off were hastily issued.

No one seems to have left a description of the scene at Botha's headquarters, but it is fair to assume that bottles that had been put aside for the occasion were brought out for happy toasts to victory. And there must have been cheering in the lines as troops who had braced themselves for battle learned that it was all over. The campaign had ended in victory, and all the marching and the heat and dust and thirst seemed worthwhile; and now they could think of going home – home to a hero's welcome.

At Khorab, the atmosphere was one of heavy gloom. The dispute between the officers over the surrender had gone on until the last moment, when, Seitz, accepting the will of the majority of the officers, agreed to accept the terms.

What would have happened if the terms had been rejected is open to speculation. A German officer is said to have told the commander of the Pretoria Regiment that preparations had been made for German troops to attack the Union position at Otavi with fixed bayonets if the surrender terms had not been accepted.[4]

The formal signing of the surrender was set for 10 a.m. on July 9 at kilometre 500. The German delegation arrived by train. With Governor Seitz and Colonel Franke were the police commissioner, Colonel Bethe, who spoke English fluently, and several other military officers.

'The Governor seemed to take defeat far more to heart than did any of the military officers who surrounded him,' Collyer says. 'He was a very different person from the alert, brusque individual who had talked at length at Giftkuppe, and now concerned himself with indicating some directions in which more exact definition appeared, to his mind, to be necessary.'

Franke said little other than to suggest that he had regarded the July 6 terms as final and would not have made his telephones available to the South Africans if he had known that they would be amended. Botha drily answered that he appreciated the use of the telephones, especially as it had enabled him to 'keep quiet commandos who would otherwise have been on the move all the time'.

Botha expressed his willingness to change the surrender terms provided the principles were not interfered with and some minor changes were made. Then Seitz and Franke signed the document for the

Germans and Botha signed for his Government.

The Germans climbed back on to their train and returned to Khorab, with the the locomotive puffing in reverse in an unavoidable bit of symbolism that may have gone unnoticed by them.

References

1. Collyer, p. 148.
2. Hennig, p. 305.
3. *Ibid.*
4. O'Shaughnessy, p. 237.

CHAPTER

34

The Bells of Victory

The news of the German surrender sent South Africa into wild celebration.

Cheering crowds took to the streets everywhere. In Pretoria they gathered outside Botha's house and demonstrated joyfully, joined more sedately by Mrs Botha.

Ships in the harbours blew their sirens, gold mines across the Witwatersrand sounded their hooters and bells were rung in churches, town halls and wherever there was a bell to be rung.

The mayor declared a public holiday in Johannesburg, bunting appeared in the streets and bands played outside the city hall. Copies of *The Star* carrying the news were snapped up as soon as they appeared in the streets.

Troops paraded and cheered on cue outside the Castle in Cape Town and elsewhere.

In Flanders, where Allied and German troops were mired in bloody stalemate, the news of the victory in South West Africa sent cheers rolling along the trenches. When British soldiers hoisted boards above the parapets informing the Germans of the surrender of their compatriots in Africa the Germans angrily riddled the boards with bullets.[1]

Telegrams of congratulation poured into Botha's office in Pretoria from many parts of the world, but especially from Britain. There he was a popular hero, not only because he had won the campaign for the British but because he had done so so soon after being defeated by them in the Boer War. If Britons felt some guilt over inflicting that defeat on the Boers they could now find absolution in this willing and splendid victory in their cause by one of the defeated Boers.

The man who had commanded the British troops who had inflicted the defeat, Lord Kitchener, was one of those who cabled congratulations. Kitchener, now Minister of War, expressed his 'sincere admiration of the masterly conduct' of the campaign. On behalf of the British

Army he sent to 'you and your force our cordial congratulations on your brilliant victory'.

Telegrams arrived from King George, from Prime Minister Asquith, from the Colonial Secretary and from cities and institutions and individuals.

Asquith asked Parliament to express the 'admiration and gratitude of the whole Empire' to Botha, who 'has rendered such inestimable service to the Empire which he entered by adoption, and of which he has become one of its most honoured and cherished sons', and to his troops, 'whether of Burgher or British birth, who have fought like brethren side by side. . .'

From Colonial Secretary Bonar Law came this tribute: 'The Germans remembered that only thirteen years ago we were engaged in a war in South Africa; they could not understand – General Botha has enabled them now to understand – that a brave foe who pledged his word would keep that word. They find that, instead of South Africa falling away from the British Empire, the forces of South Africa have won a notable victory in the cause of that Empire . . .'

In the House of Lords the tribute was expressed by the Marquess of Crewe, who praised 'the high military qualities which General Botha has shown.

The war is over for the German soldiers seen here boarding railway trucks at Otavifontein to be taken to prison camps. (Cape Archives)

'We had our own experience of him as a most chivalrous and most capable commander against ourselves. Now that he is one of us we must fully appreciate the evidence that he has shown in this campaign of the qualities of a great commander . . .'

General Smuts was to some extent but not entirely overlooked in the adulation. The Marquess of Crewe referred in the Lords to 'the admirable work done by the Defence Department in South Africa, and in particular the supreme qualities of organisation displayed by General Smuts, who presided over that department.

'Altogether we are able to state that the South African government and the generals and the officers and rank and file of the army have all contributed to add a glorious and absolutely stainless chapter to the record of this word-wide war.'

From the other Dominions came tributes to the South Africans and to Botha in particular. A cable came from Sir Ronald Munro-Ferguson, Governor-General of Australia, whose forces were now clinging in heroic misery to the slopes of Gallipoli. In London the Australian High Commissioner, Sir George Reid, declared that 'General Botha's great campaign was far more formidable than is generally known, quite apart from the great physical difficulties he had to surmount . . . Even before today, General Botha was one of the greatest and most loyal of all the King's subjects, and his latest magnificent victory will still further

German prisoners come down the gangway of the *British Prince* in Cape Town docks, on their way to the camps in South Africa where they will spend the rest of the war. (Cape Archives – E).

add to the love and admiration which all the people of the Empire feel for him.'

The Prime Minister of Canada, Sir Robert Borden, referred to the 'fantastic' hopes that had been held in Germany of the Dominions standing aloof and neutral in the war. Yet the war had strengthened the bonds of the Empire.

'What of South Africa?' he asked. 'The Prussian picture was that it should flare into rebellion at once, cut itself off from the Empire and proclaim its independence. What is the actual picture? The heroic figure of General Louis Botha receiving the surrender of German South West Africa – territory larger than the German Empire itself.'

In Germany the news of the surrender in South West Africa came as a shock to a population that had largely been kept ignorant of the advance of the South African forces. To some extent this may have been because after the fall of Windhuk and its wireless station, Germany had had to rely for news of the campaign largely on South African and British accounts, and there was no doubt some suspicion about their accuracy, given the historic propensity of governments at war to dress up facts with propaganda.

On July 15 the official German news agency issued an account of the surrender that emphasised that the German forces had been outnumbered by the South Africans:

'The bravery of the Germans was admitted by the British, who even permitted non-commmissioned officers and privates to keep their sidearms and guns.'[2]

Next day the German Colonial Secretary, Dr Solf, told a news conference in Berlin that the German forces had surrendered because they were cut off from foreign supplies and had been running short of ammunition and war materials. They were in any case only a police force equipped only for putting down native insurrections. He commended the German forces for holding out for eleven months against an enemy eight to ten times their strength. Further resistance would only have meant annihilation and would have served no purpose.[3]

Dr Solf's account is contradicted by the large supplies of arms and ammunition seized by the South African forces after the surrender.

Another German commentary published in Berlin noted with some sarcasm that South West Africa was 'the first British victory in the war and was won by a Boer general'.

Morris in his book quotes a commentary, without disclosing the source, which remarked with bitterness that 'it will strike all Germans as peculiarly painful that at the head of an English army. . . was the same Botha whom the German nation thirteen years ago took to its heart as the man who had been driven out of hearth and home by the greed and brutality of England, and whose deeds were celebrated with the same

333

The End of the African Lion Hunt.

A celebratory cartoon shows Botha as a lion licking his lips after consuming the German forces in South West Africa, whose bones and accoutrements lie before him. (SADF Archives)

enthusiasm as the achievements of our South West African heroes who put down the revolt of the Hereros and the Hottentots . . . Today Germany is receiving the gratitude of the House of Botha and his dependants.

'We could scarcely believe at the beginning of this war that the Boers would unite with the English, to whom they owe the loss of their complete independence, to break into the German colony of South West Africa, which, without the assistance of the Boers, would still be unconquerable today. And yet now Botha stands in the extreme northern part of our territory and Colonel Franke, one of our best colonial officers, whose name is still mentioned by the natives with terror and dread, must lay down his arms.'[4]

After the surrender the first official communication between Dr Seitz and Berlin was transmitted through the South Africans and then through the American Consulate in Cape Town. His telegram to the Kaiser was sent on August 1 and released in Berlin two days later.

'We inform Your Majesty that we were obliged to surrender to Botha the residue of the troops, about 3 400 men, being surrounded by far superior forces between Otavi and Tsumeb, near Gaub. All probability of successful resistance was vain, since after the enemy had taken Otavi, Guchab, Grootfontein, Tsumeb and Namutoni, we were cut off from the base of supplies, and seeing the state of exhaustion of our horses, every attempt to force the circle was impossible. All persons belonging to the category of retired soldiers or prisoners remain at work in their factories; the officers are allowed to retain their arms and horses, and on giving their parole can remain at liberty in colonial territory. The active colonial troops, about 1 300 in number, retain their guns and are to be concentrated in a place not yet determined.'[5]

Botha returned to South Africa as soon as he was satisfied that arrangements for the administration of the territory were well in hand. As Prime Minister he had responsibilities in his own country, a government and a political party to lead.

The fighting was over. Now the speechmaking would begin. At a number of parades the commander-in-chief said farewell to his troops. Leaving Lukin to supervise the execution of the surrender terms, Botha sailed from Swakopmund in the hospital ship *Ebani*.

The return of the conquering hero was the signal for a renewed outburst of celebration in the Union. A large crowd waited at the dockside in Cape Town in pouring rain for his ship to berth. As if on cue, the rain stopped and a perfect rainbow appeared as Botha's portly figure moved down the gangway while an artillery battery fired a seventeen-gun salute and the crowds cheered.

There were more cheers as he drove through streets hung with bunting and lined with people waving Union Jacks. Trumpets heralded his arrival at the city hall, where a massed choir of schoolchildren sang and politicians made endless speeches. The mayor presented him with a sword of honour inscribed with the words: 'Draw for God and the King, Justice and Truth'.

Botha said he accepted his countrymen's praise on behalf of the men he had led in South West Africa: 'They have achieved a wonderful piece of work.'

It had been a privilege to lead an army 'consisting of the two white races of South Africa.'

As he travelled northwards by train, crowds gathered at every station to cheer him, whether the train stopped or passed through. At Bloemfontein people unhitched the horses drawing the carriage taking him from the railway station to the city hall and drew it themselves through streets resounding to cheers.

The crowd that gathered to welcome Botha in Johannesburg was described as the largest ever seen there.

The celebrations reached a climax when ten thousand people crowded into the amphitheatre at the Union Buildings in Pretoria to hear and to cheer the man who at that moment symbolised what most white South Africans had accepted as their destiny: a union of Briton and Boer in one nation within the British Empire.

In putting down the rebellion Botha had eliminated all future threats to that union, it was felt, and in defeating the Germans in South West Africa with an army in which Boers and Britons were joined he had demonstrated that the Union was not only firmly cemented but capable of wielding power.

Botha was treated as a hero when he went to Europe after the campaign, and when he led the South African delegation to the peace

The conquering hero is hailed at home. Top hats wave as Botha, saluting in the centre, is cheered by an adulatory crowd at the Union Buildings in Pretoria. (Police Museum)

conference at Versailles in 1919.

But he was a sick man. His health, about which he had publicly complained at the beginning of the campaign, and which had deteriorated during it, was by this time failing. He died before the year was out, aged only 57.

In his relatively short life this son of one of the Voortrekkers who had travelled north by ox-waggon from the Cape had seen the invention of the tank and the submarine and had flown in an aircraft. So fast had technology developed.

Some believed his life had been shortened by the emotional agony of having to fight against his own people in the rebellion.

His memory was soon eclipsed by the growing stature of Jan Smuts, whom he had eclipsed while he was alive. Later generations can only wonder whether Smuts would have found it easy to flourish politically in the shadow of Botha if Botha had lived longer.

They can only wonder how differently history might have turned in South Africa after the war if Botha had been able to apply his moral strength, his leadership, his compassion and his vision to the country's ethnic problems.

References

1. Morris, p. 141.
2. Ungleich, p. 206, citing *New York Times,* July 16 1915.
3. *Ibid,* citing *New York Times,* July 17 1915.
4. Morris, p. 145.
5. Ungleich, p. 207, citing Giordani, *German Colonial Empire.*

CHAPTER

35

Homecoming

After the celebration of Botha's return came the rejoicing as the homecoming troopships began docking in Cape Town.

Arduous though it was, the campaign had been merciful in casualties. Most of those who fought in it survived, although not always with good health.

Of the 50 000 men who fought on the South African side, only 266 failed to return, 88 of them having been killed in action and 25 fatally wounded. A further 263 were wounded but recovered. Illness and accidents caused more deaths, 153, than enemy action. In addition, 606 Union soldiers were captured by the Germans.

The Union casualties were fewer even than those in the rebellion, when 131 loyal troops and 190 rebels were killed. Since the two events were related, the rebellion being a direct result of the Union's entry into the war, the casualties can fairly be added together for a total of 434 South African lives lost as a result of the decision to go to war for the British Empire.

On the German side the losses during the fighting were 103 killed, 195 wounded and 890 captured. In the final capitulation the Germans surrendered 4 740 officers and men, 37 field guns, 22 machine-guns and large quantities of ammunition and stores (other than food, of which the Germans were getting desperately short).

Compared with the slaughter on the Western Front, the casualty figures are paltry, if casualties can ever be considered paltry. They amount to fewer than the number killed in a single day at the height of the European trench warfare. But, as Whittall says, 'to measure the success of a campaign by the size of the butcher's bill is to view it from an altogether wrong standpoint.

'As a matter of fact, the reverse may often be the case. It most certainly was so in South West Africa, where the loss of life was in inverse ratio to the results achieved.'

If a less able commander than Botha had been in charge of the

338

operations, he says, not only would the casualties have been far heavier but the campaign would have lasted longer.

To some extent the light casualties were due to the Germans' strategy of seeking to prolong the campaign, knowing that they could not win it, which entailed avoiding hostilities. To a larger extent they were due to Botha's tactics.

By continually outflanking the strongly entrenched German positions with forced marches that they did not believe could be made, Botha forced them to retreat to avoid being encircled. Thus pitched battles were few.

Botha was guided by the principle that it was better for his men to lose their sweat than their blood. He would rather push them to the limits of their endurance to outflank an enemy than give them an easy march to a bloody confrontation.

Yet if it had not been for the skill with which the Germans so often extricated themselves from Botha's encirclements the campaign would have been shorter or bloodier, or both.

Perhaps an even more important factor in frustrating Botha's tactics was his lack of transport. He seldom had enough waggons and mule teams to ensure that his fast-moving troops did not outstrip their supplies. Smuts is reported to have said that if there had been enough transport the campaign could have been over eight weeks earlier than it was.[1] Collyer frequently refers to this problem and puts the blame on Defence Headquarters in South Africa.

Since General Smuts was Minister of Defence it might fairly be presumed that the buck stopped at his desk; but Collyer refrains from putting it there, and perhaps with justification, for in all quarters Smuts's planning is praised.

Collyer does, however, openly criticise the division of command, pointing out that Botha, although styled commander-in-chief, had command only over his own Northern Force and for a while over McKenzie's Central Force.

'If to some extent the intimacy of Generals Botha and Smuts and intercourse between them gave each of them an idea of the views of the other, this meant no close combination of effort, and the dual command was a cause of dissipation of resources and strength,' he says.

'Defence Headquarters, where such coordination as was ever attempted was effected, was in no position to give orders on its own responsibility while the two generals were in the field.'[2] There are other points of controversy about the structure and operations of the fledgling Union Defence Force, which had barely been established when it was flung into the war. But one aspect of the Union operations for which there was unanimous admiration – among the Germans too – was the astonishing forced marches made by the South Africans.

At the end of the campaign Myburgh's 2nd Mounted Brigade had moved 480 miles from its base and Coen Brits' 1st Mounted Brigade had marched 460 miles from its starting point. The 5th Mounted Brigade under Manie Botha had marched 420 miles and the 6th Mounted Brigade under Lukin had done 350 miles. The 1st Infantry Brigade had covered 330 miles on foot.

On its last advance Brits's Brigade marched 340 miles from Aukas to Namutoni in 20 days, averaging 17 miles a day. Myburgh's force covered the 280 miles from Wilhelmstal to Tsumeb in 220 days, averaging 14 miles a day.

In their 230-mile march from Karibib to Otavi the 5th and 6th Mounted Brigades averaged 17,7 miles a day over 13 days.

The record march of the campaign was made by Alberts's left wing of the 2nd Mounted, which began by marching 40 miles from Swakopmund to Husab in 14 hours. Then, after a 12-hour rest, it covered another 76 miles in 22 hours, marching first from Husab to Jakkalswater, where it fought a three-hour battle, and then marching back to Husab for water.[3]

In sheer human endurance, however, perhaps the most impressive effort was the 1st Infantry Brigade's 230-mile footslog from Karibib to Otavi in 16 days, averaging 14,4 miles a day. The infantry covered the distance in only four days more than the cavalry brigades.

This performance ranks among the greatest military marches in history in terms of distance covered alone. It is made even more impressive by the conditions in which it was carried out: extreme heat during the day and bitter cold at night, severe shortage of both water and food, broken terrain and thick dust. The last 80 miles were covered in four days and, when Botha asked the brigade for a final burst, it did the last 45 miles in 36 hours.

When the fighting ceased the hardships did not end for many of the troops. The trek back to the coast was for some almost as arduous as the march inland, even though it was at a more leisurely pace.

Men, horses and mules were exhausted from the sustained speed of the advance with little food or water, and many of the animals had been pushed beyond recovery.

'Before leaving Tsumeb the vets rejected many of our emaciated horses, mules and donkeys and the Remount Department substituted others almost as bad if not worse,' says Burton.

So slowly did the weary mounted brigades travel that even Burton's field hospital, which had usually brought up the rear during the advance, now got ahead of the column.

'Almost a dozen animals died daily,' Burton says. 'All we could do in their wretchedness was to remove the saddles and bridles and allow them to roam in search of any available provender.

'Burghers whose horses were not exhausted overtook small groups of comrades leading their thirsty, hungry and panting horses and as matters worsened some footsore burghers had to be put with others on a tired horse or mule.'

What had been a fast-moving, purposeful force in the triumphal advance had in the aftermath of victory become what Burton describes as 'a disordered column of stragglers'.

Some of the troops returned home on the railway line that now linked Tsumeb with Cape Town, but it was quicker and more efficient to return most of them, especially the mounted brigades with their remaining horses, on the ships that had brought them out.

Almost everybody brought back a souvenir of some kind – a German Mauser or bayonet or a piece of shrapnel that had nearly killed its present custodian, a fragment from a mine or a signboard in German. Coen Brits, not surprisingly, brought back the biggest souvenir of all : a German cannon.

When the ship carrying Brits and his men docked at Cape Town, an officious customs officer made the mistake of telling the general that he could not land the gun in South Africa without a special permit.

'Who says I can't?' asked Brits.

'I say you can't,' replied the official.

Brits raised himself to his full towering height over the official, looked down at him, and said: 'And I have fifteen hundred men on this ship who say I can.'

The customs official may not have known that he was dealing with the man who had attacked De Wet at Mushroom Valley and had chased and caught him in the Kalahari, who had fought at Pforte and who had made the dash through the desert to capture Namutoni.

But looking up at the huge hard-eyed man looming over him and at the ragged, sun-bitten band behind him, the official knew that they and their commander were not going to allow a customs official or a customs regulation to stop them from taking that cannon off the ship.

The gun came ashore and within a few weeks was occupying a place of honour on Coen Brits' front stoep.

Most of the commandos were disbanded and their members returned to their farms and occupations. Those who called themselves Afrikaners faced the business of returning to living alongside neighbours against whom they had fought in the rebellion and of trying to heal the wounds of that rift.

For many of the the troops the campaign in South West was only the beginning of their war, and they went on to fight in German East Africa, in Palestine and on the Western Front, and large numbers died there and their remains lie buried there today, often ignored by the ungrateful descendants of those for whose liberty they gave their lives.

In South West Africa the emphasis shifted from the military to the political.

Towards the end of the war the future of the German colonies became an important question. Germany had not yet been physically deprived of all its colonies; South African troops led by General Smuts were still fighting the Germans in East Africa but had not been able to force their final defeat. Botha's government took the attitude that South West Africa could hardly be handed back to Germany after it had been conquered at some cost by South Africa.

In a grateful Britain there was much sympathy with this line of thought. A British Foreign Office pamphlet issued in 1918 said: 'German South West Africa could have been included in the British Empire, not only without objection from, but with the active goodwill of, Germany. That it ever passed into German hands was due to the continued inaction of the Home Government and the government of the Cape Colony.

'It is geographically an integral part of South Africa; and, if there is to be a South African nation in the future, the exclusion of this territory can hardly be contemplated. In the interests of the natives it would be criminal to hand it back to Germany, with the ruthlessness of the Herero Wars standing on record; and, inasmuch as it was taken by the Union of South Africa, the government of that Union has a claim to its disposal which it is impossible to disregard.'

At the Imperial Conference in July 1918 South Africa made known its view that if the territory were not to be returned to Germany it should be made part of the Union. Partly because of American opposition, the German colonies were not annexed by their conquerors at the end of the war, however. At the peace conference in Paris in January 1919 the German colonies were put under the administration of the conquering nations under various classes of mandate supervised by the League of Nations.

With the assent of Britain, on whose behalf South Africa had nominally conquered the territory, South Africa undertook the administration of South West Africa. The C-class mandate allocated to the territory gave Pretoria virtually unhampered control.

Acting under the authority of the Treaty of Versailles, South Africa began deporting the civil servants, soldiers and other Germans who had no roots in the territory. Farmers, traders and other more permanent residents were allowed to stay to keep the economy growing. At the same time South Africans were encouraged to settle in the territory, and hundreds did. One result was that land claimed by indigenous inhabitants was taken over by South African farmers. The South Africans encountered difficulties with the indigenous inhabitants from the beginning. As early as 1916 South African troops were called out to put down

A new chapter begins – and one that is to be a lot stormier than Smuts might expect as he stands beside a railway carriage to formally receive the League of Nations mandate to administer South West Africa. (Namibia Archives)

defiance of authority by an Ovambo chief, and he and 100 of his followers were killed. In 1922 the Bondelswart tribe rose in rebellion and more than 100 were killed by South African troops.

Immediately before and during the Second World War the remaining German connections with the territory led to the appearance of Nazism, which South Africa firmly suppressed. During the war numbers of white residents of South West Africa, most of whom were by now South African citizens, served with the all-volunteer South African armed forces against the Italians in Abyssinia and against the Germans in the Western Desert and Italy.

After the formation of the United Nations, South Africa continued to administer the territory but refused to acknowledge the conversion of the League of Nations mandate to a UN trusteeship.

After the defeat of Smuts's United Party government in 1948, the National Party government attempted to tighten South Africa's hold on South West Africa and it became virtually a fifth province of the Union.

But the indigenous inhabitants were having none of that and, with their active encouragement, there now began a running political battle

343

between South Africa and the UN majority which saw the South African administration challenged in the World Court and increasingly hostile action in the General Assembly and the Security Council to force Pretoria to relinquish its hold on the territory. While professing an intention to respect the wishes of the inhabitants, Pretoria did little to find out what they were, let alone to implement them.

The growing demand among the indigenous inhabitants for independence led to a campaign of insurgency conducted by the South West Africa People's Organisation (Swapo) from bases in Angola. By now most South African politicians had given up hope of the territory being absorbed into South Africa, which had become a republic in 1961 and been forced out of the Commonwealth because of its government's apartheid policies and its refusal to quit South West Africa. The politicians were concerned only with ensuring that a friendly government came to power in an independent Namibia, rather than one dominated by Swapo, which was seen in Pretoria as a communist organisation.

The name Namibia was now being used increasingly in international circles in preference to South West Africa.

Attempts by the South African armed forces to suppress the insurgency escalated into a low-intensity war that spread into Angola and saw South African troops at times fighting deep inside that country, sometimes against Cuban troops who had entered the civil war in Angola on the side of the MPLA government.

By 1987 official attitudes in Pretoria had been radically changed by the high cost of the war, the increased international hostility to South Africa's presence in the territory, the disappearance of the 'Red threat' with the emergence of glasnost and perestroika in the Soviet Union and the realisation that South Africa must stop antagonising black Africa if it were to regain international acceptance.

Negotiations, in which South African diplomats played an imaginative and possibly crucial part, led to an agreement linking independence for Namibia with the withdrawal of the Cuban troops from Angola

Elections for a constituent assembly followed and on March 21 Namibia became independent and the South African flag was lowered for the last time in the territory.

It had been flying there for more than 70 years, ever since the League of Nations mandate was entrusted to South Africa.

It is doubtful whether anyone in Namibia gave any thought on that day to the men whose remains lie in the graves at Sandfontein, where South Africa's long role in the territory had begun 76 years before; or to the other South African graves – of blacks as well as whites – that were scattered across the territory as Botha's campaign rolled inland.

344

Whatever may have been the motives of their political leaders, those men entered the territory as soldiers and fought and died there as soldiers. Perhaps they felt they were fighting for their king or their people, perhaps they were there just for the adventure of it. But their deaths were brave and honourable and their graves will always be worthy of honour.

Because it was fought by relatively small armies in a relatively short time in a part of the world remote from the centre of the war, the campaign in German South West Africa was overshadowed by the larger events of the First World War. On the broad canvas of that war, the campaign was a minor detail, no more than a sideshow.

Perhaps because it was so well executed and so successful, the effects of the campaign have been largely overlooked. If the campaign had failed, or if South Africa had refused to undertake it, the consequences would have loomed much larger in history than the campaign now does.

The silencing of the German wireless stations was necessary as long as there was a prospect of German fleets breaking out of the North Sea and threatening the supply lines of the Empire, especially the vital Cape sea route. If South Africa had refused the job British or other Empire troops would have had to undertake it and it would undoubtedly have been a much costlier business. The supply routes would have been infinitely longer. The troops would have been less adept in the prevailing conditions. And it is doubtful that from any other part of the world could have come the combination of Botha's special military genius and the unique qualities of the South African mounted riflemen and perhaps even the marching ability of the South African infantry in those conditions.

Yet apart from silencing the wireless stations and raising the morale of the Allies when it was badly needed, the campaign had little impact on a world preoccupied with bloodier and more central theatres of the war.

Even after the war not much attention was paid to the historical aspects of the campaign: not only that it was the first to be fought by the armed forces of South Africa and that it saw the birth of the South African Air Force but also that it was probably the beginning of aerial warfare in Africa and certainly in Southern Africa; that it saw the first use of armoured cars in Africa, and that it demonstrated the military capabilities of the motor vehicle in desert conditions.

But as the British historian Saxon Mills observed, 'Of all the minor operations of the war, none was more marked by picturesque and moving adventure, none was carried through with swifter or more complete success, than the campaign against German South West Africa.'

The assessment can be taken beyond that. In human endeavour and accomplishment, and in military excellence, the 'sideshow' fought by the South Africans in South West Africa equals any campaign conducted in the First World War and it deserves a distinguished place in military history.

References

1. O'Shaughnessy, p. 238.
2. Collyer, p. 157.
3. *Official History*, p. 55.

Index

Imperial Conference, 342
Imperial Light Horse, 12, 13, 61, 93, 99,
    107, 108, 115, 128, 144, 148, 207, 215,
    235-239, 286
Independence, Namibian, 344
Inflexible, HMS, 137
Invincible, HMS, 137
Irish, South African
    (see South African Irish)

Jakkalswater, 181, 184, 186, 187, 188,
    247
Jameson, Sir Leander Starr, 269
Jerusalem, 58
Jones, Maj 'Fatty', 99, 209
Jones, Roderick, 149
Jordaan, Col Cdt, 264, 318

Kabus, 152
Kaffrarian Rifles, 55, 105, 121, 127
Kaizer, 89, 334
Kakamas, 57, 82
Kalahari Desert, 141
Kalahari Horse, 152
Kalkfontein (Karasburg), 24, 87, 105,
    141, 153, 154, 155, 156, 209
Kamerun, 161
Karas Mountains, 154
Karibib, 119, 141, 244, 246, 252, 254,
    266
Karroo Schuiters, 152
Karub, 240, 271
Keetmanshoop, 12, 42, 75, 141, 154, 155,
    226
Keimoes, 57
Kemp, Maj Christoffel, 42, 49, 52, 59,
    60-63, 75, 80, 81, 84, 85, 151
Kenhardt, 57
Kenhardt-Calvinia Commando, 152
Khan railway, 181, 246, 256
Khorab, 292, 298, 299, 300, 316, 322,
    327, 328
Kieriis West, 152
Kilometre 500, 322, 328
Kimberley Regiment, 115, 144, 235, 238,
    239, 284, 289, 298
Kinfauns Castle, 94, 170
King-Hall, Vice-Admiral, 136
Kitchener, Lord, 330
Klerksdorp, 50
Kolmanskuppe, 96
Kommissie Drift, 59

Kopjes, 50, 65
Krugersdorp Commando, 180, 245
Kubas, 247, 252
Kuruman, 60, 152

Landswehr, 158
Law, Bonar, 331
League of Nations, 342, 343
Lemmer, Col Cmdt L A S, 180, 245
Letcher, Owen, 108
Leursen, Dr, 304
Lichtenburg, 48, 49, 59
Lichtenburg Commando, 180, 245
Lindley, 65
Lords, House of, 331
Lucas, Sir Charles, 48
Luderitz, Herr, 161
Luderitzbucht, 7, 9, 13, 27, 41, 91-105,
    204
Lukin, Gen Sir Timson, 9, 18, 21, 23,
    25-37, 40, 68, 264, 335, 340
Lutzeputz, 73
Lydenburg Commando, 245

Mackay, Lt-Col D W, 102
Mandate, League of Nations, 342
Marico Commando, 180, 245
Maritz, Gert, 56
Maritz, Rfn O C, 301
Maritz, Lt-Col S F 'Manie', 41, 42, 52,
    53, 54-58, 73-82, 85, 86, 325
Martial law, 56
Martin, Col A C, 114
Meara, Capt William, 146, 147, 166, 289
Medding, Capt, 311, 312
Medical Corps, SA, 73
Mentz, Col H S, 245, 249, 252, 260
Middelburg Commando, 181, 245, 248,
    249
Mines, land, 129, 138, 175, 190, 210,
    247, 288, 296
Mitchell, Lt F McE, 255
Modderfontein, 189
Monarch, 102, 144
Montgomery, Lt-Col, 218
Muller, Christiaan, 64
Munnik, Senator G G, 48
Munro-Ferguson, Sir Ronald, 332
Murray, Capt C, 231
Murraysburg Commando, 152
Mushroom Valley, 67